THE IRISH TIMES

BOOK
of the
YEAR
2009

EDITED BY
PETER MURTAGH

Gill & Macmillan

Gill & Macmillan Ltd
Hume Avenue
Park West
Dublin 12
with associated companies throughout the world
www.gillmacmillan.ie

© 2009 *The Irish Times*
978 0 7171 4652 9
Design by Identikit Design Consultants, Dublin
Print origination by Carole Lynch
Index compiled by Carole C. Devaney
Printed by Butler, Tanner & Dennis, Somerset

*The paper used in this book is made from the wood pulp
of managed forests. For every tree felled, at least one tree
is planted, thereby renewing natural resources.*

A CIP catalogue record is available for this book
from the British Library.

5 4 3 2 1

Contents

Introduction

It was only in the course of considering this introduction to the 2009 *Irish Times Book of the Year* – the 10th of the series – that I noticed the subject of the first article, by Mark Hennessy (now London Editor), was the banking crisis, which burst over everyone's heads in September 2008 when the Government decided to guarantee deposits to forestall a run. Since then, we've all been living with the economic crisis and have watched our country go from boom to bust in less than a year. And book-ending the 12 months, almost exactly, are Miriam Lord's observations of the Dáil trying to come to terms with the Government's proposals for the National Asset Management Agency.

The effects of the crisis have been terrifying for most, tragic for some: jobs have been lost and dreams have gone up in smoke; pensions have vanished and with them retirement nest eggs, often held in bank shares, which for a time were almost worthless and today remain far, far below their value of 18 months ago. The extraordinary failure of the financial system, and of the regulatory authorities that failed in their duty to police it, has convulsed politics and angered voters, especially those who wonder why none of the people directly responsible is being held to account, in contrast to other countries.

These issues and many others held the attention of *Irish Times* journalists over the past 12 months, but especially those reporting politics and business, and those hired to express opinions. There are, of course, many other subjects touched upon by my colleagues whose work appears in the following pages. But the crisis remains ablaze and it will be some time before we know whether decisions taken on Nama, on the Lisbon Treaty second referendum and on the Budget make matters worse or help put the country firmly on the long road to recovery.

It has been a testing year – journalistically and commercially – for *The Irish Times*. The values of independent journalism, beholden to no one but our readers, were defended successfully by the Editor who won the unanimous support of the Supreme Court. It was a fitting triumph in our 150th year, which also saw the death of Major McDowell, the man who, in setting up The Irish Times Trust, guaranteed that independence and did more than anyone else to create today's *Irish Times*.

Few men leave such a legacy. His obituary appears in this volume.

Peter Murtagh
Managing Editor
17 September 2009

Journalists and Photographers

David Adams is an *Irish Times* columnist.

Paddy Agnew is Rome Correspondent.

Eileen Battersby is Literary Correspondent.

Arthur Beesley is Senior Business Correspondent.

Brian Boyd is a freelance journalist specialising in the pop music industry and comedy.

Adam Brophy is a stay-at-home father who writes a weekly column, a Dad's Life, in the HEALTHplus supplement.

Vincent Browne is an *Irish Times* columnist and broadcaster.

Elaine Byrne is a columnist specialising in issues of political ethics and corruption.

Sarah Carey is an *Irish Times* columnist.

Jim Carroll is a music critic with *The Irish Times* and blogs on the newspaper's web, *irishtimes.com*.

Tony Clayton-Lea is a music critic.

Stephen Collins is Political Editor.

Clifford Coonan is Beijing Correspondent.

Kevin Cullen is a journalist with *The Boston Globe* newspaper and also writes occasionally for *The Irish Times*.

Kilian Doyle works on the *Irish Times* website, *irishtimes.com*, and writes a column, Emissions, in the paper's Motors supplement.

Keith Duggan is an *Irish Times* sports writer.

Michael Dwyer is Film Critic.

Editorials are unsigned but are published in the name of the Editor.

Newton Emerson is a satirical writer whose column, Newton's Optic, appears weekly.

Garret FitzGerald is an *Irish Times* columnist.

Mary Fitzgerald is Foreign Affairs Correspondent.

Quentin Fottrell is a freelance writer and *Irish Times* radio critic.

John Gibbons is a columnist specialising in global warming and environmental issues in general.

Ciarán Hancock is Business Affairs Correspondent.

Michael Harding is a freelance writer who bases himself in Mullingar from where he surveys his life and the world about him.

Shane Hegarty is an *Irish Times* journalist and writes a column, Present Tense, in WeekendReview.

Mark Hennessy is London Editor since August 2009. Previously he was Political Correspondent.

Tom Hennigan is a freelance journalist based in South America.

Kate Holmquist writes a weekly column, Give Me a Break.

Ann Marie Hourihane is an *Irish Times* columnist.

Tom Humphries is a sports journalist and author of LockerRoom, a weekly sideways glance at the world of sports.

Róisín Ingle is feature writer, columnist in the *Irish Times* Magazine and a mother.

Morgan Kelly is Professor of Economics in University College Dublin. His several articles in the newspaper on the property bubble and subsequent banking crisis were attacked strongly by vested interest critics but others praised his analysis, including a senior judge.

Miriam Lord is a political sketch writer.

Lara Marlowe is Washington Correspondent since August 2009. Previously she was Paris Correspondent.

Seán Moran is GAA Correspondent.

Gerry Moriarty is Northern Editor.

Bryan Mukandi is an *Irish Times* blogger. He is from Zimbabwe but lives in Galway. His blog is called Outsidein.

Peter Murtagh is a Managing Editor of *The Irish Times* and edits the daily Opinion and Analysis pages.

Ruadhán Mac Cormaic is Migration Correspondent.

Fiona McCann is a freelance journalist.

Frank McDonald is Environment Editor.

Patsy McGarry is Religious Affairs Correspondent.

Harry McGee is a member of the political staff.

Ronan McGreevy is an *Irish Times* reporter.

John McManus is Business Editor.

Frank McNally writes An Irishman's Diary.

David McNeill is a freelance journalist based in Tokyo.

Yvonne Nolan is a freelance writer.

Carl O'Brien is Social Affairs Correspondent.

Ross O'Carroll-Kelly is the *nom de guerre* of Paul Howard.

Brian O'Connor is Racing Correspondent.

Fintan O'Toole is an Assistant Editor and an *Irish Times* columnist.

Michael Parsons is a local correspondent based in Kilkenny.

Conor Pope works on *The Irish Times* website and writes PriceWatch, a weekly probing of the cost of consumer durables.

Philip Reid is Golf Correspondent.

Derek Scally is Berlin Correspondent.

Kathy Sheridan is an *Irish Times* journalist.

Denis Staunton is Foreign Editor. He was Washington Correspondent until his appointment in July 2009.

Gerry Thornley is Rugby Correspondent.

Michael Viney writes Another Life, a column about the natural world, from his home overlooking the Atlantic in west Mayo.

Arminta Wallace is an *Irish Times* journalist.

John Waters is an *Irish Times* columnist.

Johnny Watterson is an *Irish Times* sports writer.

Noel Whelan is a columnist specialising in politics and the media.

Photographers and illustrators whose work features in this year's edition include *Irish Times* staff members and external contributors Alan Betson, Cyril Byrne, Aongus Collins, Brenda Fitzsimons, Matt Kavanagh, Eric Luke, Dara Mac Dónaill, Frank Miller, Bryan O'Brien, David Sleator, Martyn Turner and Michael Viney.

The Irish Times Book of the Year 2009 also features the work of freelance photographers, illustrators or photographers attached to Irish and international photo agencies, including: AP/Boston Globe; AP/The Des Moines Register, Mary Chind; AP/Doug Mills; AP/Guardia Forestale; AP Photo; AP Photo/Achmad Ibrahim; Julien Behal/PA; Patrick Bolger; Chris Carlson/AP; Niall Carson/PA Wire; Gareth Chaney/Collins; William Cherry/Presseye.com; Stephen Collins/Collins; James Connolly; Gareth Copley/PA; Courtpix; Aidan Crawley; Naoise Culhane/Maxpix; Ray Demski; Peter Dorney/Digital Post Production; James Flynn/APX; Alessandro Garofalo/ Reuters; Getty Images; Doug Hamilton; Keith Heneghan/Phocus; Tom Honan/ INPHO; Robert Jaeger/AP; Brigitte

Lacombe; Sasko Lazarov/Photocall Ireland; Justin Mac Innes/Mac Innes Photography; Don MacMonagle; Daragh Mac Sweeney/Provision; Michael Mac Sweeney/Provision; Colm Mahady/Fennells; Maxwells; Kevin Mazur/WireImage; Michael McCarthy; Eoin McGarvey; David McNew/Getty Images; Charles McQuillan/Pacemaker; MJ Memorial/Kevin Mazur/AP; Paul Mohan/Sportsfile; Peter Morrison/AP; Anja Niedringhaus/AP; Garry O'Neill; Matt Sayles/AP; J. Scott Applewhite/AP; Nikola Solic/Reuters; Pete Souza/Reuters; Dylan Vaughan; Domnick Walsh/Eye Focus; Peter Wilcock; Mark Wilson/Bloomberg.

SATURDAY, 4 OCTOBER 2008

24 Hours that Brought Irish Banks back from the Brink

Mark Hennessy

Ireland's top bankers do not usually play a supplicant's role. Sitting, however, in Taoiseach Brian Cowen's oak-lined office shortly before midnight on Monday, underneath a portrait of Éamon de Valera, there was little doubt about how much trouble they were in.

The bankers uneasily waiting there were Eugene Sheehy and Dermot Gleeson, chief executive and chairman of Allied Irish Bank (AIB) respectively, and their two counterparts from Bank of Ireland, Brian Goggin and Richard Burrows.

Four hours earlier, following a disastrous pounding for Irish bank shares on the stock markets, the four had hurriedly sought a meeting with Cowen and Minister for Finance Brian Lenihan.

Having arrived at Government Buildings at 9.30 p.m., they were taken to the Sycamore Room, once so beloved of Charles J. Haughey, and left to wait, and wait. Nearby, Cowen was chairing another meeting, involving Central Bank governor John Hurley and the chief executive of the Financial Regulator, Pat Neary.

Two hours elapsed before the bankers, who had been left on their own, were called in before Cowen and Lenihan, who asked some questions, but mostly listened. The bankers' message was not that Anglo Irish Bank was about to collapse; or that Irish Nationwide was on the brink, though both had cash shortages to face on Tuesday and Wednesday. Instead, it was that they themselves were facing a crisis.

'(They) made it clear to us that liquidity was drying up in the Irish banking system and the

Cartoon by Martyn Turner.

maturity dates for the various loans they need to fund their business were shortening all the time and reaching dangerous levels of exposure in terms of time limits,' Lenihan would later explain to the Seanad.

The air of crisis had mounted on Monday as the collapse in the banks' share value became more brutally evident on the stock markets. David Doyle, secretary general of the Department of Finance, Hurley, Neary and others were in close contact throughout, before heading to Government Buildings after the 4.30 p.m. close of markets.

The option eventually chosen – to guarantee 'the deposits, loans and obligations' of the six Irish banks – had been circulating within the Department of Finance, the Central Bank and Government Buildings for over two weeks. The idea was also circulating elsewhere and economist David McWilliams argued strongly for it in a column in the *Sunday Business Post* last Sunday. McWilliams also spoke to the Green Party leader, John Gormley, four days before the article. Since then, he has claimed credit for the idea, to the quiet fury of State officials.

In the weeks leading up to the decision, the Government had also considered nationalisation of one of the banks, whereby it could be run as a going concern with new capital, or simply run down. In the fortnight before the eruption of the crisis, Department of Finance officials favoured getting new investors for any crisis-hit bank, rather than a State takeover.

Indeed, AIB and Bank of Ireland were asked by, or before, last weekend by the Central Bank to inject capital into Anglo Irish, according to numerous sources. However, the two baulked, frightened by Anglo's €110 billion loan book. The proposal looked less attractive in light of institutional investors' reactions and the Government's refusal to underwrite the deal, and guarantee them against losses.

After markets closed on Monday, Lenihan came from the nearby Department of Finance at 6 p.m., and was soon closeted with Cowen; Attorney General Paul Gallagher; Central Bank governor Hurley; Tony Grimes, the Central Bank's director general; Financial Regulator Neary; the department's second secretary general, Kevin Cardiff, and assistant secretary, William Beausang. Key advisers, such as Joe Lennon, Peter Clinch – a relative newcomer to Government Buildings but already known as 'The Prof' – and Eoghan Ó Neachtain were also on hand.

By then, it was clear to those in Government that some of the institutions could be facing disaster if they were to sustain another such day, but hope remained that the US Congress would pass the $700 billion bailout and restore stability, if only for a time.

Up until then, Cowen and Lenihan had decided that radical action had to be taken, but they hoped that it could be delayed until the weekend when markets were closed. However, a note sent into the meeting detailing the result of the Washington vote ended any such timetable. A second note followed shortly afterwards telling of AIB and Bank of Ireland's call to meet urgently.

A number of Ministers, including Micheál Martin, Mary Coughlan and Noel Dempsey, were put on notice that a Cabinet decision would have to be reached over the telephone later that night, which are known as 'incorporeal' meetings when Ministers cannot be brought together in time.

By then, the European Commission had learned 'something serious was up in Dublin'; but not its detail. Cowen fretted that the press would learn details early.

Once brought into the meeting, the four bankers made their stark presentation and left. The actions to be taken next were not discussed in front of them. But the next move was not long in coming: all six Irish banks would be fully underwritten. Other non-Irish banks operating here would be considered on a case-by-case basis.

Brought back into the meeting, the proposal was put to the bankers, but they were given time

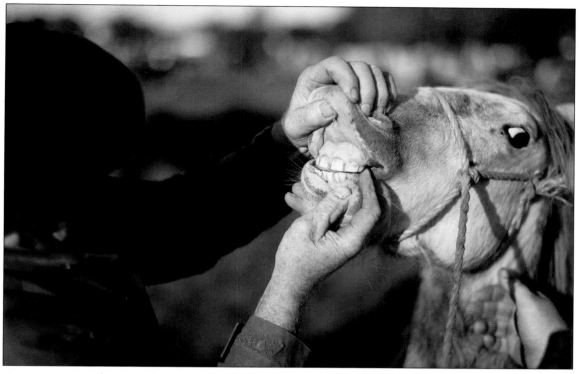

A man examines a horse's teeth at the Ballinasloe Horse Fair. The oldest horse fair in Europe attracts thousands of traders and visitors to the Co. Galway town every year. Photograph: Julien Behal/PA.

'to reflect', and to consult with colleagues. Sheehy and Gleeson returned to the Sycamore Room, while Goggin and Burrows held hushed calls on the corridor, before they were ushered into the building's dining room for privacy. Grimes and Neary, for the Central Bank and regulator respectively, were in contact with other bank chief executives.

By now, the occupants of Government Buildings were without food or bottled water. The crate of Spar sandwiches that had been brought in earlier had long since disappeared while officials watched RTÉ's *Questions and Answers*.

The issue of the foreign-owned banks operating here has been highlighted by the Opposition since, as they argue that the Government has unknowingly written a blank cheque. However, the Attorney General had raised the issue of those banks; and of the dangers posed by foreign subsidiaries owned, or part-owned, by the Irish banks themselves during Monday night's talks.

'Our first obligation was to the Irish banks but it was always known that we would have to consider foreign-owned banks,' said one figure, closely associated with the events.

Preparation on a press release had begun shortly after 9 p.m. – even before the bankers had arrived in Government Buildings. It was drafted and redrafted throughout the night but the substance did not change. During this work, the phrase 'serious disturbance in the economy' was removed before it was hurriedly returned because it could offer some protection in time against any European Union challenge on state aid rules.

Under EU law, member states have the freedom to intervene to prevent a 'systemic' collapse in the national banks, though the Irish action has not been met warmly there. However, mergers valued at €5 billion or over must be approved by Brussels, leaving a question mark over Lenihan's powers to approve unions.

While a number of senior Ministers had already been put on notice, the Cabinet secretariat contacted the remainder, telling them to be ready for the 'incorporeal' meeting between 1 a.m. and 2 a.m. Even then, most Ministers were not told exactly of the decision's scope. Willie O'Dea was woken shortly after 1 a.m. by his ringing mobile, but it had gone to voicemail by the time he got to it. The landline by his bed rang seconds later.

Green Party leader John Gormley had more knowledge than most of an imminent banking crisis but, up until then, the secretariat had failed to make contact with him because his mobile had run out of power. In the end, Irishtown Garda station was called, and they sent a garda to his Ringsend home to wake him and ask him to ring the Taoiseach's office.

Thereafter, the secretariat rang all the Ministers again, and detailed the proposal, asking for their decision. All agreed to it. Martin was in Newark Airport returning to Ireland from the United Nations General Assembly, when he went to a private room to take the call.

Once the bankers left at 3.30 a.m., Cowen told Lenihan to go home to bed for two hours to ready himself for the crucial round of early-morning press interviews and calls, before he too left at 5.45 a.m., also for little more than two hours.

Back in his office, before 6 a.m., Lenihan called the French finance minister and the current chairwoman of EU finance ministers, Christine Lagarde, and the Luxembourg prime minister, Jean Claude Juncker, who heads the group of euro zone member states, and, mostly in French, briefed them on Ireland's decision.

An advance copy of the decision had been sent at 4.30 a.m. to the European Central Bank, followed by a call from John Hurley to its head, Jean-Claude Trichet. Lenihan called Fine Gael leader Enda Kenny, while the latter was walking around TV3's *Ireland AM* studio, waiting to go on air for a pre-arranged interview.

Lenihan also called Labour leader Eamon Gilmore. Conversations later took place with Fine Gael finance spokesman Richard Bruton and his Labour counterpart Joan Burton.

A call to RTÉ's George Lee rang out, so, with time of the essence, his colleague David Murphy was called instead, getting the interview with Lenihan on to the airwaves first.

The statement entered the public arena at 6.45 a.m., causing consternation among the banks not immediately included along with the six Irish institutions. And the consternation made itself heard very, very quickly – and directly to the man next in line for the throne of England.

Furious at the news, Sir Fred 'The Shred' Godwin, chief executive of Ulster Bank's parent, Royal Bank of Scotland, called Prince Charles, as well as the British prime minister, Gordon Brown, sources say.

Brown's chancellor of the exchequer, Alistair Darling, quickly called Lenihan. 'He was very unhappy, let's put it that way,' said one closely involved in the night's events. Demanding a reversal of the decision, Darling warned that money would flood out of British banks. Lenihan listened, but gave no succour and said he had to protect Ireland's interests. Later, he called again.

Brown rang Cowen later. Though he expressed concern, he did not ask for the guarantee to be stopped, but he did urge Cowen to do something for UK bank subsidiaries operating here. Replying, Cowen, no doubt conscious of the lack of warning by London when it nationalised Northern Rock 12 months ago, said Ireland had to look after its own banks. However, Brown has not left the issue rest, speaking twice against it in telephone calls this week to the President of the European Commission, José Manuel Barroso.

Now empty of bankers, the Sycamore Room hours later hosted Fianna Fáil Ministers for their usual pre-Cabinet breakfast meeting at 8.30 a.m. Some were clearly stunned by the night's events. Exhausted, Cowen made no effort to hide the situation's gravity. One of those present reported the Taoiseach saying: 'We came very close to the brink.'

By then, Cowen had already become annoyed by the response of Labour's Joan Burton, and he became even more irritated by her as the week progressed. But the markets had opened and the tidings were good: 'That helped to settle people. We took heart from that,' a Government source said.

Lenihan dropped in briefly, adrenaline-pumped. 'I was surprised at how sprightly he looked,' said one colleague, impressed by his performance since the decision was made.

One senior banker turned up at the Department of Finance offices in Merrion Street without an appointment, demanding to see Lenihan. Sources say he declared: 'You're trying to screw us.' It had been reported that the banker was Ulster Bank chief executive Cormac McCarthy, but that is not the case.

Once Cowen had met Gormley and Mary Harney for their usual pre-Cabinet tête-à-tête, the full meeting of Ministers began, about 45 minutes late. Here, Lenihan and A.G. Gallagher went through the draft legislation line-by-line, facing questions quickly from Tánaiste Mary Coughlan and Minister for Agriculture Brendan Smith.

Both representing Border constituencies, they had already been contacted by mobile phone by infuriated officials in Ulster Bank on their way to the meeting in their ministerial cars.

The issue of foreign subsidiaries had not been raised with other Ministers before they had given their assent in the earlier 'incorporeal' contacts. But both Smith and Coughlan raised it now.

Lenihan said the Irish-regulated banks were first and he would 'wait and see' about everybody else. Asked about the emergency plan's possible cost, Lenihan told colleagues that banks will be levied if one of them does collapse, and that these payments would be used to settle the defunct bank's debts before the State will have to face any bill.

'An awful lot is about confidence,' said one Cabinet Minister. 'Bankers around Dublin were doing as much damage as anybody outside them because they were all trying to get their own advantage . . . It is all right as long as the guarantees are not called in.'

MONDAY, 6 OCTOBER 2008

No Reason to Expect Bank Chiefs to be Held to Account

Business Opinion, by John McManus

Imagine, if you will, that you are Brian Cowen. You are in your office in Government Buildings, it's coming up to midnight and the heads of the State's two big banks are standing cap in hand on the carpet.

They have told you in no uncertain terms that if the Government does not guarantee the Irish banks before the markets open in the morning, there will be a catastrophe. You have no choice but to take them at their word; no government can let the two biggest retail banks fail. Your first question is pretty simple: 'How much do you need?' They tell you: '€400 billion.' You say: 'Okay.'

You would like to think that your next question is: 'Tell me, Mr (Eugene) Sheehy and Mr (Brian) Goggin, about the arrangements you have put in place to minimise disruption caused by your resignations.'

Was the question asked? I doubt it. Were the resignations tendered unasked? I doubt it even more. And that is a problem.

There is, of course, a need to be pragmatic in the sort of circumstances in which we find ourselves. This is not the time for pointless gestures and the unpalatable truth is that the people who steered the banks into this mess may be the best people to get them out of it.

This argument applies to all the actors in the drama, from the regulators right up to the Taoiseach himself, who was minister for finance when the property market went into hyperdrive.

Indeed the extent to which everybody in the State bought into the property boom makes it hard really to single out one or two individuals without making them into nothing more than scapegoats. I for one am not aware of anyone writing to Sheehy or Goggin and refusing mortgages on the basis that they were concerned that AIB and Bank of Ireland's capital bases might not be able to sustain them.

More pertinently, we all bought into the property market story. Along with our banks and our Government, we happily lived the fairy tale whereby a semi-detached house in Dublin was worth more than a castle in Bavaria. Indeed, you could almost go as far as to say there is something rather honest about the lack of heads rolling in the Irish bank rescue package.

In pretty much every major bank rescue that has taken place on both sides of the Atlantic in recent months, the heads of the chief executives of the banks have been demanded as part of the price. But the people who demanded these heads are the same regulators and politicians who failed to rein in the banks. The point is most neatly illustrated by US treasury secretary Hank Paulson. Having seen what was happening from the inside as the head of Goldman Sachs, he joined the Bush administration two years ago, but failed to take action.

Unfortunately, it's not really credible to argue that the reason no one is being held to account in Ireland for what happened to the banks is because

An Indonesian trader reacts on the trading floor of the Jakarta stock exchange as the country's benchmark stock index plunged 10 per cent. Photograph: AP Photo/Achmad Ibrahim.

of our unique national insight into the complexities of the moral hazard argument. Rather, it is just another manifestation of one of the less than attractive aspects of Irish political and business life: We don't do personal accountability.

Brian Cowen and his colleagues could hardly ask Sheehy and Goggin to pay the price for the near collapse of the banks, having let his predecessor as taoiseach off the hook for years over his increasingly bizarre explanations about how he bought his house and where he got his money. If that sorry episode is any yardstick of the Cabinet's views on personal accountability and standards, the chief executives of the Irish banks can sleep easy.

Equally, Sheehy and Goggin belong to an elite business culture that didn't and still really doesn't understand why Jim Flavin had no option but to resign after being found to have broken the law on insider trading. Whatever pressure comes for them to take responsibility for the effective failure of their banks will not come from their peers.

And you would have to wonder if that is not one of the reasons we got ourselves into this whole mess to begin with. The failure to hold the chief executives of the banks accountable for their near collapse sends a signal that they had no obligation to manage their banks in a way that might be loosely termed responsible. They did not have to take regard of the national interest, despite knowing that when it came down to it — as it did last Monday — the taxpayer would back them up.

It also says that you can draw down a massive salary, make a mess of things and not only keep your job, but probably earn a bonus for sorting out the mess. Possibly the only justification for the massive salaries paid in banking is that if you screw up you lose your job.

We will hear a lot in the coming days about public interest and how much the banks will be paying for the guarantee. It would be nice to hear something about accountability, but that is not the Government's strong suit.

Playing King for a Daybreak

Displaced in Mullingar, by Michael Harding

I stayed in a chateau in France, which was built hundreds of years ago and is still in the hands of the same family, though the interior needs some re-plastering and a complete overhaul of the electrical system.

I was there for a wedding. The groom, and heir to the estate, works in Paris, but he made his vows in the local village church and carried his bride away on the back of a bike. Later in the afternoon, we drank champagne on the lawn, served by waiters in tuxedos.

A little boy directed traffic on the avenue. He wore an armband and blew into an ancient bugle as he marched up and down. I asked him why he made so much noise. He told me he was calling the deer.

The banquet, by candlelight, was in the main hall. Baroque plasterwork adorned the ceilings and the walls were covered with canvas tapestries, painted more than a century ago by the groom's great-grandfather, an eccentric artist who had a passionate interest in Joan of Arc.

We supped at long tables, warmed by a huge log fire, above which was a mantelpiece of stone, hand-carved to depict a hunter with his hunting hounds, all in a state of shock as they confronted a stag with a Christian cross sticking out of its forehead.

The dinner was a stew of 50 chickens, served in crocks, followed by trays of cheese. Everyone poked each cheese and discussed its merit. The bride put three varieties on my plate and suggested I eat the mild one first, so that I would not blunt my palate with the stronger cheese. I did her bidding, to the letter.

Then some guests began to sniff and poke at a lump of Irish Cheddar, as if they were surprised

Veronika Volkova models a Donna Karan dark green, silk evening dress at the Harvey Nichols Autumn/Winter Collection launched in Dublin. Photograph: Eric Luke.

that Ireland did cheese. I felt a bit uneasy, socially, for a moment, until the boss man at the top table took a few nibbles and declared that indeed the Irish cheese was excellent. After that I relaxed and took to the drink, while the other Irish guests produced their fiddles, flutes and concertinas and let loose a fury of jigs and reels.

I suppose there is only so much refinement human beings can endure, and there is nothing like a few jigs to rip asunder the affectations of a highly mannered society. Men with delicately perfumed wrists and manicured fingernails, and women who use binoculars and wear silk shawls at Fontainebleau in the evening sun, lost the run of

themselves completely, as polkas bounced off the high ceilings. The climax came when two little girls from Co. Clare stepped on to the floor with sweeping brushes and danced the broom dance.

My bedroom, flooded by moonlight, was at the end of a long corridor, and it occurred to me that in Mullingar I often gaze at the very same moon when I wake in the night and go down to the kitchen to get a glass of water.

On my way back upstairs in Mullingar, I have a choice of three toilets: one under the stairs, one at the top of the stairs, and one en suite. But in the grand chateau of Beauregard there were only two lavatories, both far from my corridor, and I was obliged to go down the winding staircase to the front hall at five o'clock in the morning, unlatch the ancient doors and step out into France.

Solitude is a great consolation for those who are always lonely in a crowd, and so the morning mist and the empty lawns were a great comfort to me after a night of such society.

In west Cavan years ago, there was nothing more splendid, after a night of music and drink, than to go out the door into the fields at dawn for relief, and hear the birds at it in the trees, like the Berlin Philharmonic under Karajan.

France, too, looked good at dawn: a soft September fog floated over the duck pond, though there was no birdsong. I crossed the gravel forecourt and found a spot well hidden by foliage, where I relieved myself, like any king or peasant of ancient days who might find himself alone in the universe when all the music is over.

Nothing moved; not even the big stag that eyed me from across the duck pond.

SATURDAY, 11 OCTOBER 2008

Cashing in on the Global Crunch

Arthur Beesley, in New York

Sam Pande (45) owns a bar in New York. In 1992, when the city's property market was in one of its periodic downturns, he bought an apartment in a foreclosure auction for $40,000 upfront and $327 in monthly maintenance fees. The deal worked fine.

'It was an amazing bargain,' he says. 'The same apartment was worth about $200,000 a year ago, before the market collapsed.' Pande is still well ahead on his investment, however, and now he's back for more. He's not the only one.

On Wednesday, in courtroom 130 of the New York state supreme court, about a dozen people have turned up for the weekly round of foreclosure auctions. Mobile phones buzz and there is agitated talk in different languages.

Manhattan properties are sold off here at 1 p.m. every Wednesday in auctions announced in the classified columns of newspapers. It's a dusty room, with filing cabinets lined up against wooden panelling. There's no judge here, no jury. In God we trust, reads the legend above the bench.

As the US economy slides into recession, not even the New York property market stands aloof. The city suffers to a lesser extent than outlying boroughs, but the market is coming down all the same. In places such as Syracuse and Buffalo, in upstate New York, foreclosure is widespread.

The loss of a home is painfully disruptive and marks the beginning of a traumatic and uncertain phase of life. Stories circulate here of stressed-out property owners, unable to make repayments, handing keys back to their lenders in despair. Some remain in their homes in desperation as banks take action against them. Many have nowhere else to go.

But other people are taking advantage of the situation. Although such purchases are not without risk, deals can be struck at 20-30 per cent less than the open-market value.

The foreclosure market thrives when the regular market goes down badly, but despite the bargains, the process is not without friction. 'A lot of time when these foreclosures happen the people are still in the house. If it's sold then they have to leave,' says Bill Mannion, an auctioneer and advertising agency owner who for 30 years has specialised in the sale of foreclosed property.

'They [the purchasers] have to get a marshal or a sheriff to evict them. On some of these co-op apartments I sell, they're sold to a third-party, somebody who shows up at the gate . . . People buy them with someone still living in them – the debtor or the shareholder are still living in there – and it's their responsibility to get them out.' While there are professionals who engage in foreclosure purchases for a living, there are also newcomers chasing an easy profit.

Keith Siilats, an Estonian hedge-fund executive, is one of those waiting for the action to begin on Wednesday. Aged 30, and living in New York for 10 years, he's on the look-out for his first investment property 'to hold or sell later'. Siilats is disappointed, however. He has his eye on a four-lot auction of properties in Manhattan and Brooklyn. But when Michael Gould, the attorney handling the transaction, arrives, he says the sale is off. 'It is postponed,' he says. 'It won't be happening today.'

A dwelling at 6 Convent Avenue is auctioned. Apart from the bid from the bank that foreclosed on the property's previous owner, there are no other bids.

The sum in question is $527,036. The process couldn't be more informal. The man who announces the start of bidding wears trainers and it is all over within a minute. As those in the courtroom look on in silence, a lawyer present attempts a joke. 'I'm going to do a dance later,' he says.

The collapse of the US housing market is at the root of the financial turmoil sweeping through the world. What started as a serious problem with subprime mortgages granted to people with little ability to pay back their loans has evolved into a deeper problem.

Although the weekend papers here still carry glossy adverts for multi-million-dollar apartments perched in towers high above the city, research points to ruinous decay in the US market at large.

The latest estimates from the Mortgage Bankers Association suggest the number of loans in the foreclosure process rose to 1.47 million in the April-June period this year. This was twice the number in foreclosure compared with the same period last year and almost three times as many as in 2006.

According to the *Wall Street Journal*, nearly one in six home-owners owe more on their mortgage than the property is worth. In some US areas, values are down 30 per cent from their peak. With

An estate agent's sign of the times in Pasadena, California. Photograph: David McNew/Getty Images.

job losses last month at their highest level for five years, the risk of mortgage defaults is rising by the day.

There's worse to come, Bill Mannion says. 'Over the last 20 years I've probably done at least 10,000 of these types of auctions. It's been getting busier lately. There's a lot more defaults, I think, coming around.

'It's trickling down slowly. I know that there's a lot of people in foreclosure now, but it seems that it takes a long time for these things to go through the works . . . It's easily a year delay from when you go into default before you actually have an auction.'

Mannion's office is on Broadway, not far from the supreme court building. On the bookshelf behind his seat, there's a huge gavel. Sirens wail intermittently from the street two floors down. Many home-owners are frantically engaged in efforts to stay afloat, he says. At present, about half of all foreclosure auctions are cancelled because owners retrieve the situation through renegotiation of their loan terms.

'You can pay up at the last minute. A lot of people do that. The banks are more than ever willing to work with you. The banks do not really want to do the foreclosure. It's expensive for them and, especially in this market, the last thing they want to do is take any non-performing loans back on their books,' he says. 'What the government is trying to do is make it easier for lenders to rewrite the face of a loan or to renegotiate the interest rates. I don't know how that is going to affect things yet; it's too soon to say. Nobody really knows how it's going to help.'

Mannion says the foreclosure market facilitates the churning of property, creating an opportunity for another owner. Asked, however, if he ever ponders on the difficulties encountered by people who lose their homes, he says it can be a 'nasty' enterprise. 'I do think about that sometimes,' he says. 'Sometimes it's sad. It really is. There are genuine hard-luck stories out there. There are people who have lost jobs, or through traumatic illnesses or even separations in their marriage and what have you.

'There's also some scam artists, some people who invested and they bought more than they could afford. There's a lot of that over there too. I've seen people that file bankruptcy to stop the sale – just a stalling tactic.

'I saw a woman bring a small child once and pinch the child to make the child cry to get sympathy. I literally saw her lean down to pinch the kid to make the kid cry so people would feel sorry for her that she was being foreclosed on. She needn't have done that, but it's a nasty business.'

TUESDAY, 14 OCTOBER 2008

The Mother of All Debs' Seasons

Give me a Break, by Kate Holmquist

It's Debs season and parents on Hysteria Lane are on stress alert. There's the cost of dresses, tuxes, hairdressers, spray-on tans, waxing, brow-shaping and make-up, plus the challenges of dealing with emotionally overloaded teenagers embarking on university, job searches or gap years, but that's not what's really worrying them.

It's the alcohol, the sex and the prospect of having to pick up a psychologically-frazzled child from the hormone morass in time to focus on real life with some semblance of organisation. And no one's more worried than the parents of boys – especially the mothers.

'She's got him twisted around her little finger. She calls and he jumps. He's totally unfocused. I'm convinced it will cost him a hundred points in the Leaving Cert. Wouldn't say that to him, though. I have to be nice to her.'

'Have you noticed that they're more well-endowed these days? Did you see them in those dresses at the parents' reception the night of the debs? It nearly convinced me to have a breast enhancement. We weren't that big. No way.'

'It's the nutrition. Hormones in the meat, maybe.'

'It's the push-up bras!'

'And the hair! Teased up about a foot high and slicked back. They all looked the same!'

'The Stepford Debs.'

'I know! The Dublin 4 debs more like.'

'That little tease is not getting her hooks into my son.'

'Thank God my son isn't serious about the girl he brought.'

'How do you know?'

The tinkling of a coffee spoon serves as a dramatic pause at this point. 'He said he was only bringing her to the debs because he wanted to get drunk and have a snog.'

A cappuccino cup lands heavily on its saucer. 'He actually said that? What sort of girl is she?'

The name of a posh south Dublin girl's school is mentioned. 'They're not all like that, of course. I'd hope that he would treat her properly.'

'Did [husband's name] have a talk with him?'

'I don't like to get involved in that. It's between father and son.'

'I know what you mean. But I still have the urge to toss a couple of boxes of condoms into the cart in Tesco and leave them lying around. I don't want my son to be – you know . . .'

A silence then.

'They're good boys. Mine came home at 7 a.m. and he wasn't drunk.'

Roberta Rowat and Ben Kelly O'Brien (5) from Gorey, Co. Wexford, help launch Trick or Treat for Temple Street at the Botanic Gardens, Glasnevin, in aid of the children's hospital in Dublin. Photograph: Colm Mahady/Fennells.

One of the mothers pulls her mobile phone/camera out of her bag and shows it to her companion. 'There they are.'

'Oh my God! That's not natural. Couldn't BE! You think she's had a boob job?'

'No – her hair! Those are extensions, definitely. And look at the way she's draping herself over his shoulder. OH MY GOD!'

'Pure Hollywood. I know. That's what's freaking me out.'

'We weren't like that, sure we weren't?'

'Not even in our dreams.'

The other mother pulls out her phone and shows it to her friend. (It takes total self-control on my part not to sneak a peak.)

'Ahhh, look at him!'

'It's not a great picture.'

'So handsome . . . they were babies only yesterday . . . remember when they were in Montessori? The little hand-prints they gave us on Mother's Day?'

'I still have mine.'

'Me too.'

Another silence. My waiter appears. I've finished my espresso and should be going but I need to know how this story ends, so I order another coffee.

'I always swore I'd never be one of those possessive Irish mothers,' one of the women says.

'So did I, but look at the reality. I've been married for 20 years to a man with a possessive Irish mother and, damn it, I'm going to give as good as I got. My baby boy is mine. He's not going anywhere.'

Then she produces her own mobile phone/camera. She shows the screen to her friend, who says, 'She looks familiar.'

'Please tell me you haven't seen this girl advertising on Facebook.'

What is it about mothers and their sons? That night, I watch TV with my 11-year-old son and enjoy every precious moment when he decides to snuggle up beside me. I can already feel the goodbyes.

New Generation of Kung Fu Crazy Chinese Discovering Bruce Lee

Clifford Coonan, in Beijing

Bruce Lee's compact body is coated with sweat and ripples with muscles; he seems impervious to the razor slashes across his midriff. Glaring from beneath fierce eyebrows at the fool who has chosen to cross him, he tenses those legendary fists before striking out. Scores of villains are no match for him. Lee always prevails.

A sign outside Huangpu park in Shanghai saying 'No Dogs or Chinese' causes unbearable anger. His lip curls and the man born in the Hour of the Dragon in the Year of the Dragon tears down the sign and smashes the offending warning into pieces with an overhead kick.

'I am Chinese,' he yells as he defeats another would-be oppressor, very often a Japanese or Russian villain.

The Way of the Dragon has never been so popular in China. Bruce Lee is a national hero in kung fu crazy China for the way he embodied Chinese pride and nationalism in his movies, but many in mainland China missed him the first time around in the early 1970s because films like *Enter the Dragon* and *Fists of Fury* were banned by Mao as spiritual pollution and rightist sentimentality.

China's state broadcaster, China Central Television, is setting the record straight this week with the start of a 50-part prime-time series on him, *The Legend of Bruce Lee*.

It was shot in Lee's ancestral home in Shunde, in southern China's Guangdong province, as well as Macau, the US, Italy and Thailand, and took nine months to make at a cost of 50 million yuan (€5.35 million). It has pride of place in the evening

Defence minister Willie O'Dea at the PDforra conference in Westport, Co. Mayo. Photograph: Keith Heneghan/ Phocus.

schedule, with two hour-long episodes shown consecutively every night.

Bruce Lee is largely credited with reviving interest in the ancient art of kung fu in Hong Kong, and subsequently China, and the whole country is crazy about martial arts. China wanted to include kung fu in the Olympics in August but was turned down, instead staging a separate kung fu competition.

The quick-fire kung fu moves and often sur-really dubbed dialogue, combined with Lee's incredible athleticism, transformed the martial arts movie and his films quickly achieved cult status.

In his films he is always called Little Dragon and his association with the powerful dragon symbol is central to his philosophy.

What Lee himself would have thought of his fame in China is hard to say. He was certainly a nationalist, but he was also a Hong Konger. During his heyday the Cultural Revolution was at its height and there were a lot of tensions across the border with Hong Kong. Until Hong Kong was returned to China in 1997, many in the colony had an uneasy relationship with the People's Republic, the antithesis of its free-wheeling capitalism.

Lee was born in November 1940 in San Francisco and raised in Hong Kong, before his father sent him back to the US after a brawl as a youngster. As well as his martial prowess, he was also a ballroom dancing champion.

He made 46 kung fu movies, and his popularity around the world paved the way for stars like Jackie Chan and inspired film makers like Quentin Tarantino. But he could have been even bigger. Lee was just 32 when he died in 1973, while starring in and directing the *Game of Death* in Hong Kong, less than a month after the release of *Enter the Dragon*, the movie which turned him into an international star.

His death is a source of some mystery and

there were all kinds of rumours. The discovery of cannabis in his blood led to speculation of a drug overdose. Triad crime gangs were rumoured to have poisoned him; another popular theory was that he was simply too fit and his veins burst under the sheer strain. The official version is he died of a brain haemorrhage.

Mainland Chinese only started watching Bruce Lee films in the 1980s, when videos of classic movies like *The Chinese Connection* became available, but his legend has not ebbed. A theme park, complete with a statue, a memorial hall, conference centre and martial arts academy, is being built in Shunde.

Lee is a resonant figure for the Chinese because he always emphasised power and resolve in the face of adversity, particularly from foreign oppressors. He reserved much of his wrath for the Japanese — post-second World War humiliation was felt even more strongly in the 1970s.

The television series is attracting keen worldwide interest, both in places with a large Chinese diaspora like Malaysia and Singapore, and further afield in the US and Korea. The producers are confident they can sell the series abroad at $100,000 per episode. The website for the show has already received two million hits.

'The previous versions made in Hong Kong and Taiwan were too commercial. We hoped to make a good version,' said Zhang Hua, general manager of China Film Television Production Corporation. Lee's daughter, the actress Shannon Lee, has approved the script and is credited as an executive producer.

The series was originally scheduled to be aired before the Olympics, but was postponed because of the mourning period following the Sichuan earthquake.

Expect the Bruce Lee love affair to run and run. The latest news is that China's top director Zhang Yimou, who made *Hero* and directed the Olympic opening ceremony, has said he is keen to shoot a film version.

FRIDAY, 17 OCTOBER 2008

Dáil Hails Three Marys not so Full of Grace under Opposition Fire

Dáil Sketch, by Miriam Lord

With the help of God and a young policeman, Tánaiste Mary Coughlan made good her escape from Leinster House. It hadn't been a good morning.

The Taoiseach and his Minister for Finance were away in Brussels and the Tánaiste had been left to mind the shop. But she couldn't cope on her own with the rowdy Order of Business. So in the absence of the Two Brians, Dáil Éireann got the Three Marys.

As it turned out, this provided scant comfort to fretting Fianna Fáil backbenchers — not to mention all those anxious pensioners in their constituencies. At this stage, they were well into Three Hail Mary territory over the medical cards fiasco.

Coughlan should have expected fireworks at the Order of Business. She should have been ready for the best the Opposition could throw at her. But she didn't inspire confidence.

Tuesday's abolition of automatic medical cards for all citizens over the age of 70 provoked a furious reaction from pensioners and their families. Their anger saw Opposition politicians emerge as among the few winners from the Budget.

As the hostile public reaction intensified, it didn't take a genius to work out that, come Thursday, the Opposition would be enthusiastically wielding the cudgels on behalf of the 'angry' and 'confused' pensioners. Which is exactly what they did. With gusto. 'Expect a rolling maul this morning,' whispered a Labour adviser before the off.

Those Fianna Fáil backbenchers who had the stomach to turn up sat disconsolately. Perhaps they were only there to get some respite from their mobiles. A striking feature around Leinster House from early on was the sight of deputies from all parties talking animatedly into their phones. They were fielding calls from both their constituency staff and overwrought pensioners.

'What ages are they?' 'How much?' 'I understand.' 'Ring her back.' 'Write this down quick.' 'Tell him he's grand.' 'I'll get back to you on that.' 'It's not finalised yet.' 'Oh, for Jaysus' sake!'

In a way, the numbed Fianna Fáil backbenchers could empathise with the old folk. They too were angry and confused. What on earth was happening? How in God's name had their party upset the pensioners? They love the pensioners. They've always been great with the pensioners. Since when did they become so out of touch, for a measly €100 million?

Fine Gael got the maul rolling. 'Stupid, callous, own goal,' said Enda Kenny. 'You've put the fear of God into the old people,' said Jim O'Keeffe. 'Trampling on the old people of this country,' said

Dinny McGinley. 'You made a hames of the driving testing,' said James Bannon. 'Shush James!' said Fine Gael.

Labour piled in behind. 'Old people are worried,' said Eamon Gilmore. 'The banks will claim a €100 million back from their customers, but the old age pensioners won't be able to claim their money back from anybody,' said Joan Burton.

Fine Gael's Michael Ring, who regularly regales the Dáil with heart-rending tales of the latest 'poor wida woman' he's met while traversing the byways of Mayo, was near apoplectic. 'They put the old people on bicycles and took the medical cards off them!'

Across the floor, Government deputies sighed. They didn't need the Opposition to tell them the situation was a shambles – they were living it.

Mary Coughlan tried to explain. But she was contradicted at every turn. She whispered constantly to Mary Harney, who was sitting beside her. When a vote was called, Mary H had to move to

Cartoon by Martyn Turner.

her designated seat in the next section. She stayed there when hostilities resumed and Mary C was grilled again about the legislation underpinning the medical card measure.

The Tánaiste looked over at Mary H with pleading eyes. The Minister came back to sit beside her. Mary C, apparently unaware that Charlie McCreevy had made changes to the eligibility threshold in 1999, seemed to be seeking guidance from Mary H.

After a quick confab with the more experienced Minister for Health, she began talking about 'the context of a methodology'. The Opposition berated her for what they saw as her lack of understanding.

Coughlan, after another consultation with Mary Harney, then said that Minister for Social and Family Affairs Mary Hanafin would be looking after the legislation. Hanafin, you can't blame her, said nothing.

'Too many Marys!' taunted the Opposition. Some of them have now taken to referring to Mary Coughlan as Sarah Palin. As in 'I understand foreign policy – I can see Derry from my window.'

'The problem with the three Marys', chortled a Labour deputy in the corridor afterwards, 'is that Mary Harney started it, Mary Coughlan doesn't understand it and Mary Hanafin is trying to run a mile from it.'

Straight after the Order of Business, Mary Palin had to face another unruly group of politicians at a Fianna Fáil parliamentary party meeting. She told fuming backbenchers that she would make Brian Cowen put manners on them if they spoke out publicly about their disquiet.

Afterwards, the Government chief whip took to the plinth to give a briefing on the meeting, which had been addressed by Mary Harney. 'Very businesslike,' said the emollient Pat Carey. Over 30 people spoke over the course of two hours. They were 'very rational'. 'Fianna Fáil parliamentary party meetings don't do angry,' said Pat loftily, even though everyone knows they keep a pressure

hose handy for when they need to wash the blood off the walls.

Tánaiste Palin wasn't around to witness Pat's magnificently low-key performance. She didn't talk to the media. She was asked if she would by a reporter as they both went through the revolving doors. Instead, when she reached the exit, she looked to her left, saw a uniformed garda and requested him to escort her straight to the gate.

Dem pensioners can be vicious when riled.

WEDNESDAY, 22 OCTOBER 2008

Down and Outs the Order of the Day in Leinster House

Miriam Lord

The OAPS put their foot down. Brian Cowen climbed down. Bertie Ahern fell down. Mary Harney tried to calm them down. Fine Gael put a motion down. And after all that, everyone needed a lie down.

Which means they'll be fresh and ready for the fray today, when Fianna Fáil backbenchers face their worst nightmare: waves of belligerent pensioners marching on the Dáil in protest at the Government. They're dreading it. Then there's the former taoiseach.

The brother Maurice sniffed ruefully on radio the other day that if Bertie were still in power, the medical card debacle would never have happened. As it is, Bertie will be qualified and able to take his place among the retired and the lame today, waving his crutches with the best of them. He has broken his leg. Needless to say, once the news broke in Leinster House, the jokes started.

How did it happen? He was upstairs in St Luke's when he saw Michael Wall coming up to the front door carrying a bulging briefcase, and ran down the stairs so quickly that he lost his footing.

When he went to the Mater Private to get a plaster cast on his leg, guess the doctor's name? That's right, it was Paddy. Paddy the Plasterer. And did he jump, or was he pushed?

Bertie, we hear, is in plaster up to his knee. If he walks among the OAPs tomorrow, he'll be besieged by admirers asking to sign it. Although, judging by the sulphurous mood among the elderly medical-card holders who packed out St Andrew's Church in Westland Row yesterday morning, even Bertie's stock has plummeted.

They met after Brian Cowen's snap decision to convene a press conference just after breakfast to announce details of his climb-down over the medical cards. The announcement did little to assuage the anger of the pensioners.

For them now, it's a case of 'universality' or nothing. In the course of a few strange weeks, the population has taken to discussing solvency, liquidity and universality like it was the most normal thing in the world to do.

The press conference was a downbeat affair, after a shambles of a week saw Brian Cowen and Brian Lenihan go from being the heroes of the midnight hour during the banking crisis to the Bungle Brothers of Irish Politics.

If the Taoiseach, his Health Minister Mary Harney and Green leader John Gormley thought that their significantly revised medical card scheme for the over-70s would get them out of hot water, they were mistaken.

Junior Minister John Moloney discovered this to his cost when he was dispatched to calm the furious pensioners at their meeting in Westland Row church. It was to have taken place in a near-by hotel, but such was the crowd, they had to change venue.

And so, to add to the Government's misery, they were faced with the bizarre spectacle of a church full of raging OAPs, booing one of their Ministers off the altar. That scene will go down in history. Or maybe not. Wait until we see what happens today.

But back to yesterday's light relief. It would have been provided by Jackie Healy Rae, who gave a most entertaining press conference on the plinth explaining why he would now continue to support the Government despite the medical card debacle.

'It's sorted now. The people of Kerry have nothing to worry about,' soothed Jackie. As far as he was concerned, all of his constituents would be covered by the much higher eligibility threshold. It might be a problem for some people up in Dublin, but not where he comes from. 'We have nothing down in South Kerry, only bogs and turf and rushes,' he declared. Nobody believed a word, but it sounded lovely.

Meanwhile, the Fianna Fáil parliamentary party had met and had its ears soundly boxed by Biffo. Deputies crept outside, keeping a wary eye out for members of the media. None of them wanted to be seen talking to a journalist. They were already shell-shocked after the weekend back in the constituencies.

Yesterday, the sight and sound of the pensioners singing 'We Shall Overcome' put the fear of God into them.

Good old Bertie saved the day.

It may sound callous (it's all the rage in Government, if the Opposition is to be believed) but news of the former taoiseach falling down the stairs and breaking his day was treated with a certain amount of levity. Once, of course, it was ascertained that poor Bertie was not in any danger.

The information about what actually happened to him was scant. As evening gave way to night, reporters worked feverishly to try and uncover the circumstances surrounding his accident. It didn't help that the brief statement issued by his office was very short of detail.

Depending on who was canvassed, Bertie either broke his leg at his home in Beresford, Drumcondra, or in his office, St Luke's. St Luke's was the scene according to a party spokesman. One of his brothers said he thought it happened at his home.

Tommy Bolger from Ringsend in Dublin covers his ears and shouts as minister of state John Moloney attempts to speak at the Age Action Ireland protest meeting in St Andrew's Church in Westland Row, Dublin. Photographer: Dara Mac Dónaill.

Then the plot thickened when it emerged that the former taoiseach may have spent the later part of last weekend at a luxury hotel in the west of Ireland. Enquiries to sources close to Bertie would neither confirm nor deny this but they did say he attended the Mater Private (good pension) and he broke his leg.

This lack of clarity bug seems to have invaded every part of Fianna Fáil. It makes people suspicious, and they start to ask questions and read things into situations they shouldn't.

This is what has the pensioners in such a tizzy. They suspect, with the new measures to be introduced, that their medical card eligibility thresholds will be lowered, year on year, by a needy Government.

It's like the last decade or so never happened. We're back to the days of briefings on the plinth from a party elder, assuring the media that all is well within the ranks. This time, instead of 'The Yellow Rose of Finglas' – the late Jim Tunney – we have his constituency successor, Pat Carey. He's more mellow prose than yellow rose.

Then there's the return of dragging in the lame and the infirm for important votes. In 1983, Fianna Fáil's Seamus Kirk was brought from his sickbed for a leadership vote, and Dick Spring once struggled in on crutches.

Today, Bertie will hobble in to vote against Fine Gael's motion to restore medical cards to all the over-70s. Unless the pain gets too much, or the OAPs hold him hostage. Lucky him, if that's the case. Then, unlike his colleagues, he won't have to endure the embarrassment.

Enda Kenny said yesterday that the budget is now becoming 'a discussion document'. As Cowen legged it to China, hoping to catch a slow boat on the way home, the prospect of more climb-downs looks certain.

Fine Gael's Charlie Flanagan summed up the situation: 'It's the politics of headless chickens.' And the pensioners are out to pluck a few today.

MONDAY, 27 OCTOBER 2008

Spurs Unlikely to Strike it Rich with this Geezer

LockerRoom, by Tom Humphries

This column will eventually be about Tottenham Hotspur. I have seen how the column ends and if you plough through the powdery guff heaped at the front there will be, thrown in toward the end, some incredibly acute observations about Spurs being a metaphor for modern football. These observations are so startlingly perceptive and so on the button that it would be irresponsible to just begin a column with them. So . . .

I awoke the other morning through a gauze of dreamy semi-consciousness and beneath a looming mountain of work convinced myself I had the 'flu – not that spluttering, snotty, common-cold type of thing most of you people pass off as 'flu these days, but the real, chilled-marrow, two-weeks-off-school 'flu I used to get.

Except in my doziness the other morning I felt I was a young fella again and nobly suffering from this real 'flu and was reading, for the first time, Jack London's *Call of the Wild*.

As a very sick 11-year-old I had *Call of the Wild* on the floor beside the bed as the read of choice between shivers and sweats. Why? One of those parental gifts 'with a message'? There are plenty of people in the world colder than you are now, Sonny Jim.

Anyway, Jack London sparked a brief, boyish obsession. I consumed everything there was to

consume about Alaska and the Klondike and all places cold and shivery. Indeed, later in life one of my major triumphs as a sportswriter was persuading the Sports Editor to let me go to Alaska for a week to cover a sleigh race. I stayed in the Anchorage Hilton. Gold rush, my ass.

Anyway, the other morning (Brace yourself, Bridie! This paragraph may cause palpitations) I lay naked and cold but sweaty 'neath the eiderdown as memories of the Klondike segued into another favourite mental game I play when I am bored: the game I call 'Times and Places In History Where SportsWriters Would Be Even Less Useful Than They Are Now'.

The game is premised on there being no such thing as an anxious crowd that would part like the Red Sea upon hearing the words 'Let me through. I'm a sportswriter.'

If a plane-load of people came down in the Andes and the survivors were forced into cannibalism those who would get eaten first would be the disc jockeys and the sportswriters.

At the storming of the Bastille the sportswriter is the one saying, 'Non, non! You go ahead, mes amis. I'll mind the buffet and come in and get the post-storming quotes from the winners and the losers. D'accord?'

And as for the Gold Rush? We wouldn't have got past Soapy Smith.

Just about every prospector started the trek toward the Klondike in the town of Dyea rather than in its neighbour Skagway because in Skagway there was a man called Soapy Smith who would steal all your gear with his cunning swindles. Soapy ran the town.

(When I get a year off and €125 million I am going to make a movie about Soapy Smith, once described as 'the most gentlemanly crook that ever scuttled a ship or cut a throat'. Soapy is believed by many to have ordered the murder by Edward O'Kelly of Robert Ford, aka 'the dirty little coward who shot Mr Howard, he laid poor Jesse in his grave' – Mr Howard was the alias Jesse James was using at the time Ford shot him in the back of the head.)

Anyway sports hacks would have opted for Skagway every time. For the mileage. Those that were spared by Soapy would perish on the Chilkoot Pass, a place where an NUJ card bought precisely nothing in terms of privileges.

The Chilkoot Pass should in this current chilly economic climate be a metaphor for almost everything. The pass came at the end of a bleak and treacherous 33-mile trek and rose 1,000 feet in its last half mile.

There is a famous photograph of this section that shows a long, black line of hunched prospectors queueing like ants to climb the so-called Golden Staircase, 1,500 steps carved out of snow and ice and leading to the top of the pass.

This section was too steep for pack horses so you hid all your belongings (including the ton of food you were legally required to bring to avoid famine in the Klondike) down at the bottom of the pass and climbed up in that long, black line, bearing as much of your gear on your back as you could. You cached that at the top and then slid down the hill sitting on your shovel and began again. And again. And again. Many just went home after their first ride on the shovel. They made lives for themselves as sportswriters and disc jockeys.

The Chilkoot Pass is how football should be. All struggle. Many climbs up the mountain and many slides back down the mountain. No sugar-daddy syndrome like we see at Chelsea or Manchester City.

Spurs, once an elegant and serious club, have now abandoned all pretence at Continental sophistication after a long series of flirtations with men

Grape-munching Sibu, a 30-year-old male Bornean orang-utan, back in Dublin Zoo after seven years at Rhenen Zoo, in the Netherlands, for breeding purposes. Photograph: Alan Betson.

like Ossie Ardiles, Christian Gross, Jacques Santini, Martin Jol and Juande Ramos and have handed the club over to a man, 'Arry Redknapp, hewn out of the geezer tradition of El Tel Venables. They are sliding down the mountain on their shovel.

Perhaps they will have begun the next climb toward the top of the pass from the valley of next year's championship. If so it would be poignant but it would be meet and just.

Daniel Levy's stewardship of the club has been as thuggish and dopy as that of any of his recent predecessors. How is it you need a certain Fifa badge to coach a football team but no qualifications or guarantees at all to own one? Levy, in cahoots with the director of football, Damien Comolli, a bright man with an unclear role, has presided over the asset stripping of his own first team and ushered out (certainly in terms of Jol, Chris Hughton, Ramos and Gus Poyet) some of the smartest men in football. The solution is Redknapp, whose respectable tenure at Portsmouth was preceded by periods of mixed attainment which included guiding Southampton and Bournemouth to relegation. He is a punt.

It is a pity to find Spurs in such a position. They have always been one of those clubs with a distinct character of their own, and despite long periods without success they have always given off an aura of being prepared for success when it came, but perhaps a little too desperate to get it.

I can still remember the surprise I felt when they got relegated about 30 years ago. They just always have had the feel of a top-flight club. Back then they promptly sold Pat Jennings to Arsenal but somehow they got back up the next year. Not long afterwards they purchased Ardiles and Ricardo Villa, a sensational thing to do at the time.

That little glitch in their character, the need to gamble, the desire to skip around Chilkoot Pass, keeps undoing them though. They run back and forth from the arms of crafty geezers (Venables, Gerry Francis, 'Arry, Alan Sugar, etc.) to slick Continentals for whom they lack the patience.

They look around at Arsenal and Chelsea and the ache they feel must be pitiful.

Spurs have always been a pleasing club to observe, White Hart Lane a decent place to visit. It would be nice if they accepted that they aren't going to be part of the distant gold rush but that the style with which they climb the steps counts for something.

SATURDAY, 1 NOVEMBER 2008

Mum's the Word . . .

Róisín Ingle

I've just found out that over the past five years my mother has been writing 'a little story' about me and my boyfriend and his little brother. This fascinating fact comes to light as I give orders and the boys ferry boxes from our house to her apartment, which is to be our home until February.

She drops it in, casual, like, as my boyfriend and I get into one of our many heated discussions about whether we should bring the boxes up to his granny in Keady, Co. Armagh, or deliver various bits of furniture to Dublin-based siblings first. As usual, his sensible little brother comes up with a solution that calms us both down. 'It's just like in my story,' says my mother enigmatically.

I say nothing, thinking I must have heard wrong, but later, after she serves Sunday dinner – mother's chicken, roast potatoes, home-made gravy and string beans, followed by expertly sliced Viennetta; ah, it's good to be home – she brings up the subject again. 'I can't believe you haven't asked about my story,' she says, sounding put out. I tell her I thought she was joking, but she goes off and returns with two pages of neat print. (Two pages. In five years. My mother appears to be channelling John Banville.)

She begins to read. It's the story of 'Sinéad' and 'Brian' and 'Brian's' little brother 'Robbie'. It

Eve Rochfort (10), of Mary Help of Christians National School in Dublin, holds a thorny devil stick insect at the launch of Science Week. Photograph: Eric Luke.

soon becomes clear that it's not so much a story as a blow-by-blow account of our interminable quest to transform the house into a home. Listening to her was kind of like a car crash. I want it to stop but at the same time I want to stand by the side of the road and watch the nightmare of seeing myself and my relationship unfold through my mother's all-seeing eyes.

It begins as 'Sinéad' and 'Brian' move out of their 'rented modern apartment' to the house they have bought. 'Now they would have to begin the enormous task of making the old house they had just bought habitable. They needed help,' our intrepid narrator says, setting the scene.

'Our wee Robbie would come from Portadown for a few days and give us a hand if I asked him,' Brian said. 'Och, to be sure, he spends

most of the day in bed anyway just now, so he does.'

'They were an unlikely trio for this mammoth task. Sinéad was a successful journalist, outgoing and full of life – provided it was the kind of life that involved lots of parties, openings of art exhibitions and alcohol. Brian was an administrative officer, really more like a secretary to a set of very demanding businessmen. He was not as outgoing as Sinéad but liked her gregariousness, for now anyway. Robbie spent a lot of time in bed and was refusing to do his A levels.

'The North-South divide did not figure greatly in the relationship between Sinéad and Brian, at least not in the political sense. It did, however, become more apparent when work began. Brian was hard-working but sometimes lacked logic.

Sinéad was lazy but better at organising big events, although she lost her purse, mobile phone and credit card on a regular basis. Robbie was an easy-going young boy, but it soon became apparent that he had more sense than both of them.'

It went on (and on), but in case you're hooked I'll provide another highlight: 'One of Brian's main preoccupations was cleaning. He came from a household where order was maintained and the smell of bleach hung permanently in the air.' See? Not so much a work of creative fiction, I suggest to my mother, as an exploitation of the minutiae of our domestic lives for her gratification. 'Isn't that a bit like the pot calling the kettle black?' asks my mother. I can't think what she means.

Anyway, she reckons she is going to continue the story while we are living with her, but, at the rate of a paragraph every three months, I am not too worried. It turns out moving in with my mother is the best idea I've had in years. With my carousing days behind me, having just about grown out of my extended, petulant adolescence, I now seem to be in tune with her.

We sit and listen to Terry Wogan and Jonathan Ross on BBC Radio 2 and *The Archers* on Radio 4. We read our book-club books in companionable silence. She whips up perfect meals out of seemingly nothing. We watch *Little Dorrit* on the BBC, escaping into the Dickensian slums and splendour. At times it feels as though we are in a nursing home. In a good way.

I'm going to leave my mother with the last word. I'm not being funny, but it might just be the only way she'll ever get this story published.

'So the work was to proceed, and Sinéad checked with her mother that it would be all right for her and Brian to move in with her mother while the builders did the job. "Just from November to February, Mum," said Sinéad. Everything had to be removed from their house and taken up to Brian's granny's house in Keady, and Robbie was roped in again for the stressful move. Sinéad, however, was unable to assist. She wasn't being lazy this time. She had just found out that she was expecting a baby.'

Tolerant, Humorous, Intelligent: Obama is Different

Vincent Browne

Frank was an elderly black poet. The young man's grandfather used to visit him. The grandfather and Frank drank together, talked and then, usually, the grandfather would fall asleep. The young man went there occasionally just to talk and one evening did so just before he was to leave home for college. Frank spoke of the 'price of admission' for college. The young man asked what he meant.

'Leaving your race at the door . . . Leaving your people behind . . . You are not going to college to get educated. You're going there to get trained. They'll train you to want what you don't need. They'll train you to manipulate words so they don't mean anything anymore. They'll train you to forget what it is you already know. They'll train you so good, you'll start believing what they tell you about equal opportunity and the American way and all that s★★t. They'll give you a corner of the office and invite you to fancy dinners and they'll tell you you're a credit to your race. Until you want to actually start running things, and then they'll yank on your chain and let you know that you may be a well-trained, well-paid nigger, but you're a nigger just the same.'

The well-trained, well-paid nigger may have been elected president of the United States by the time you read this. The story is taken from *Dreams from My Father* by Barack Obama, first published in 1995, long before he thought of a political career. It is an extraordinary work of autobiography and of literature. Beautifully written, stunningly honest, moving, even painful. It reveals a man, not just of such a varied and turbulent background, but of insight, humour, self-deprecation, intelligence, tolerance, awareness. This fellow, Obama, is different.

He tells of the racism he encountered.

'The first boy, in seventh grade, who called me a coon; his tears of surprise – "why'dya do that?" – when I gave him a bloody nose . . . The older woman in my grandparents' apartment building who became agitated when I got into the elevator behind her and ran out to tell the manager that I was following her . . . Our assistant basketball coach, a young wiry man from New York with a nice jumper, who, after a pick-up game with some talkative black men, had muttered within earshot of me and three of my team-mates that we shouldn't have lost to a bunch of niggers and who when I told him – with a fury that surprised even me – to shut up, had calmly explained the apparently obvious fact that "there are black people and there are niggers. Those guys were niggers" . . . "There are white folks and then there are ignorant motherf★★★★★s like you", I had finally told the coach before walking off the court that day.'

After one of his friends had been arrested for drug possession, his mother berated him about those he hung around with, his declining grades, his general lassitude. He hadn't yet told her he planned not to go to college in Los Angeles, instead to hang around Hawaii, working part-time. She said: 'Bar, you can't just sit around like some good-time Charlie, waiting for luck to see you through.' He writes: 'I suddenly felt like puncturing that certainty of hers, letting her know that her experiment with me had failed.'

He tells of hearing his grandparents arguing one morning. His grandfather, Gramps, was refusing to drive his grandmother, Toot, to work. She had been threatened by a man on the street the previous evening. This didn't seem to explain her alarm and then Gramps said it was a black man.

'The words were like a fist in my stomach and I wobbled to regain my composure . . . I knew that men who might easily have been my brothers could still inspire their rawest fears.'

He went to talk to Frank about the incident. Frank said: 'Your grandma's right to be scared. She's at least as right as [Gramps] is. She understands that black people have a reason to hate. That's just how it is. For your sake I wish it were otherwise. But it's not. So you might as well get used to it.'

Frank fell asleep and Barack left. 'The earth shook under my feet, ready to crack open at any moment. I stopped, trying to steady myself and knew for the first time that I was utterly alone.' Throughout his youth he tried 'to reconcile the world as I'd found it with the terms of my birth'.

That speech he made in Philadelphia last March when the Jeremiah Wright controversy broke showed how he had achieved that reconciliation.

The troubled meeting with his Kenyan father; the year in Indonesia with his mother and her lovely, disturbed, Indonesian second husband; the solace his mother, Gramps and Toot brought to his childhood: all are narrated vividly in a book that must be the most extraordinary self-revelation of anyone who has attained such political prominence.

This guy is of a different order to anybody who has attained the White House and because of that he brings to it hopes not just of the Americans, and particularly black Americans, who voted for him, but of hundreds of millions around the world, who, understandably, see in this remarkable man a hope of serenity, justice and fairness in the world. An expectation surely to be disappointed, even by this extraordinary man, a man who no doubt now, even in the moment of this transformative achievement of reaching the US presidency (this is written in the expectation – yearning – that he makes it), is grief-stricken by the death of that loving grandmother, who was so fearful of black men.

THURSDAY, 6 NOVEMBER 2008

Obama Tells Rally: 'America Is a Place Where All Things Are Possible'

Denis Staunton, in Chicago

As we streamed into Chicago's Grant Park on Tuesday evening in our tens of thousands, we knew we could be on the verge of a history-changing moment, but when it came on the stroke of 9 p.m. local time, nobody seemed to be prepared for it.

'I think I'm still in shock,' said Ann Marty, a 25-year-old architecture student, after Barack Obama's victory was announced. 'I've been working for this and waiting for it and thinking about it for two years. Now I just can't believe it.'

It was a crystal clear, unseasonably mild night in Chicago, the city's magnificent skyline curving around the park where, 40 years earlier, baton-wielding police and armed national guardsmen had staged a bloody battle with anti-war protesters.

Many of those who came to Obama's election night party had been waiting for hours and some had camped out all night on the edge of the park. As the election results came in on giant screens, however, the crowd was strangely subdued, watching in silence as the numbers crawled upwards, the outcome remaining unclear.

The first big cheer went up when Pennsylvania was called for Barack Obama after 7 p.m., cutting off John McCain's best route to the White House. When Obama claimed Ohio at 8.30 p.m., we knew the election was over but the crowd at Grant Park remained muted, cheering briefly but waiting until CNN called the entire race for the Democrat when it erupted into wild jubilation, hugging one another, weeping or calling friends and family.

Tino Barber, a short, stocky African-American in his mid-30s, was sobbing as he hung up the phone after a call with his mother in South Carolina.

'I said I wasn't going to get excited until it happened because I thought Karl Rove was going to orchestrate something in the background and screw things up in Florida again,' he said. 'My mom is 70 years old. She's been out working for Obama every day but she said she didn't expect to see this in her lifetime.'

One of the biggest cheers went up in Grant Park when Virginia, which last backed a Democratic presidential election in 1964, fell into Obama's column. There was little trace of triumphalism, however, and the crowd cheered when McCain's concession speech was broadcast on the giant screens and applauded each mention of the defeated candidate's name in Obama's victory speech. McCain's supporters in Phoenix, by contrast, booed every time the Republican mentioned the new president-elect.

Madeleine Molyneaux, who had travelled to Chicago from upstate New York, put the subdued atmosphere in the crowd down to Obama's own cool temperament. 'He's like a Zen master,' she said. 'He just commands that sense of calm.' The moment the reality sank in for me was when the announcer introduced 'America's next first family' and four African-Americans – Obama, his wife Michelle and their two daughters – walked out onstage.

This family which, half a century ago, could not have eaten at the same lunch counter as their white neighbours in parts of the US, was about to move into the most prestigious address in the country – and their success seemed to elevate all of us.

The moment he started speaking, standing before 25 American flags and looking out over the vast crowd and the city lights beyond it, Obama identified the significance of the moment for all Americans, regardless of their race.

'If there is anyone out there who still doubts that America is a place where all things are possible; who still wonders if the dream of our founders is alive in our time; who still questions the power of our democracy, tonight is your answer,' he declared.

'It's the answer spoken by young and old, rich and poor, Democrat and Republican, black, white, Latino, Asian, Native American, gay, straight, disabled and not disabled – Americans who sent a message to the world that we have never been a collection of Red States and Blue States: we are, and always will be, the United States of America.'

The new president-elect paid tribute to his late grandmother, who died in Hawaii hours before the polls opened, thanked his wife Michelle and offered a special word to his two daughters. 'Sasha and Malia, I love you both so much,' he said. 'And you have earned the new puppy that's coming with us to the White House.'

As celebrations broke out everywhere, from Dublin to Berlin and from South Africa to Sydney, Obama addressed directly the world beyond the US.

'To all those watching tonight from beyond our shores, from parliaments and palaces to those who are huddled around radios in the forgotten corners of our world – our stories are singular, but our destiny is shared, and a new dawn of American leadership is at hand,' he said.

'To those who would tear this world down – we will defeat you. To those who seek peace and security – we support you. And to all those who have wondered if America's beacon still burns as bright – tonight we proved once more that the true strength of our nation comes not from the might of our arms or the scale of our wealth, but from the enduring power of our ideals: democracy, liberty, opportunity, and unyielding hope.'

Munster's Rua Tipoki and Jeremy Manning (left) engage in the Haka before facing New Zealand at Thomond Park in Limerick. Munster lost narrowly by 18-16. Photograph: Eric Luke.

THURSDAY, 6 NOVEMBER 2008

Supporters Bristle as Gracious Loser Hails Significance of Verdict

Mark Hennessy, in Phoenix

The Frank Lloyd Wright ballroom in the Biltmore Resort in Phoenix can seat 895 people on the numerous occasions when it plays host to Arizona's rich and powerful.

Shortly after 9 p.m. on Tuesday night, it barely needed to offer standing room to several hundreds by the time Senator John McCain conceded defeat.

Several hundred more, admittedly, had gathered outside on the lawn to watch the McCain speech.

The day had never been other than a preparation for defeat: even if stallholders were selling McCain Palin Victory Rally, November 4th T-shirts earlier for $15. Shortly after lunchtime some 4,000 Republican supporters, the ladies already in evening wear, began to gather in the Biltmore, the hotel where McCain married his wife, Cindy, 28 years ago.

The crowd illustrated, perhaps, some of the reasons for the Republicans' declining fortunes: it was almost entirely white, with a few Hispanics, but no blacks, bar the hotel staff.

It was also rich and conservative; and in many cases scared — and that is not too strong a word — of the man who will become the 44th president of the United States, Democrat Barack Obama.

Throughout the early evening, they tried to keep their spirits up, cheering to the rafters as Fox News declared meaningless victories for McCain in Tennessee and Mississippi. Hank Williams Jnr, who accompanied McCain for much of the last part of the campaign, came on stage; as did a parade of other local country and western musicians.

Frank Kasha, likeable, chatty and one who came from Iraq in 1968, said despondently: 'These people don't know what socialism is. I do, and I don't want it here in the United States.' Fiercely proud of his adopted home, he joked, nevertheless: 'I told my wife: if Obama wins, we're going to Ireland where they keep the taxes low.

'He shouldn't have run for president. He doesn't love the United States, not with the people that he associates. I have a few friends who are Democrats; but they are borderline.'

In the end, the declaration of Obama's victory came in a rush and took many in the crowd by surprise; and many of them had left even before McCain came on stage outside to end his bid for the White House. Sarah and Todd Palin emerged first; with the Alaskan governor slightly unsure of herself, and with the glint of tears in her eyes. Moments later, John and Cindy McCain followed.

It was, and will remain, perhaps, his finest hour in a career that has had many fine hours. 'Today, I was a candidate for the highest office in the country I love so much. And tonight, I remain her servant.

'That is blessing enough for anyone, and I thank the people of Arizona for it,' said the Vietnam veteran, who has represented the state for 23 years.

However, McCain, who has often braved unpopularity to bring unwelcome ideas during his political career, once again voiced thoughts uncomfortable for a partisan crowd to bear. He congratulated his opponent, paid tribute to him for the campaign that he ran and for the millions, black and white, young and old, that he inspired and he pledged to work with him, and called him 'my president'.

The crowd fidgeted, and many bristled with unhappiness, particularly when he noted 'the special significance' Obama's victory would have for African-Americans.

'What?' said a young, impeccably well-groomed and dressed woman, shaking herself with temper as she turned for encouragement to her friends behind her. He bade the crowd to be quiet on a couple of occasions as they booed following references to vice president-elect Joe Biden 'my friend of 35 years'.

Later, the gathering made no attempt to watch Obama's acceptance speech from Chicago: 'I can't believe that I have to call that man my president,' said a woman, on the point of tears.

Another, Patti Ramsey, said the Republican had fallen beneath the tide of economic bad news, and a retaliation by some for George Bush's victory – not, so much, for the one in 2004, but his first one eight years ago. 'I feel wounded, but optimistic. The US is still the land of opportunity, but I am scared that Obama will destroy all that our parents and their parents sacrificed to build,' she commented.

Paying tribute to Palin, McCain turned to her and said to the woman who must now see herself with hopes of running in 2012 that she had been 'one of the best campaigners I've ever seen, and an impressive new voice in our party'. Turning to her husband, Palin, who received as she has done so often during the campaign the loudest cheer of the night, said, 'That's nice', struggling by now to keep back the tears.

For a while, some of the crowd went back to party; but their heart was not in it and by midnight the caterers and clean-up staff were already busy at work. In the foyer of the Frank Lloyd Wright ballroom, the stallholders still had a pile of McCain Palin Victory 2008 T-shirts unsold in front of them. The price now, though, had gone down to $5.

MONDAY, 10 NOVEMBER 2008

As with All Irish Wakes, the PDs Departed in Sadness and Passion

Harry McGee

What made it strange was that nobody knew until the final moment if it was a funeral or a resurrection they were witnessing in Mullingar on Saturday.

In the end, only 40 votes separated those who believed in a dignified end for the PDs after 23 years and those who believed that, Lazarus-like, its fortunes could be miraculously revived.

As it turned out, reality prevailed. And delegates who swarmed out of the hallway of the Mullingar Park Hotel just after 4.30 p.m. did speak of sadness and of a wake-like atmosphere. Those in the majority spoke of the futility of continuing the project.

If it was a wake, it was an Irish wake – evoking as much passion and argument as mourning. Ironically, after 18 months of aimless drifting and an utterly pointless leadership contest, the death scene of the PDs was played out with the kind of vigour and conviction that reminded you of its earlier days. The will of the leadership – that the party had no viable future – was confirmed but not before an intense internal debate and a too-close-for-comfort vote.

Those two senses – loss and passion – were encapsulated by Mary Harney, who personified the PDs in the second half of its existence in the same way Des O'Malley had in its early years.

The meeting was closed but most of the details filtered out. Former senator Tom Morrissey's outspoken criticism of the organisation; party leader Ciaran Cannon's rationality in saying they had to call it a day; and the call-to-arms by young Meath PD Serena Campbell who insisted the party did have a future.

But the one speech that everybody referred to was the one given by Harney. She spoke without notes for half an hour and was given a standing ovation. Her performance was, by all account, a *tour de force*.

'Mary Harney was head and shoulders over everybody else in what she said,' said Aodhán Mac Donncha from Galway West. 'She spoke with great passion.'

Fergus Kennedy from Longford said that she 'yet again had proved her quality as a leader and as a politician. There was tremendous sincerity and

Royal Marines bugler Alaine Shakespeare at the funeral in Westport, Co. Mayo, of Robert McKibben, who was killed in November 2008 while serving in Afghanistan. Photograph: Keith Heneghan/Phocus.

tremendous passion in what she said. I suppose it underscored what the PDs stood for.'

Harney began by saying it was the saddest political day for her because 23 years before, to the day, she was in Des O'Malley's house planning the formation of a new party. She likened the excitement back then in 1985 to the excitement now in the United States. And with it the clear inference that the hope and energy had gone from the PDs.

'When we were formed, Des O'Malley was a year younger than Obama is today. Bobby Molloy had six successive elections behind him. Pearse Wyse had five and I had three.

'In order for the party to continue, you need people of that calibre that have a political track record. I don't see that in the party today.'

Former general secretary John Higgins, speaking after the vote, said that what had ultimately clinched the argument is that those who argued for continuity could not point to a leadership figure. 'Where is the strong leadership coming from? That was not apparent in the hall,' he said.

Behind the scenes, the PDs knew that even the winding-up of the party could backfire. There was a spirited group who wanted to keep it going. And part of the exercise during the week was trying to convince people who thought the party had no future to turn up. In the end, the turnout was more than respectable.

Most of the party's former TDs and senators were there, but with a couple of absentees – Liz O'Donnell and Michael McDowell, Des O'Malley and Bobby Molloy (but the latter two did not attend on health grounds). A letter from O'Malley was read out, saying the party should be wound up. But the talking point about the letter was O'Malley's omission of McDowell's name from those deserving praise.

There were mixed views from delegates. Serena Campbell said she was disappointed and 'quite angry' and hinted at forming a new right-of-centre party. 'We might have a new political party in the future hopefully with similar beliefs,' she said.

Others like Edward Delahunt from Laois-Offaly shared the sense of disappointment. 'A huge amount of people coming out of that room still have a huge interest in the PDs and in PDism.' But Galway delegate Mac Donncha summed up the majority view. 'The party had too much baggage and was associated with Fianna Fáil for too long and had lost its way slightly,' he said.

It was a strange coda in Mullingar on Saturday. The battle was won so the war could be lost.

WEDNESDAY, 19 NOVEMBER 2008

Don't Let Rupert Murdoch Decide Ireland's Future

Sarah Carey

Although I spent four years obtaining a degree in history, I really only learned one lesson: when reading anything – newspaper, essay or biography – it's wise to ask oneself: 'Who is behind this and what is their agenda?' Sometimes the answer is easy. Everyone has an agenda of some sort, and most of the time they'll be upfront about it. Other times the stated agenda is only a cover, and one has to hunt for hidden motives.

For anyone relying on the *Sunday Times* for information on its continuing coverage of the Lisbon Treaty, they would do well to ask themselves those two questions. For over three years, I worked for the Irish edition of the *Sunday Times*, which, like other British newspapers the *Sun*, *News of the World* and *The Times*, plus Sky television, is owned by Rupert Murdoch's News International. During my three years with the Irish edition of the *Sunday Times*, I was only vaguely aware that it was a distant outpost of Murdoch's empire.

We seemed to be like the hobbits in *Lord of the Rings*. The eye of the evil Lord Sauron was rarely fixed on our petty domestic issues and we got on with the business of political and social opinion without any comment from Wapping. Except for Lisbon.

Some months before the date for the referendum was announced, I told Irish editor Frank Fitzgibbon that I was eager to write a piece in favour of Lisbon. At the time, we seemed to be in agreement on the political imperative that the treaty be passed, though it's possible I misunderstood his views. We also discussed the fact that Murdoch's well known pro-US, hawkish views would obviously be the opposite, but we shrugged our shoulders.

Time passed, the date was set and I staked my claim to the pro-treaty column. But something had changed. Fitzgibbon told me that not only would I not be writing a pro-treaty column, but no other writer anywhere in the paper would either. This was not a matter for Sarah's precious little ego, but a cover-to-cover ban on any pro-treaty comment. Apparently since our first conversation, Fitzgibbon had looked into his heart and discovered the democratic deficit. From seemingly being in favour of Lisbon, he was now cheerfully banning all opinion favourable to Lisbon from the paper.

He argued that only broadcasters were legally required to present balanced coverage, and that as a privately-owned newspaper the *Sunday Times* was under no legal obligation to offer opposing views. I countered that while this was legally correct, he was under an ethical obligation to provide an alternative view, especially when that view tallied with the extraordinary political consensus that Lisbon was good for Ireland. He claimed he was under no such obligation – and that was that.

I should have written the column anyway and resigned if he refused to print it. But I was in no financial position to go around resigning on a point of principle, and I backed off. So no kudos to me. Part of me accepted that Fitzgibbon had a point: everyone is entitled to their agenda. The problem

only arises – which it did in this case - when it's not really your agenda at all.

In Britain, buying a particular newspaper title is an explicit statement of political allegiance. Here, the lines are blurred and so our sensitivity to the political motives behind editorial policy is dulled. Sure, *The Irish Times* has its whole Dublin 6-intolerant-liberal thing going on. There is also the problem of a 'newsroom culture' in which without any actual coercion, journalists will eagerly adopt each other's views. The *Sunday Independent* runs brazen campaigns such as the one to canonise Bertie Ahern and demonise Brian Cowen. But even the Sindo has Gene Kerrigan, so regardless of what paper one buys, Irish readers can expect that writers' political agendas will be both upfront and balanced out, allowing them to casually absorb different opinions across the political divide.

This was not the case with the *Sunday Times* referendum coverage.

When I mentioned to people that there was no pro-Lisbon comment, most professed disbelief but also an admittance that they hadn't really noticed. This lack of awareness was a big part of the problem. It thwarts our ability to process what is honest opinion, what is consensus and what is fact. Context is everything when processing opinion, and only hard-core political Irish readers could place the coverage in the right context.

But the real question is the motivation behind the policy. Politicians and commentators who argued for the Lisbon Treaty did so because they believed it was in Ireland's best interests. Of those who argued against the treaty, some believed they were also acting in the national interest, even if I personally disagree with them. But others cannot say the same. In whose interests did the *Sunday Times* campaign against the Lisbon Treaty to the exclusion of all favourable comment? Was it because they really believed that Ireland is best served by wrecking the treaty or because Eurosceptic views were imported, or worse, imposed, from Britain?

*Minister for Integration Conor Lenihan and Djamal Tirab from Chad at the 2008 Metro Éireann Media &
Multicultural Awards (Mamas) presented at a ceremony in the Abbey Theatre in Dublin. Photograph:
Alan Betson.*

I'm not saying that anyone who voted No didn't care about Ireland. But I am saying that certain constituencies who argued against Lisbon did so not because they believed it to be the right thing, but for other reasons. If our entire political establishment was dismayed because Lisbon was defeated and the cheers from Wapping were ringing in our ears, doesn't that make anyone wonder whether No was the right answer to the question?

If we're lucky we might get to vote twice on Lisbon, and this time I'll be allowed to argue whatever my opinion happens to be. When reading other people's opinions, it would serve you well to think twice and ask that old Latin question: Cui bono? Who benefits? Us or them?

Let that answer aid your reply to the next question: Yes or No?

TUESDAY, 25 NOVEMBER 2008

Japan Still Hooked on King of Fish

David McNeill, in Ishiki, Japan

On a gloomy day pregnant with rain and the weight of past expectations, Minoru Nakamura is welcomed back to port like a conquering hero. Three family generations, including Nakamura's father Toshiaki and newborn child Misaki wait ashore, smiles wide and cameras primed, as his boat sails into harbour. 'Good for him,' says a beaming Terutaka Okubo, head of the local fishing co-operative. 'That's wonderful to see.'

On this remote island off southern Japan, where rusting boats wait for fishermen who increasingly stay at home, few sights excite more than Nakamura's precious cargo: a 172kg bluefin tuna, splayed across the deck of his small trawler.

Dubbed Japan's king of fish, at peak prices Nakamura's single catch will fetch more than 1.5 million yen (€12,100) at the world's biggest fish market in Tsikiji, Tokyo. By the time it is carved up and sold as thousands of sushi, sashimi and steak cuts to restaurants across the city, it will be worth at least three times that much – the price of a luxury family car.

But today's celebrations are likely to fade as fast as the watery afternoon sun. Among many of Ishiki's 32,000 people, one in eight of whom depends on the sea to survive, the talk is of one thing: the extinction of their livelihood. 'In 40 years on a boat I've never seen it so bad,' says Yoshiju Kukeya. 'Nakamura-san is lucky today. The fish are not there anymore.'

Atsushi Sasaki, a fisherman-turned-conservationist who sounds increasingly desperate alarm bells about Japan and the world's free-falling tuna stocks, speaks of imminent extinction. 'If the situation continues, it is inevitable that tuna will disappear from the seas,' he says.

Sasaki is not alone. A string of doomsday predictions about the fate of the Pacific tuna forced Japan's largest fisheries co-op this summer to announce an unprecedented suspension of operations.

Last week, an international preservation group meeting in Morocco warned that once-teeming stocks of bluefin tuna in the Atlantic Ocean and Mediterranean Sea have plummeted by 90 per cent and may shortly be put on the official endangered list.

Most of the blame has been heaped on Japan, which consumes about three-quarters of the world's bluefin, according to Greenpeace, and increasingly imports what it can't catch (about 44,000 tonnes a year).

But the global spread of healthy Mediterranean and Japanese cuisine and exploding consumption in China and Russia are also helping to drive the species off the extinction cliff.

Rocketing prices for a fish that until 30 years ago was considered so worthless by many trawlers that it was thrown back into the sea or converted into cat food have attracted the attention of the Italian and Russian mafia, who control much of the Mediterranean trade, according to Daniel Pauly, one of the world's top fisheries experts. 'Most Japanese people have no idea where their tuna is coming from,' he says. 'If they did, they might eat a lot less.'

Around the coast of Japan, in fishing communities like Ishiki, boats are returning to port empty. Co-op manager Okubo shows a spreadsheet in his office charting the stunning decline in tuna catches: down to one-quarter of the 2005 figure. Nakamura's haul is the first 150kg-plus tuna to be caught this year; last year there were more than 100.

'It began a few years back but it is now really striking,' he says. 'Smaller fish are coming in because they're all that are left.' Sasaki explains the implications: 'Tuna under 36kg are incapable of producing babies, so the fishermen are cutting their own throats by catching immature fish.' But they need to survive. 'It's a vicious circle: the more younger fish they take, the more likely it will be that they go extinct.'

Tough and sinewy at 61, with the leathery skin of a veteran seadog, Sasaki has circled Japan in his 15m (49ft) trawler on a one-man research mission, which has made him deeply pessimistic that voluntary suspensions will succeed. 'The government must bring in much tougher regulations. At the moment, it's a free-for-all,' he says.

Later, he sails his boat into the choppy seas an hour off Ishiki, to a narrow channel where Pacific tuna shoals have navigated for millennia – south in the winter and north in summer. The area, one of the Pacific's key natural signals of the health of tuna stocks, is crowded with boats like his, sinking single lines into the sea.

At peak prices a single catch of bluefin tuna – like this one – can fetch more than 1.5 million yen at the fish market in Tsikiji, Tokyo. By the time it is carved up and sold, it will be worth at least three times that.

Tsushima Sasaki bitterly condemns net fishing, which he calls 'the enemy' because they haul in babies and smaller tuna, and are virtually unregulated. 'We can't do much damage with single lines,' he says as he rigs up the first of several rods. 'This is the only way that tuna fishing can be sustainable. We catch one at a time.' Like all the fishermen here, he speaks of the 'romanticism' of the tuna. 'It's big and powerful and it stirs boys' imaginations. There's no other fish like it.'

Seven hours later, he returns to port empty-handed, his worst fears again confirmed. 'If the fish are no longer there, Japan will starve,' he says.

The disappearing tuna and rising fuel prices are keeping fishermen at home and putting youngsters off the industry, imperilling its future. Kukeya says the average age of the men in the co-op is 61 and membership is falling year by year. 'In six or seven years the number of fishermen will halve,' he predicts.

Many of the men work 12 or more hours a day to make up for the declining catch. Some have shifted to other fish like sauries or sardines in an effort to make a living. 'Last year I earned five million yen [€40,400]; this year it's down to about half,' estimates Koji Harada.

'Nobody wants to really face up to what might happen,' says his colleague, Hiroyuki Yoshihara (38), who like Harada has a young family. 'We joke about it but if something doesn't change we won't be here in 10 years, but we don't know how to do anything else.'

The ripples from the crisis around Japan's coastline are already being felt on the nation's restaurant tables. Some sushi chefs have switched to using alternative fish and ingredients, a move that made worldwide headlines and a smug editorial in the *New York Times*, which said Japan is 'merely reaping the whirlwind it and other nations have sowed'. The newspaper called the tuna drought 'a wake-up call to consumers'. Some restaurants outside the country have already removed the bluefin from menus.

Few Japanese want to contemplate the disappearance of the beloved dinner-table staple, but unless the country takes drastic action, they may have no choice, warns Sasaki.

He says alternatives to fishing, such as raising tuna artificially, are making the problem worse because they entail robbing the seas of young stocks.

'We have to learn to hunt sustainably and eat less,' he says. 'There is just no other solution.'

TUESDAY, 25 NOVEMBER 2008

The Naked Truth about Gok Wan

Give me a Break, by Kate Holmquist

I hate Gok Wan. Well, I don't actually hate him in the sense that I'd like to see him die a slow death by having his intestines squeezed by a high-top thigh-length panty girdle. I suspect he wears one of those already. It's more the sort of hate that would have him suffering the constant ache of arthritic toe joints as a result of stiletto-wearing.

He's judgmental, oppressive, manipulative – your worst nightmare. He's a man that no sensible woman would invite to a party because he'd be following you upstairs on your potty-break, sitting on the side of the tub, telling you that your trousers are the wrong cut for your thighs. Then he'd go through your closet, toss your clothes onto the bed with a wry comment about each, then go back downstairs to dominate the party without even offering to help you hang all the clothes back up in the closet.

How vulnerable are we that we're watching his TV show and buying his book? As for the women who actually agree to strip to their underwear for him in front of the camera, how incredibly insecure and shame-based are we to believe that getting naked for Gok will lead us to self-image nirvana (as in, better job, better boyfriend, better life)? In a recent show, one of the women was so distressed about baring herself that she refused to do it – she was eventually convinced by Gok to go naked anyway. From the expression on her face as she did, it wasn't a life-transforming moment.

At least Trinny and Susannah exposed their own bodies – even if that meant Susannah flashing her boobs and tummy flab in increasingly pathetic demands for attention. Gok shows as little skin as possible, like a buttoned-up, black-suited New Age priest on holiday. He hides his face with mask-like spectacles – like Yves St Laurent on a bad day.

Gok's only trying to make a living. It's what he represents that I loathe – the mewling slavery of women who still believe that they need a man to tell them how to dress.

When men go to work, funerals, weddings and other places where they have to make an impression, they wear well-cut suits. The suit, shirt and tie combo is a classic that men haven't veered from for about a hundred years. Their dry-cleaning and shirt-ironing bills are doubtlessly large, but they spend about two seconds every morning deciding what to wear. Well-cut suit, clean pressed shirt, tie, polished shoes, done.

We women make what should be simple so much more complicated. There is nothing in our fashion symbolism that translates into 'pressed shirt, tailored suit, discreet tie, polished shoes'. Instead, we buy fashion magazines and wake up every morning wondering what we can choose out of the closet (or, more likely, the discarded pile on the bedroom floor) that will transform us into powerful, managerial, creative, adorable, in control.

Dressing for work, for women, is a nightmare. If you wear the classic suit, you're boring. If you wear your weekend clothes, you're feeling comfortable but you're still wondering whether the boardroom will ever accept you as a member.

Women are expected to express their power, creativity and efficiency through a complex puzzle of fashion semaphores that only other women understand. Wearing a power suit means 'I'm

headed for management'. Wearing an arty skirt and top means 'I'm content to work 9 to 5 but I have to be home to help my children with their homework'. Which brings me back to Gok and why I hate him.

He has no idea how real women actually live – trying to succeed rather than seduce. There is always an implication with Gok that for women to succeed they must seduce, and he teaches women that they are holding themselves back from success until they flaunt their bodies and receive his approval. He assumes that we women are universally ashamed of how we look and that we need a man to affirm us.

And women buy into it – that's the scary part. And even when they do what he wants, Gok punishes them. When Gok asks his 'girls' to organise their own photoshoots showing themselves at their liberated, most powerful best, they do what they think he wants. They have themselves photographed naked or nearly – and then Gok tells them that they are wrong, wrong, wrong! The whole point of being naked for Gok was to show the world that you could dress like a slob and not care! You weren't supposed to be naked at all!

We real girls, who work and manage and try to mix caring for our families with being authoritative at work, will not promote our careers by getting naked. We need the school uniform of success dressing. Because our success has nothing to do with being sexy and we don't want to look that way. We just want clothes that last. The sort men have.

FRIDAY, 28 NOVEMBER 2008

Suite Success

Ciarán Hancock

At 80 years of age, Dr Billy Hastings, doyen of Northern Ireland's hotel industry, doesn't stand on ceremony. Sitting in the bar of his Europa Hotel in

Belfast, famed for being Europe's most-bombed hotel, he gets straight down to business on meeting me.

'An important man like yourself, from *The Irish Times*, doesn't come to Belfast just to see me,' he says with disarming frankness. Age might have dulled his hearing a touch and whitened his hair, but the veteran hotelier and publican has lost none of his perceptive powers.

I had got another appointment later that day and before I could say we had three hours to chat, he said: 'Have you got some questions for me? What would you like to do? Would you like some lunch?'

Before I knew it, we were sitting in his Rolls Royce Seraph – registration BIL1066 (the year of the Battle of Hastings) – and on our way across the city to his five-star property, the Culloden, for a bite to eat. En route, he chats about the many changes to Belfast he's witnessed, his family's involvement in the business and the various twists and turns in his life, liberally sprinkled with some questions for me.

'Have you not got some questions for me?' he asked as we drive past Belfast City Airport. 'I thought you were going to have a list of questions for me.'

Later, in the Culloden, he proclaims to the hotel's manager and his daughter Julie that I must be the only journalist in the world without a pen. It was a fair point, but it's hard to take notes in the passenger seat of a car, even one as comfy as Dr Billy's. And balancing a notebook on my knee, on a couch at a relatively low table, while we both scoffed fish and chips just wasn't a runner.

At one point, the Culloden's manager comes over to inquire about our fish. 'It's not great,' says a no-nonsense Dr Billy. It killed the conversation stone dead and freed me of any obligation to praise the dish.

While still involved in the affairs of Hastings Hotels as chairman, Dr Billy is now one step removed from the day-to-day decision-making within the business, which comprises six hotels in Northern Ireland and a half share in Dublin's Merrion Hotel. His son Howard is managing director, while his three daughters have key roles in the business.

Dr Billy admits that the current recession has made life more difficult for Hastings, but he remains unfazed by the challenges ahead. 'You must be prepared for more challenging times,' he says. 'If you can't get ready for more competition, then you won't reap the benefits of the better times.'

This is true but much of the trade of the Europa, the Culloden and his Stormont hotel in Belfast is made up of business people. The same goes for the Merrion. Won't these properties be squeezed from the inevitable reduction in corporate trade during the recession?

'You tell a guy who has been going to a five-star hotel that he's going to Dublin next week and he's going from the Merrion down to a three-star. He'll look at you with a cross face . . . he's not going to pull in his horns.'

Having survived the Luftwaffe and 25 years of the Troubles, which saw a number of his hotels bombed, Dr Billy isn't particularly fazed by the current economic slump. 'I'm not waking up in the middle of the night due to the credit crunch,' he says, matter-of-factly.

He bought the Culloden, which overlooks Belfast Lough, in 1969 when he was in bed with the mumps. It had just 13 bedrooms. It now has just more than 100 rooms and is considered the best five-star hotel in Belfast.

He bought the Europa in 1994 when it was a bombed-out shell and turned it into one of the busiest hotels in Belfast city. At the time, he was recuperating from a quadruple heart bypass.

'The last number of years have been taken up with developing that which we have now,' he says. 'They [the hotels] haven't been developed to their ultimate and there are still plans in the pipeline.

'We are not actively seeking opportunities, but

Billy Hastings as seen by caricaturist Michael McCarthy.

I believe that over the next year, there will be bargains worth looking at.'

He said Hastings' turnover this year would be flat at around £34 million. 'That in itself is an achievement,' he said. 'The year was satisfactory, but we were under pressure because of expenses, primarily energy.' He describes bookings for 2009 as 'very healthy'.

He did make a bid of €70 million to buy the Portmarnock Hotel and golf links a couple of years ago, but missed out. 'I reckon it would have needed the same again to refurbish it. Under the present circumstances, I'm glad we didn't get it,' he says.

Not surprisingly, given the business he's in, Dr Billy likes to travel and stay in top-class hotels. Each summer for the past eight years, he's enjoyed the sunshine in Barbados from the plush surroundings of Dermot Desmond's Sandy Lane property.

Every February, he sets sail on a cruise. 'I'm fed up with the Caribbean, so I haven't made my mind up on next year.' Fair enough.

His favourite hotel used to be Claridges in London and he loves the Ritz for afternoon tea. He also has a soft spot for the five-star Burj Al Arab in Dubai. 'It was the only suite I've stayed in where I had my own private billiards room.'

It could all have been so different for Dr Billy. He worked in the timber business for two years as a teenager before joining the family firm. His father owned a handful of pubs, which passed on his death in 1940 to Roy, his eldest son. Roy died at 30 from a kidney disease and the baton passed to Billy, who was then just 27.

Dr Billy admits that he was one of only a small number of 'Prods' working in a business then dominated by Catholics. The pub business was a cash cow and provided the funds for Hastings to make a serious foray into the hotel trade in 1971 with the purchase of six properties from the Ulster Transport Authority. He hasn't looked back since and Hastings is now comfortably the biggest hotel operator in the North.

In 1997 he teamed up with businessmen Martin Naughton and Lochlann Quinn to develop the Merrion in Dublin, his first foray south of the Border. 'I have great respect for both of them as people,' he says. 'I think we have the best hotel in Ireland . . . in Dublin, anyway. I don't think you will hear any horror stories about the Merrion. None of us is greedy. We like to put into the proposition what we take out of it.'

Ironically, it could have been Jurys in Ballsbridge – now in the ownership of Seán Dunne – that marked his entry down south. 'Jurys hotel was for sale in 1969 and I had a look at it,' he recalls. 'If memory serves me, it was sold for £700,000, which at the time was too much for me.'

It's been something of a rollercoaster ride since then. He was kidnapped by the UDA and locked up at gunpoint by the IRA. He plays down both episodes. 'That didn't happen every day or every week,' he says, without fuss. 'If it happened to you one day, you had a year to get over it.'

But why not sell up and do something else? 'Who was I going to sell to? There weren't many buyers around.'

After 60 years in business, Dr Billy says that he has no regrets. 'I'm still looking forward to tomorrow . . . regretting the past would be a useless exercise.'

Nor has he any intention of quitting work, cashing in his chips and enjoying his millions. 'I don't like working in the garden and I don't like DIY. I play a game of golf, but once a week does me. They [his children] run the business now. I enjoy the business so much that if they ever wanted to dispose of me, I would feel it very much. Sure what would I do with millions?'

FF Cheers Up as Biffo Comes Back from the Dead

Miriam Lord

Aah, the Christmas. It's for the little ones. Not long now – just seven sitting days before the Dáil rises for the festive season. The tree will be going up soon. Outside, there's a lovely Christmassy nip in the air. Inside, there's the return of old Nipper Cowen to warm the cockles.

It had been so long since they saw him last, the little ones were beginning to doubt his existence.

'Do you still believe in Nipper Cowen?' the bolder ones dared to ask as a terrible year neared its end.

'There's no such thing as old Nipper Cowen,' they whispered. 'Bertie told us. He knows everything.' But the more innocent little ones, refusing to let go, continued to proclaim his existence.

'I saw him, so I did. Loads of times. Mammy O'Rourke says she left a pint out for him once and he drank it. You're very bold and I'm going to tell Scary Carey on you.' Yet, you could hear the doubt creeping into their fearful little voices. What a difference a day makes.

Outside Leinster House on Tuesday, they poured salt on the icy plinth. Inside, vinegar poured from a sour Taoiseach. But yesterday, Cowen breezed into the chamber and opened a window in the political Advent calendar. Joy was unconfined on the Fianna Fáil backbenches.

We looked at those happy little faces during Leaders' Questions: full of hope for what the future might bring and beaming with joy at the sheer wonderment of it all. With their bright eyes and the excited way they clapped their tiny hands, the backbenchers were a joy to behold. For there he was – their main man. Doing what he does best.

All together now. Opposition nuts roasting on an open fire, Cowen cross and nipping at their toes . . .

It's what those poor little mites were waiting for. The last few months have been difficult for them in the Dáil. Disaster piled upon disaster. It began to resemble Mishap Central in Government Buildings and the Cowen of old, the one they adored, was missing in action.

Day after day, they sat in the Dáil chamber while their hero underperformed spectacularly before their eyes. To their unfolding horror, Eamon Gilmore was trouncing him and he was even making Enda Kenny look good.

The days of Nipper Cowen, battling Biffo, the man who caught the last election by the scruff of the neck and set Fianna Fáil back on course for victory, appeared to be gone. In his place, a downbeat

leader spouting cold statistics in place of inspiring words and fighting talk.

There was no reason to believe that yesterday would be any better. The little backbenchers trooped disconsolately into their places, pulled on their tin hats and waited for the Opposition barrage. Kenny lined up his sights and let fly at Biffo. 'We have been led into the middle of an economic swamp by the most disastrous government in 40 years,' he boomed.

Just how was the Taoiseach proposing to cut €5 billion from the public spending bill? The little backbenchers shrank further into their seats as the Taoiseach rose to reply.

But what's this? He was making sense, in a way that ordinary people, as opposed to economists, might understand. He began talking about his Government's strategy. He hadn't his head buried

The aftermath of the ram raid on McCullagh's Garage at Bagenalstown in Co. Carlow on the morning in which a 4 x 4 vehicle was used to steal an ATM. Photograph: Dylan Vaughan.

in briefing notes and, wait a minute, yes, he was making sense. They perked up a little, bless them.

Enda hit him with job losses and VAT increases and that plan to cut public spending. 'There isn't any plan, or any coherence, or any strategy,' he countered. Strategy? Brian told Enda he'd give him strategy, rubbishing the Fine Gael leader's idea of an economic plan.

He started his reply with four words that had the little backbenchers hugging themselves with delight. 'To answer Deputy Kenny directly . . .' And he did, without bamboozling and without much recourse to notes, waving his arms and pivoting on his heels: the pugnacious Nipper of old. Enda tried to interrupt, but he wasn't given the chance. The Taoiseach said he was in no humour to argue. 'I want to be straight and outline where we're at,' he insisted, and so he did.

'We will bring forward an approach that will best guarantee our way through this problem. We have done so for the last 20 years, in good times and in bad. We are the authors of the partnership programme which Fine Gael has always decried. We will prove you wrong on this one as well.' Nipper was back. 'Hooray!' cried the little ones.

Gilmore tried to take Nipper out. But he stood his ground. He had a strategy and was pursuing it because 'it's the right thing for this country'. 'Hear, Hear!' cried the little backbenchers, as little Hallelujah choruses broke out in the ranks.

Never mind the nitty-gritty of Eamon's argument. The Taoiseach, with rare passion, was going toe-to-toe with the Opposition. His Government was working to recapitalise the banks in a way which would not see the first call for capital made on 'Joe Taxpayer'. The backbenchers were in winter wonderland.

Later on Deputy Gilmore made a veiled comment on Cowen's return when he smilingly observed he had been quite the expert that morning. 'I'm more resilient than he thinks,' grinned Cowen.

Christmas is looking up for the little ones. A glimpse of old Nipper is far better than a trip to Lapland. (The country, not the club.)

Just What Planet Are Economists on?

John Gibbons

Brian Cowen and Enda Kenny suffer from this. So does Gordon Brown and at least nine in 10 other world leaders. All are labouring under the same crippling psychosis. This is their shared conviction that, whatever the problem, the solution lies in economic growth.

So deeply ingrained has the notion of relentless, limitless growth become that to suggest it may be the cause of, rather than the solution to, our greatest challenges borders on heresy.

Growth and the pursuit of growth is the secular religion of the western world, and its dogma is gradually infecting every society on Earth via globalisation. Every cult needs its clergy, and the high priests of growth are our economists. Purporting to understand such magic as the 'hidden hand of the marketplace', economists have been fêted by presidents and parliaments as the new alchemists, with their dazzling theories suffused with the promise of technological transubstantiation that will somehow lift us beyond the mortal limits of our fragile blue planet.

These sorcerers have led politicians and populations alike to believe that they alone understood and could tame the raging marketplace, while extracting from it an infinity of goods to satiate our ever-expanding appetites. Perhaps their greatest sleight of hand has been in selling the notion of infinite growth within a finite – and sharply declining – ecosystem. Take Robert Solow, a Nobel Prize-winning US economist. 'The world can, in effect, get along without natural resources,' was his breathtakingly myopic analysis.

Ask an economist to value a forest, and he'll tell you how much timber sells by the tonne. The Amazon releases 20 billion tonnes of water into the atmosphere every day, free of charge. Forests control floods, purify water, protect biodiversity and keep the planet habitable, but what does this matter to a hedge fund manager? Another trick, called temporal discounting, allows economists to sell our children's future down the heavily polluted river in favour of short-term profit.

Yet this analytical vacuity is the norm, not the exception, among the economic elite. Alan Greenspan, former chairman of the US Federal Reserve, dressed up political ideology and passed it off as rational economics, while cheerfully choreographing the world's greatest financial crisis since the 1930s. None of this has dented the collective self-confidence of the ruling cabal of economists, nor cooled the media's love affair with them.

Tune in to RTÉ or Today FM any day of the week to hear the very economists who sold us the poison during the boom years; now they are peddling their repackaged 'cures' in the form of the latest economic elixirs of growth. Heavy drinkers will be familiar with this logic: it's called the hair of the dog.

In nature, growth is a phase, leading to the equilibrium of maturity. An adult that continues growing can only do so by becoming obese. Within the body, cells that multiply exponentially in an otherwise stable organism are more commonly known as a cancerous growth or tumour. The World Wildlife Fund's Living Planet Index has tracked the ecological health of the world since 1970. Its 2008 report found that total planetary resources have been permanently depleted by 30 per cent in well under four decades.

'The possibility of financial recession pales in comparison to the looming ecological crunch,' said the fund. The report found that three in four people live in countries that have exceeded their own ecological limits. Ireland is well up the debtor list. We consume resources requiring three times the amount of land actually available globally per person. We are ecologically as well as economically in hock. You really wouldn't want to be around when this debt is called in.

For now, we continue propping up our house of cards by rapidly running down the ecological capital of other countries to maintain our astonishing bubble of affluence. In famine times, this was called eating the seed corn. When our political elite, guided by their hierarchy of economics, believe they can cure the recession by 'jump-starting' the consumption-driven economy and so plunge us deeper into ecological debt, you see just how the cancer cult of growth economics has metastasised throughout the body politic.

Capitalism, in the words of John Maynard Keynes, an economist now back in vogue having been deemed passé by the seeming triumph of right-wing political ideology, 'is the astounding belief that the most wickedest of men will do the most wickedest of things for the good of everybody'.

Many people who live in man-made environments like cities may wonder what ecology has got to do with them. Put simply, our environment is to human survival and wellbeing what water is to a fish. If growth is toxic, what about the alternatives? In 1972, a group called the Club of Rome published its prescient book *The Limits to Growth*.

Reaching what they call equilibrium would require hard choices. We would have to trade some freedoms, such as the right to have unlimited population growth and resource consumption, 'for other freedoms, such as relief from pollution and crowding and the threat of collapse of the world system'.

In the 36 years since its publication, Earth now bends under the burden of an additional 3.3 billion people. As we fret about declining property prices, philosopher Henry David Thoreau's observation was never truer: 'What good is a house, if you haven't got a tolerable planet to put it on?'

Boyd Rankin in Napoleonic period uniform as a sergeant major in the Royal Artillery at the inaugural firing of replica cannons on the Millmount battlements in Drogheda, Co. Louth, for the opening of a new military exhibition in the tower. Photograph: Alan Betson.

MONDAY, 8 DECEMBER 2008

A-shrinking and A-thinking on Roy in the Tub

LockerRoom, by Tom Humphries

Brace yourself, Bridie. I am in the bath. Gloriously and colossally naked. I have the mobile phone welded to my ear. I am holding forth. I am sweating. I am quite the spectacle.

In the 37 years or so of his turbulent existence Roy Keane has spent maybe 10 hours in rooms with me, trapped there in the fraught and unnatural circumstance of being interviewed for this paper. This I feel qualifies me to be an Explainer of Roy Keane to the English.

I have no real clue as to why Roy Keane left Sunderland. I am in the bath. I have the mobile phone welded to my ear. I am holding forth to the BBC. My views have the substance and value of the frothy bubbles hiding my modesty. Me and the Beeb are wondering whether Roy Keane is mad.

I should say to the BBC first off that I am a fraud. My 10 hours with Roy Keane have been far more interesting for me than they have for him. I should say I find Roy Keane way more interesting than he finds me. I should say it stands to reason that anybody who has spent enough time with

Roy Keane to be able to offer a qualified opinion on what makes him tick wouldn't be going on the radio to peddle that opinion. Instead I am holding forth happily. And anyway the BBC wouldn't care. Today it's all Keano, all the time.

'What is Roy Keane thinking?' asks the voice on the other end of the phone. In the bath I pause as if tuning in telepathically to Roy Keane's thought process.

He could be thinking that he'll have the pepperoni 12-inch with garlic bread. He could be thinking the dog needs walking but the world has seen enough photos of Roy Keane walking the dog in times of trouble. Hopefully he isn't thinking, 'there's that fraudulent tosser on the radio telling people what I am thinking'. I burble on happily with my half-baked theory that modern football is a halfway house between circus and asylum and perhaps the most ringing act of sanity a man can make is to walk away from it all.

'He doesn't seem very well liked,' says the BBC man to the Explainer of Roy Keane to the English. I am in the bath with a towel over my head so my voice won't echo off the white tiles and the gentle lapping of the water on my gut won't be audible to the English. There is a lot of steam. Some from the water. Lots from me. This is my fifth interview of the day as a Keanologist. I am a full-blown geyser of steam.

I first interviewed Roy Keane in late 1993 in the Four Seasons Hotel near the airport in Manchester. He walked into the hotel and everything froze like a four-star Pompeii until he had passed through. I asked the usual dumb questions. He gave the usual thoughtful answers. He was young and considered mad, bad and dangerous to know back then. I asked him what he had spent the previous night doing. He said he had gone to bed early with tea and biscuits. He said that's how mad he was.

He asked me: How did I get to Manchester? Had I kids? What was the job like? What time was my flight home? What would I do between now and the flight home? Would I like to come to his house? Could he give me a lift?

Footballers never ask these things. They never wonder about the workings of the world. I have a friend who travelled to London once for an arranged interview with an Irish international. The player had forgotten he had arranged the interview and asked could it be done the next day. My friend explained he had just flown there. The player said, 'Well, get in the car we can talk on the drive home.' So they did and when it was finished the player pulled in on the hard shoulder of the motorway and said, 'Cheers, mate. I'll let you out here.' He wasn't being a bastard. They just don't think.

I was disappointed Keane wasn't driving the big red Merc he had been reported as owning. It had a registration something along the lines of Roy 1. I asked him about it and he blushed. 'Yeah. I was driving around making a complete fecking eejit of myself,' he said. We drove and he said to me he would never have driven about at home in Cork in such a thing. He was embarrassed to think he had driven around Manchester in it.

He doesn't seem very well-liked? I venture that being well-liked by the populace isn't the point of Roy Keane's existence. Being faithful to himself seems more important. Being the guy who left Mayfield. Every ending he has experienced since then has been ugly and messy and painful. Being well-liked wouldn't be a currency he would place a lot of faith in.

'Hmmm,' says the BBC man.

There is a radio silence. A solecism in itself. I have run out of things to say. Me, a fat man in a steamy bath in another country with a mobile phone to his ear and no opinion worth anything more than the radio callers from their motor cars, I have dried up.

Is Roy Keane mad? Football is mad. Several times today while waiting for the disc jockey to come to me on air and ask me to pour my bucket of steam down the phone I have heard little audio collages of Royisms played. Everything parsed and analysed to an inch past reason. I am just a little fragment of the Tower of Babel over Roy Keane's head, a contributing voice to the madness of media which feeds into the madness of crowds which underpins the madness of modern football.

Ron Atkinson made some crass racist remarks into a live mic a few years ago and has spent the rest of the time telling the world firstly, that he is sorry and secondly, that he has said sorry enough. Can he please get back into football? Alex Ferguson announced his retirement but could not retire. Terry Venables throws his pearly king hat into the ring for every job there is. Bryan Robson, God love him, is working they say as 'an ambassador' for Manchester United.

Football is full of men who live by the tabloid and die by the tabloid. Full of broken-down adrenalin addicts who accept the absurdity of the world they live in without question. Football is full of managers who fret 24/7 for their teams and for their jobs and never for their sanity. They are on a rollercoaster. Wheeeeeeeeeee! A rollercoaster which has a paying audience. Woooooooooooooo! An audience which obsesses as much as they do.

Football is mad. The attention we give it is mad. The importance we accord it is mad. The pretence at there being binding loyalties is mad. The clammy desperation to extract meaning and morals is mad. The thin line between the winners' steps and the bacon slicer is mad. The fickleness. The cynicism. The money. Mad. Mad. Mad.

Roy Keane decided it wasn't for him and stepped off the rollercoaster and went home with his wife.

I'm in a bath talking to a man I've never met before and feigning an expertise I don't possess for a radio audience who are all either angry or disappointed with Roy Keane. I'm just a little vibrating atom in this raging, boiling body of noise.

Roy Keane is at home playing with his kids. Is he mad? Too darn right he is. Mad as a fox, Bridie.

Food Supply Has Become a Social Time bomb

Ann Marie Hourihane

Ate rasher sandwich. With mustard. Feel okay. Drive through frost-filled, fog-drenched Irish countryside, admiring Ireland in December. Arrive home to find that all pork products have been recalled. That the owner of our corner shop is binning all his ham pizzas. As a good consumer try level best to feel worried about own health but even my top-performing hypochondria isn't up to this. More worried about pig farmers. Sleep well.

Sunday. Discover that we have no pork products in our fridge to throw away. In any event that old salami was not made from Irish pork, having been bought in evil foreign supermarket. Feel a bit left out. Ring Food Safety Authority's (FSA) helpline (1890 33 66 77) in an effort to participate in national drama. Ring at 11.44 a.m., noon and 12.15 p.m.

A young female voice says that all their lines are busy at the moment, but if I leave a message they will return my call as soon as possible. Then spooky English voice comes on to the FSA helpline and says: 'Record your message at the tone. When you are finished hang up or hold for more options.' God almighty, even our phone services are imported. More angry about this than about the pork being recalled.

Still worried about pig farmers. More responsible adults are talking about traceability and are busily binning all their bacon. But what's the point in having traceability if, as the FSA has stated, all pigs are slaughtered in the same factories, and you can't separate the contaminated pork products from the uncontaminated ones? Have terrible desire for a sausage.

Dimly remember suggesting that we have a pork steak for dinner on Friday, and having been overruled by the catering committee which, although low in numbers, is high in aggression, quite a row ensued. We had spaghetti instead. Today both members of the catering committee are looking pretty pleased with themselves. Still cross about that.

Of course the recall of all pork products from pigs slaughtered since 1 September is very serious. But the thing about consumers is, we're flighty. Oh, we're flighty. We are inclined to get scared and bolt. Our decisions about what food to buy are emotional as well as economic.

There is no logic to us really, which is just as well, because the consumer authorities don't have any logic to them either. On the one hand they're saying that there's absolutely nothing to worry about; on the other hand they've instituted what is in effect a blanket ban on pork products. This is the kind of behaviour any five-year-old child could see through, and habitually does.

About the pig industry your average consumer knows absolutely nothing. There are times, after a couple of glasses of wine in a foreign country, that we might drunkenly say 'Irish ham is the finest in the world' but these statements are embarrassing and made from a position of total ignorance, shortly before we burst into our version of *Spancil Hill* and cry about emigrating, even though we never have.

What your average consumer does know, though, is that food has become a sort of social

Stockman Martin Sheehan tending animals in the O'Brien piggery near Mitchelstown in Co. Cork as Irish pork products were removed from supermarket shelves due to fears that animal feed had been contaminated with harmful toxins. Photograph: Daragh Mac Sweeney/Provision.

bomb, which can explode at the most unfortunate moments; and surely no moment can be more unfortunate than the weeks coming up to Christmas. We've lived through quite a lot of food scares over the past two decades, giving up eggs and then beef as the UK had its salmonella and then its BSE scares. There was foot and mouth. There was blue tongue. To non-farmers these outbreaks were mysteries; we still don't know exactly how or why they started or finished.

The Irish farming industry is regarded by most non-farmers, rightly or wrongly, as a series of scams perpetrated by cute country people who have been getting away with it for years. This makes farmers understandably furious; but even they might admit that consumers only hear about farmers and farming when things go disastrously wrong.

The last time pig farmers intruded on the public consciousness in any significant way was when a couple of them were fined for destroying rivers by releasing slurry into them. And the bovine TB scandal (is it over yet?) never did much to instil public confidence in the agricultural authorities. Then there is the whole organic movement, which is founded on suspicion, and a sure-fire method to guarantee that food became even more of a class indicator than it already was.

The children of the privileged munch their way through appallingly expensive organic chicken and organic vegetables and the children of everybody else are, it is assumed by the organic movement, negligently filled with toxins and growth hormones and will consequently, it is also strongly implied by the organic movement, die screaming. A scare like this one over pork products only reinforces this food apartheid.

For the pig farmers, of course the FSA ruling is a catastrophe. But if the ban is shown to have been justified, and if it leads to better practice in the feed factories — which seem, to the untutored eye, to be the source of an awful lot of food scares — then perhaps it will be seen to have been a good thing. It will go some way to restoring consumer confidence in the safety of Irish produced food, and the consumer might be recaptured sooner than we think.

Share Price Says the Game is up for Anglo Irish Bank

John McManus

It is clear from the share price of Anglo Irish Bank that no one — apart from its board, presumably — believes management when they say the bad debts in its €73 billion loan book will amount to a manageable €879 million while the economy shrinks by up to 4 per cent next year.

But this alone is not the sum of Anglo's difficulties. The truth is that nobody believes the management of any of the Irish banks when it comes to their bad debts and thus the scale of capital write-offs to come in the next few years. It also follows that no one believes the Financial Regulator and PricewaterhouseCoopers (PwC), its adviser, who both say the banks are solvent and adequately capitalised to meet projected losses.

Investors, however, have disregarded the banks, the regulator and PwC and have done their own back-of-the-envelope calculation based on their assessment of the economy, the banks' loan books and whatever other secret ingredient they use to try to get a handle on what is going to happen next.

The problem for Anglo is that, when you do this sort of worst-case exercise on it, there appears to be little chance that it can attract sufficient capital to allow it to absorb its losses. Hence the collapse in its shares relative to the other banks.

The Anglo share price reflects a consensus — justified or otherwise — that the situation at the bank is so serious, it is either beyond rescue or current shareholders will be obliterated whatever

Players from St Pius X Boys National School, Terenure in Dublin, celebrate their defeat of Terenure College in the Corn Mhic Caoilte final at the Allianz Cumann na mBunscoil finals in Croke Park. Photograph: Eric Luke.

happens. The share prices of the other banks reflect a greater degree of hope that existing shareholders will not be entirely decimated in the coming restructuring.

The reasons why Anglo is seen to be in deeper trouble than its peers have been well ventilated over the past six months, and boil down to its exposure to property investment and development. Put simply, the argument is that, if all Anglo's chickens come home to roost in this regard, the amount of capital required to save it is beyond the resources, or the appetite, of any of the current players in the Irish bank recapitalisation game: the Government, the domestic fund managers and the various private equity funds.

Last night's statement from the Government talked of €10 billion in new capital in total for the sector. And Anglo will be standing behind AIB, Bank of Ireland and Irish Life Permanent in the queue.

That said, the bank remains open for business and solvent thanks to the Government guarantee. And much of the negative comment and the various apocalyptic scenarios being presented should be seen in the context of the manoeuvring by the other banks and prospective investors as they jostle for advantage in the recapitalisation stakes.

But even allowing for all of that, Anglo's share price is saying it is a broken business. The acid test

– whether it can raise more money in the market – seems to have returned a negative result, with the mooted State-underwritten rights issue all but abandoned, notwithstanding the Minister's statement last night.

If there really is the black hole in Anglo's balance sheet that all of this implies, then its directors have no option but to ask the Government to take it over. In truth, even if the management are right and losses are in fact manageable, it probably does not matter, so firmly is the opposite view entrenched in the market.

The game appears to be up and it would be irresponsible of Anglo's board just to ignore the share price and limp on under the Government guarantee. To do that would court insolvency as deposits will start to leave the bank – and that could see the Government guarantee called in. Something nobody really wants to see. Anglo's pivotal role in the property market – and the consequences should it collapse in a disorderly fashion – also means that a wider view has to be taken.

By this analysis, the least-worst option is for the board to ask the Government to step in. It would put the Minister in a position to stabilise it, minimise systemic problems and still include Anglo – or its assets – in the wider co-ordinated recapitalisation of the banks.

It would, of course, still be a disaster on a colossal scale, firstly for the people who work at the bank and made careers there, as many of them could lose their jobs. And, secondly, it would be a hammer blow to the reputation of the Irish banking industry and, indeed, to business confidence, to see the once-shining star of Irish banking fall so low. It is obviously a disaster for shareholders too and, lastly, for the generation of entrepreneurial bankers who built the bank from almost nothing but their brains and sweat.

But when you put all of that in balance against the consequences of an Anglo Irish zombie running around until it falls over, this option may be the lesser of several evils.

THURSDAY, 18 DECEMBER 2008

Nation Plunged into Mourning after Death of the Good German

Berlin Diary, by Derek Scally

Life as a Derek in Germany is never dull – it just takes some getting used to. Mentioning that your name is Derek can elicit anything from a sly smirk to, in extreme cases, shouts of 'Get the car, Harry!' followed by gales of laughter. It turns out that we poor Dereks share a name, if not the spelling, with Germany's most famous television detective.

Beginning in 1974, the popular drama series *Derrick* related the adventures of Munich detective inspector Stephan Derrick for 24 years and 281 episodes.

News that Horst Tappert, the actor who brought Insp. Derrick to life, had died this week aged 85 plunged Germany into mourning and introspection. Nearly every newspaper in the country carried a picture of the actor, with his penetrating, heavy-lidded gaze, staring out from the front page. Just as distinctive as its lead actor was the show's penetrating, claustrophobic atmosphere and stories often set in the seedy Munich underworld.

Unusually, for a crime show, there was no violence and not so much as a raised voice. Derrick solved the crimes without a gun or DNA scrapings, relying instead on reason and empathy to unravel motives in scripts which often addressed the social aspects of crime.

Equally compelling was the deliberate decision not to give the humourless detective a personal life. The only personal touch was Derrick's interaction with his assistant, Harry Klein (played by Cabaret star Fritz Wepper). Umberto Eco memorably described the series once as 'electrifying mediocrity'.

A huge hit at home and sold to 108 countries, the reaction to Tappert's death in Germany makes clear that *Derrick* was much more than just another television show: the detective was, for many, the best ambassador the country has known.

In the 1970s, as the scars of war began to heal, *Derrick* was a civilised investigator, a democrat and gentleman who gave villains a just punishment and viewers the closure they sought. The lead character was a compelling new role model for European audiences who may have had another kind of German seared into their memories.

'Tappert represented the kind of person we could be proud of, and by "we" I mean "we Germans",' said Hans Janke, a former executive at public broadcaster ZDF. 'He was the fearless German one didn't have to fear.' Sadly, like nearly all German television shows, *Derrick* never sold to Britain or the US.

Even if it had been shown, it's unlikely that *Derrick* alone could have neutralised the Nazi clichés kept alive in *Allo Allo*, *Dad's Army* and *Hogan's Heroes*, not to mention endless reruns of war films. But perhaps the most important side-effect of *Derrick* was not its reception abroad, but attitudes at home to its international success.

Germans tell proudly of how the series was shown in 100 countries, 108 countries, 120 countries. How the late pope John Paul was a fan. How Italians kissed Tappert's feet on the streets of Rome or how funny it was to hear Insp. Derrick speaking Mandarin during their holiday in China. They tell of how *Derrick* had fan clubs in the Netherlands and Norway, despite deep-seated resentment to all things German.

Perhaps the most amusing *Derrick* effect is the polite but firm refusal of many Germans to accept that the series is an unknown quantity in most of the English-speaking world – except Australia, where it aired for a time, with subtitles.

Behind all this *Derrick* enthusiasm, of course, is a cautious pride and the hope that the welcome for the Munich police inspector could be extended to all Germans. It was in recognition of this that Tappert was awarded Germany's highest civil honour, the Federal Cross of Merit.

Now, a decade after Derrick handed in his badge, Germany has a new generation of goodwill ambassadors, particularly since the 2006 World Cup introduced millions to modern Germany.

The millions of foreign visitors who descend on the country's Christmas markets this month are witness to that positive vibe. But few of these visitors sipping their Glühwein will know that the goodwill groundwork was done three decades ago by Stephan Derrick, the good German.

SATURDDAY, 20 DECEMBER 2008

'We Put People in Dog Boxes. We Put Them in Ant-Farms beside Motorways. We Put Them in Villages that Weren't on Any Map'

Ross O'Carroll-Kelly

I saw it on *Six One* but it was one of those things I knew I was going to have to see with my own actual eyes? Hook, Lyon and Sinker has become the first major estate agent to go under as a result of the blahdy focking blah blah. George Lee is standing outside the place, predicting a new ice age, and in the background I can just make out JP and his old man, bringing out the furniture and dumping it into this humungous skip out front.

I'm suddenly feeling weirdly emotional? I spent six months of my life in that building, doing the only real work I've done in the ten years since I left school. When I see them carrying out the big neon scoreboard that me and JP used to use to keep track of our commission, I hop straight into a Jo and head for Ballsbridge.

President Mary McAleese and her husband, Dr Martin McAleese, with Irish actor Colin Farrell, when the President attended a reception hosted by the Irish Film Board at Warner Brothers studios in Hollywood, Los Angeles. Photograph: Maxwells.

People are openly weeping on Merrion Road – men and women, though it's the saucepans who'd actually break your hort. They're going, 'Mummy, Daddy – what's going to happen to us?' and the parents are there, 'Nobody knows,' not even bothering to lie. Because if Mr Conroy is pulling down the shutters, then the country really is focked.

I have to fight my way through a ruck of people outside. I bang on the window. JP sees me through the glass and opens the door just wide enough for me to, like, squeeze through. We high-five each other, both of us wondering, I'm sure, whether that's going to be the next thing to go.

Mr Conroy is sitting on the floor, with his back to the wall, a bottle of Glenfiddich beside him. He pours me, like, a large one. I sit on one side of him, JP on the other, none of us saying anything, all of us staring at the last thing left in the office – the 40-inch plasma television that Mr Conroy bought to celebrate JP leaving the priesthood.

We watch the ads. People skating up and down outside Brown Thomas. 'A nightingale sang in Berkeley Square,' I go. 'The focking nerve of these people!' It just feels like the right thing to say?

'No,' Mr Conroy goes, 'that's not how we're going to go out – all bitterness and recrimination. Make hay while the sun shines, they say. And we made hay. Oh, that's as sure as I'm going to be in Leggs of Lower Leeson Street at four o'clock tomorrow morning – where women with a past meet men with no future . . .' I offer them a toast without knowing what I'm actually toasting.

'Everything on earth has its own time and its own season,' JP suddenly goes. 'A time to be born and a time to die, a time to plant and a time to reap, a time to kill and a time to heal . . .' and there's no prizes for guessing who he's quoting – in other words, God? I'm wondering will he be angling for a return back to Him now that the arse has fallen out of the property game.

'If these walls could talk,' I go, suddenly all nostalgic. 'I mean, some of the shit we got up to in here. Doing whatever it took to bleed that extra five, ten, twenty grand out of people. "You have things you can sell, don't you? You have children? Can they not work?"'

Mr Conroy laughs. 'You were good,' he tells me. 'You were one of the best, Kid,' which is always nice to hear. 'We put people in dog boxes. We put them in ant-farms beside motorways. We put them in villages that weren't on any map and we called it a commutable distance . . .'

'Athlone,' JP goes, 'the gateway to Dublin,' and we all laugh at the famous *Irish Times* ad and the memory of him trying to, like, justify it to even the Advertising Standards crowd. You'd have chanced anything in those days.

I'm there, 'You know, I used to invent motorways that were going to be built to supposedly slash commute times. I'd go, "Yeah, it looks a good distance away on the map – but the M57 is going to change all of that." And I'd have put some poor focker in practically Kerry . . .'

JP goes, 'It's a wonder none of us ended up in jail.'

'People bidding against themselves,' Mr Conroy goes. '"Sorry, my friend – better offer

came in. You'll need to give us another twenty Ks and sell us your non-vital organs to stay in the game. You can always let the spare room. No, that's not damp – it's a water feature . . ." You know, it breaks my heart to think that the next generation aren't going to know any of this.'

There's, like, a sudden flash of light outside. Someone has set fire to the skip. The three of us walk over to the window and watch it burn – thirty years of work, literally up in smoke. I notice Mr Conroy's old suit – his Lucky Louis – on top of the fire. Someone has stuffed it with something to make it look like a Guy.

I'm there, 'What are you going to do now?'

'The new craze', he goes, 'is to drive to Dublin Airport, leave the keys in the car and fly some place no one will ever find you. Mad, I never thought about doing it in the eighties. But now . . .'

His voice breaks. JP puts his orm around his shoulder and I sort of, like, slap him on the back. 'It was the Klondike,' he goes, wiping his eyes and taking one last look around. 'And this . . . this, my friends, was Bonanza Creek.'

He flicks the switch and the lights go out.

SATURDAY, 20 DECEMBER 2008

O'Brien Made People of Ireland Reassess Nationalism

Stephen Collins

Conor Cruise O'Brien was one of the most influential public figures in Ireland in the second half of the 20th century. Although he served as a TD and a minister he exercised his greatest power through the force of his ideas, as expressed in books and newspaper articles for more than half a century.

His greatest achievement was to get the people of his country to reassess the meaning of Irish nationalism. Even many who regarded themselves as being utterly opposed to his political views were influenced by him and, well before the end of his life, his basic position of utter rejection of IRA violence and the promotion of the principle of consent with regard to the future of Northern Ireland had become accepted as the political orthodoxy.

When he began to propound his ideas about nationalism and challenge the notion that a united Ireland should be the supreme political goal the atmosphere was completely different.

The emergence of the Provisional IRA after the loyalist pogrom of 1969 put the country into a dangerous position, and outright civil war and the destruction of the economy was a real possibility.

The collapse of Yugoslavia into appalling ethnic violence in the 1990s shows what can happen when nationalist sentiments are whipped up to a frenzy and used by cynical politicians. Something similar almost happened in Ireland in 1969 and 1970, but thankfully the Fianna Fáil taoiseach, Jack Lynch, managed to see off the forces that wanted to push the country over the brink.

O'Brien, though, went a step further and gave intellectual force to the argument not simply that a united Ireland could not be achieved by force, but that it was wholly inappropriate and dangerous to seek to include in a state a substantial number of people who did not wish to belong.

Although many of his views came to be accepted over time O'Brien showed enormous courage in propounding his principles in the late 1960s and early 1970s in the face of deep-seated hostility not only from Sinn Féin/IRA but from most mainstream Irish politicians who could not face the fact that Northern unionists were British, and entitled to remain so for as long as they remained in a majority.

In the end even the IRA accepted the consent principle. While it galled O'Brien to see Sinn Féin involved in a powersharing arrangement in Northern Ireland his pen proved mightier than the

IRA's sword even if it took 30 bloody years for his message to sink in.

Of course, he also made political mistakes. His determination to defeat the objectives of Sinn Féin/IRA led him to ignore the faults on the unionist side, and his venture into Northern politics in the 1990s as a member of Robert McCartney's fringe unionist party devalued his real achievements.

In party politics he made a considerable impact on the country in the period from 1969 to 1977 when he was elected to Dáil Éireann as Labour TD for Dublin North East. It was the same constituency as his prime opponent in the politics of the Republic, Charles J. Haughey. The arms crisis of 1970 in which Haughey was directly involved was one of the factors that caused O'Brien to reassess traditional nationalism and he was a bitter opponent of Haughey thereafter.

In the Labour Party O'Brien's views caused huge dissension, but with the support of the party leader, Brendan Corish, he swung the party behind his policies despite intense opposition. That opposition came not only from a number of traditional party TDs like Seán Treacy and Stevie Coughlan but from the other two well-known media figures, Justin Keating and David Thornley.

As Labour Party spokesman on the North, O'Brien had a platform to air his views at every available opportunity, attacking the IRA campaign and all those who supported it.

One direct consequence of the arms crisis was that Labour reassessed its opposition to coalition with Fine Gael and the party dropped its anti-coalition stance. When the two parties came to power under Liam Cosgrave in 1973 O'Brien was appointed as minister for posts and telegraphs which meant he had responsibility for broadcasting.

There were regular spats with the media over the implementation of Section 31 of the Broadcasting Act, originally introduced by Fianna Fáil, which banned Sinn Féin from the airwaves.

Ornithologist David MacPherson from Clontarf in Dublin took advantage of yesterday's bright sunshine to record wildlife movements on Bull Island. Photograph: Matt Kavanagh.

O'Brien alienated some of his old liberal allies by defending the ban to the hilt.

While he was a minister he also made regular speeches on the North, frequently stirring up a hornet's nest. While some of his cabinet colleagues were furious with him for courting controversy, Cosgrave never attempted to rein him in. As far as Cosgrave was concerned, O'Brien was Labour spokesman on the North and entitled to express his views in that capacity.

While many expected that O'Brien would be a maverick as a minister he showed absolute loyalty to the taoiseach, and that loyalty was reciprocated. The devout Catholic Cosgrave was at the other end of the political spectrum to O'Brien on many issues but, on the North and the defence of democracy, they shared the view that the IRA campaign had to be defeated at all costs.

O'Brien lost his Dáil seat in the Fianna Fáil landslide of 1977 but that did not quieten his voice or his involvement in Irish political life. Throughout the 1980s and 1990s, as well as writing powerful and influential books about history and ideas, he also wrote regular and influential newspaper columns. His overriding theme was the national question and the preservation of tolerant democratic values. Of Conor Cruise O'Brien it can truly be said he did the State some service.

TUESDAY, 23 DECEMBER 2008

Better to Incinerate €1.5bn than Squander it on Anglo Irish Bank

Morgan Kelly

For the current Government, a month without a catastrophic policy error has come to seem like a month wasted. After the bank liability guarantee in September and the medical card fiasco in October, the Government had a quiet November but has now come roaring back to form with the bailout of Anglo Irish Bank. Attempting to recapitalise Anglo Irish is not only expensive and economically pointless, but futile.

Some simple arithmetic shows the hopelessness of what the Government is trying to do. In the typical property bust over the last 30 years, US banks have lost on average about 20 per cent of what they lent to developers. Let us suppose that Anglo Irish is no more incompetent or dishonest than the average bank and will also lose up to 20 per cent of what it has lent. Then, given lending of about €80 billion to developers, it follows that Anglo Irish is facing losses on the order of €15 billion. The true figure could easily turn out to be twice as large.

With likely losses of this magnitude, the Government's proposed investment of €1.5 billion will vaporise in months, forcing it either to continue pouring good money after bad, or to repudiate Anglo Irish's liabilities. For all it will achieve, the money might as well be piled up in St Stephen's Green and incinerated.

Anglo Irish epitomised the Irish bubble economy. Its rise began a decade ago as the boom created a demand for houses and commercial property. As prices started to rise, banks made a miraculous discovery: the more they lent, the more prices rose; and the more prices rose, the more people wanted loans to get into the booming market. And the more loans that bankers made, the bigger the bonuses they could award themselves.

It was brilliant while it lasted. One of Bank of Ireland's stable of developers would buy an office block for €100 million, and sell it on a year later to one of Anglo's for €120 million, and so on: a process known to bankers as adding value. Everyone was a genius and nobody could lose.

As a senior executive of Anglo Irish once assured me, there was no risk involved. All of the loans were guaranteed by the enormous property portfolios of the borrowers. What concerned me at the time was not that he was spouting transparent nonsense – that, after all, was what he was paid to do – but that he clearly believed it himself. Sadly, like any pyramid scheme, it contained the seeds of its own destruction.

Once banks stopped lending, as they were forced to do earlier this year, the market collapsed. Developers were left holding properties whose rental incomes were a ruinously small fraction of their interest payments, and banks discovered that their collateral was worthless.

All Irish banks have been injured by the collapsing property pyramid, some fatally so. Unfortunately, as international experience shows, banks that have been overwhelmed by bad property loans do not simply fade away. Their final act typically has three scenes.

First, the bank starts to admit that a certain fraction of its loans are receiving active management, it increases its bad loan provision but by an unrealistically low amount, and its share price collapses.

In the second scene, evidence of malfeasance starts to appear, as senior bankers are found to have had difficulties in distinguishing the bank's assets from their own, and to have been acting as poachers as well as gamekeepers in their dealings with developers.

It is to be hoped that any Irish bankers in this situation have heeded the cardinal rule of Irish

Members of the Ward Union, the only remaining stag hunt in Ireland, on the outskirts of Navan in Co. Meath. Photograph: Alan Betson.

finance and kept their more imaginative dealings within the jurisdiction. As Patrick Gallagher discovered, the British judicial system takes a less indulgent view of lapses of fiduciary responsibility than does our own, and seems to harbour a particular antipathy towards charming Irish rogues.

In the final stage, as the bank slides over the brink of collapse, senior managers loot its assets. Looting a bank involves nothing so unsubtle or easily traceable as driving away with carloads of cash. Instead, each bank has a filing cabinet with personal guarantees written by borrowers and deeds to property pledged as collateral (large property deals involve surprisingly little paperwork); and these documents have a tendency to find their way into the briefcases of departing executives who can later negotiate their return to their original owners.

So much for the future. Right now, in the 'nothing in the last six months has really happened' world of the Government, the bailout of Anglo Irish follows a compelling political logic. Anglo Irish funds developers, and developers fund Fianna Fáil.

By any other criterion, a bailout of Anglo Irish is senseless. Institutions such as AIB and Bank of Ireland fulfil an economically vital role of clearing payments and lending to households and businesses; Anglo Irish and Irish Nationwide were purely conduits for property speculation. They fulfil no role in the Irish economy and their absence would not be noticed.

By using taxpayers' money to acquire Anglo Irish's portfolio of dingy shopping centres and derelict development sites, the Government is squandering scarce resources that are needed elsewhere. Just as the State is putting too much money into Anglo Irish, it is putting in too little to recapitalise AIB and Bank of Ireland on which, whether you like it or not, large sectors of the Irish economy depend.

Governments tend to forget whose interests they are supposed to serve. Our Government was not elected to look after the managers, shareholders and bondholders of recklessly mismanaged banks. Its sole duty is to Irish taxpayers: to ensure that banks that serve a useful economic purpose continue to operate, while those that serve none are swiftly closed down.

SATURDAY, 3 JANUARY 2009

Reflecting on a More Private Life

Shane Hegarty

Ryan Tubridy suggests we meet at a five-star hotel in Stillorgan, just up the road from RTÉ. Inside, the lounge is busy with business types and groups of women, catching up over €4 euro pots of tea.

The room is dominated by a large, blazing fireplace that is carefully scattered with Christmas decorations. It appears oddly artificial, like the studio set of a seasonal television special. Or like the cover of the Christmas edition of the *RTÉ Guide*, on which Tubridy was among those pictured in a kitsch 1950s set-up, yet looked more natural than anyone else in it.

He has texted ahead to say he's running late, 'but I will be there'. He has presented that morning's radio programme from Roundwood,

Co. Wicklow, doing it with a giddiness that always seems to grab him when his show hits the road. Once he's ticked this interview off his to-do list he will go to see his daughter in the school nativity play. He has wavered a little on the exact time that it starts, maybe giving himself an exit strategy from the interview, should he want it.

He arrives, very apologetic about the delay. We agree to have the pictures taken first. 'The show was great this morning, Ryan,' a woman shouts to him as we pass her in the corridor. 'We had great fun. I'm so glad you liked it,' he replies, deploying a grin while walking sideways without breaking stride. It's a politician's trick, giving someone a moment without letting them take up his day. He's clearly a master at it, lessons perhaps learnt from a couple of years of pressing the flesh at the Rose of Tralee or from a political family (his mother is of the Fianna Fáil Andrews). Or maybe from how popping to the shops can mean several such encounters.

The exception is teenage boys, who he good-humouredly calls 'baboons' due to their general demeanour. From way off, he'll spot them, loose-limbed, excitable, gathered outside a shop, nudging, egging each other on ('Tell him he's shite'). Until eventually, once he's 10 yards past them, one of them will yell after him, 'Tubridy, you're shite!'

We find a private lounge for the interview, because in the tearoom some of the patrons would be too close to resist earwigging. And people will earwig. There is currently something of an appetite for his personal life, as there has been in the three years since the break-up of his marriage to RTÉ producer Anne Marie Power, with whom he has two daughters. His dates currently make national news. Occasionally, he hasn't helped himself, such as a recent 'I love a girl who appreciates darkness' cover interview in the *RTÉ Guide*, for which he got an awful slagging.

'There have been two articles in the last 10 days saying Let's Find Ryan a Wife, one naming five girls, and marks out of 10 for suitability. Mad!

Ryan Tubridy. Photograph: Aidan Crawley.

That I laugh at. It's pure comedy.' He tried to deliver a punch line himself when he asked a young model to accompany him to the Bond movie premiere in October, partly because they both agreed that her name, Laura Toogood, was too apt to resist.

It was a one-off, and he remains single, but he admits that he was also 'curious to see what the reaction would be if I brought someone to something. And the reaction was, in my world, very large and interesting to see'. She ended up being profiled in a national newspaper. 'As an exercise in journalism-watching, I was quite taken aback that they were dying to know who was that and who is he going out with. I didn't know there was so much interest, that it was intense.' He insists it was not a PR stunt; that there would be nothing for him to gain through that.

At the very least, though, it proved that his arm will offer a publicity boost to any ambitious young woman who attaches herself to it. 'Well, now I know. Now I know what happens when I go somewhere with somebody. I never knew, because I never did it. If anyone benefits from being seen with me, well done to them. I can't help it,' he says. 'There is great naïvety on my part I have to say. I mean I always say I am in a constant state of learning, but still I keep going.

'But if it was somebody else in the future, if I was to see somebody — and I very much hope to go out with somebody at some point — I would be careful because somebody else would be less able for it. And it would require more commitment, because if you're seen with somebody you don't want to play games with them or hurt them. And this weight of expectation on you, people are following you and your relationship asking, "Well, how's it going now? Is it still there?"'

He pauses just a beat. 'Do people really give a damn about this? Do they really though?' Here's the thing: they do. Almost everyone who knew I was interviewing Tubridy asked one thing: 'Are you going to ask him about the marriage break-up?' He levitates a little out of exasperation. 'Why? It's three years ago. Three years ago.' For the usual reasons that the Irish love rummaging through the lives of others.

'I would challenge anyone to talk to their brother or sister or auntie or uncle or anyone who had been through a marital break-up and ask them how easy it was for them to discuss it with anyone. And then ask them how easy it might be to discuss it in a public forum. Or to have it discussed. It's like a violation. It's such an intensely private scenario, and a very painful scenario and one that's nobody's business. But people still talk about it and they still add it as a tabloid line on top of an article

and it's a pity because it's private. Some things have to be off limits, some things have to be out of bounds and that's one.'

We immediately reach the out-of-bounds marker when I ask him if any of his family first learned of the break-up through the newspapers. 'That's too personal,' he says, firmly but not angrily. 'That's what I mean. The point I'm making is that I've never discussed it at any great length because it's not fair, there are other people involved, children and other people. It's not fair of me to discuss such a deeply intimate matter in the newspapers.

'And I hope that even by talking about it, it doesn't sound like I'm talking about it, if you know what I mean. That's behind a door. And I think it does come down to gossip, it does come down to squinting windows. People want to know more. My private life should be just that in some respects. And what I do is I present a TV show and

Cartoon by Martyn Turner.

a radio show. They're good, I enjoy doing that; I hope they're ok. Why do you want to come into the dressing room?'

It wasn't so long ago that the press focus was almost solely on his professional life. His had been a rapid rise; within 10 years he went from being Gerry Ryan's teaboy to having a daily Radio One show, a Saturday night chat show and a couple of years doing the Rose of Tralee under his cummer-bund.

The step up proved painful, with criticism of his radio show coming even from Gay Byrne. Tubridy gets less stick now, growing his radio ratings as his competitors begin to leak a little, and on recent Saturday nights his TV show has battled gamely against the rating beast that has been *The X Factor*. 'We had to run to stand still,' he says. He still had half a million viewers each week.

He's not one of them; can seldom bring himself to watch it. 'I sometimes get embarrassed. For me.' His brother recently announced that he can finally watch him now after five years of glimpsing it through his fingers. 'He said, "You were too odd, too weird. You weren't great." Which is bizarre, because you have half a million people watching you, if you're lucky, and all it takes is one to give you that little boost.'

But there must be vanity. Otherwise he wouldn't be in the job. 'Absolutely. And ego. You have to think you're pretty cool, which is pathetic. I don't know, my feeling is this is all I can do. This is probably the only thing in the world that I'm halfway good at. I'm pretty bad in every facet of my life. I'm a pretty bad human being.'

Does he mean he's a bad person or just not very good at doing things that most humans can do? 'I think I've got more flaws than the average fellow. I think that I'm bad at fixing things in the house. I'm not great at paying bills. I'm bad at keeping an eye at myself. I'm bad at all these mundane elements of my life. And in other elements of it I'm pretty shoddy too. And when I'm in the radio or TV studio I just think I'm really happy and

comfortable. In that red-lit moment of live, no one can get you. You are the beast and no one has a key to that cage. You're untouchable by people and life. And I like that. It's like scoring a goal. It's a very strange feeling.'

If he could eliminate one flaw as a radio presenter, he says it would be to stop saying things that he believes are funny but nobody else does. It gives him 'out-of-body' moments in the studio, when he looks at himself and thinks 'what a tosspot'. He has corrected other flaws, his biggest lesson being that 'the conversation you have in the pub or at the breakfast table or in the back of a taxi is utterly allowed on radio or television, because that's human speak'.

Occasional lunches with Gay Byrne, Gerry Ryan and Harry Crosbie act as extra-curricular lessons in life and broadcasting. 'Gerry, Harry and Gay have what they call the grumpy men lunch and they invited me as an honorary grump. And we get on well. There is no initiation ceremony other than to come, drink a glass of wine and talk complete nonsense. But it's lovely because it's essentially three generations of broadcasters, and Harry is the arbiter; he's like Hans Blix coming in to investigate the whole mess. And it's just three guys shooting the breeze, no shyness and very honest and everything comes out, whether it's about broadcasting, whether it's about private life. Everything is up for grabs.'

Among the more valuable lessons was one delivered by Byrne after Tubridy told him how Christmas of 2007 had been a 'pretty, pretty sad time', when he was alone, away from work, and with too much thinking time available. Byrne told him how, at the end of each *Late Late Show* season, his wife Kathleen would send him out for a few days of walking to get it out of his system.

'Gay said, when the lights go off and all that clapping and attention and your ego and everything stops and suddenly you're at home, in my case home alone, it's very quiet and very eerie and you've suddenly gone from full-on assault on the senses to thinking time. And thinking time isn't good if you're on your own, thinking about stuff.'

Expect the comedown, Byrne told him, and manage it. 'Because I worry about it. I worry about my children and their happiness and making sure everything is in order in the world. And their happiness is paramount.'

Since turning 35 last May, he has undergone a bit of a reassessment. It wasn't anything as intense as an epiphany, but a 'gentle realisation' that certain things don't matter. 'Health matters. Beauty doesn't matter in physical terms. Intellect matters. It's more interesting. Good conversation. Going for pints with your brothers. Being nice to your mother and sisters. Doing favours. Hugging your kids a bit closer if you've had a long day.'

Is his self-awareness a sign of confidence born of experience? 'Yes. When my private life became of great interest to people three years ago, it shook me to the core, and my confidence was rattled and it took a huge amount of puffing up my chest in the morning to get out there and do the chat show and everything. And I hid behind personas and all that, and it did me a favour – it was a help. But the confidence I have now is more natural. It's not being driven by an emotional vulnerability. It's being driven by an enjoyment of life.'

He thinks it may have something to do with no longer being the new guy, with all that golden boy stuff attached to it. Certainly, in the seven years since I last interviewed him, there is less of the giddy ambition, the bouncy gait of a young man heading off on a big adventure. He is more introspective, and clearly more experienced. He still talks a lot, in an articulate but slightly breathless fashion, but he is more calculated, perhaps more tactical than before. He is more serious. And there is a toughness, although it coats a definite vulnerability.

Good ratings have helped the confidence, as has a new three-year contract. How much he'll earn he won't say, but it'll be public in a couple of years anyway (for the record, he earned €346,667 in 2006). He'd prefer it wasn't, but what can he do? It's public money. Was there pressure to take a pay cut, given RTÉ's straitened circumstances? 'No. I think the 3 per cent levy is enough, my contribution to the Government.'

Tubridy says he loves it in RTÉ, and is working on a couple of projects that he hopes will stave off a tendency to get bored easily. He wonders if a growing exhaustion from working six-day weeks will gnaw at him, but says that high ratings prove there's room for two weekend chat shows.

He insists there was no tweak of envy when Gerry Ryan stood in for Pat Kenny on *The Late Late Show*, because he knew his Saturday night show ruled him out of the job anyway. He won't pretend that *The Late Late Show* doesn't play on his mind, but says that right now he'd be happy if he could take his show to Fridays and see *The Late Late* given to a 'deserving host on a Saturday night, someone who isn't presenting a radio show five days a week'.

The recent appointment of Claire Duignan as head of radio in RTÉ is welcome, he says, and guesses a shake-up will come to the schedules. On a career level, it's his one wish for 2009, because the one-hour slot is chafing. 'Did you ever get a duvet and give it a good rattle and then it feels really nice when you put it down? I want that slightly with my career.

'I want those, what do you call it, the jump leads to kind of go: come on, here we go again. In radio terms I'd like more time, to allow for more fluidity, because I just feel the show keeps ending abruptly. I keep feeling I'm ending in the middle of a sentence.' That, he clarifies, is meant as a metaphor.

'I'd like to breathe please. For ages I used to think an hour was enough; the show wasn't formed yet. But I do believe we're formed, nearly formed, and with that in mind I think it's time to flex it a bit.'

And on a personal level, what is his one wish for 2009? 'I would like if my private life becomes a bit more private.'

THURSDAY, 8 JANUARY 2009

Mourners Told They Would Get Gregory Sardonic Look

Kathy Sheridan

In St Agatha's, the church where Tony Gregory was baptised and once served as an altar boy in his beloved north inner city Dublin, the State's political establishment gathered for his funeral Mass.

What they heard yesterday was a pointed message about his life-long exclusion by much of that same establishment, and a message directed at certain publicity-conscious politicians who might lay claim to his mantle.

'He was for 25 years systematically excluded by every political party from the position of lord mayor and any other position on Dublin City Council. Just as for the most part of his years in the Dáil, he was excluded . . .' said his long-time friend, Cllr Maureen O'Sullivan, in a eulogy delivered before a coffin draped in a stylised version of the Starry Plough.

Only a few weeks from death, he had made the effort to enter the Dáil to speak on the education cuts, she added, but was not allowed speaking time.

'So,' she asked to sustained applause, 'how would he have dealt with certain politicians and their lavish tributes and praise in the last few days?

Noel Gregory (right), brother of Tony Gregory, with Annette Dolan, partner of the late Independent TD, followed by Cllr Maureen O'Sullivan, after Mr Gregory's funeral mass at St Agatha's Church, North William Street, Dublin. Photograph: Matt Kavanagh.

Or those people speaking profusely about him in death, but during his life when he came looking for help, never so much as put a leaflet in a letterbox? I think they would all be getting the Gregory look – you know, the sardonic one . . .'

In fact, she implied, he had anticipated this. 'At Tony's wishes, the burial and after the burial are private. They are for his relatives, his close friends, canvassers and supporters who maintained their loyalty towards Tony over the years – and for those politicians, regardless of their politics, who had a genuine friendship with Tony over the years. His funeral is not a photo opportunity,' she said emphatically to a congregation headed by President Mary McAleese, Taoiseach Brian Cowen and former taoiseach and local TD Bertie Ahern.

She distinguished between 'Tony the politician, who didn't do much smiling' and 'Tony the personal friend, who did'. This was the Tony with 'the great sense of humour, who was great company, a great teller of stories . . . An outdoor person who loved the sea, who loved walking, and enjoyed his trips to Cape Clear . . . one who loved cooking and loved eating'.

The simple, moving service, much of it celebrated by An tAthair Piaras Ó Duill in Irish at Tony's request, included the traditional May hymn, 'Bring Flowers of the Rarest,' sung in a church still garlanded with Christmas wreaths, a twinkling tree, and white altar flowers. The prayers of the faithful were read by Tony's partner, Annette Dolan, in a clear, confident voice that wavered only at the end.

The first burst of applause – and an intimation of the feeling among mourners – came earlier, during Fr Peter McVerry's homily, when he said: 'Politicians come and politicians go and although they won't thank me for saying it, politicians get forgotten.'

He continued when the applause faded: 'Tony Gregory will not be forgotten . . . Tony was my idea of a true Christian; a person who imitated Jesus in giving everything he was, for the sake of his brothers and sisters.'

To a murmur of amusement, Fr McVerry recalled Tony the iconoclast who 'made open-necked shirts respectable, much to the consternation of the establishment of that time – but Tony never sought to identify with the establishment, and indeed, I think the feeling was mutual . . .'.

Noel Gregory also drew sustained applause when he preceded a passionate rendering of Joseph Mary Plunkett's 'I See His Blood Upon the Rose', with the suggestion that 'Tony would want us all to be mindful of the Palestinian victims of the brutal Israeli aggression . . . in Gaza'.

Outside, four senior gardaí – Assistant Commissioner Michael Feehan, Chief Supt Pat Leahy, Supt Seán Ward and Supt Ray Barry – stood to attention.

Bishop Eamon Walsh, who concelebrated the Mass, remarked, 'We preached; Tony was the sermon.' Later, Joe Higgins, the Socialist Party leader and former TD, delivered the graveside oration, partly through Irish, saying that for more than 30 years, Tony Gregory 'stood out as a rock of political integrity and independence . . . In 2003, the record of the Dáil will show that he moved the first comprehensive motion in opposition to the then impending criminal invasion of Iraq. Everything he said then has tragically been vindicated'.

Those present also included Minister for Foreign Affairs Micheál Martin, Minister for Social and Family Affairs Mary Hanafin, Minister for the Gaeltacht Eamon Ó Cuiv, chief whip Pat Carey, the Lord Mayor of Dublin Eibhlin Byrne and the leaders of all the main political parties including Enda Kenny, Eamon Gilmore, John Gormley, Gerry Adams and Ciarán Cannon.

The attendance also included politicians Cyprian Brady, Seán Haughey, Trevor Sargent, Michael Woods, Finian McGrath, Aengus Ó Snodaigh, Caoimhghín Ó Caoláin, Mary Lou McDonald, Ciaran Cuffe, Dan Boyle, Joe Costello, Patricia McKenna, Christy Burke and Clerk of the Dáil Kieran Coghlan.

Also present were David Begg, Fergus McCabe, John O'Shea, Hugh O'Flaherty and his wife Kathleen, Alice Leahy, Padraic Ferry, Bill Cullen, Nicky Kelly, Rose Dugdale, Nell McCafferty, Theo Dorgan, Maol Muire Tynan, Máirtín Ó Méalóid, Liam Ó Maonlaí, Vincent Browne, Shane Ross, Michael Farrell and Seán Dublin Bay Loftus.

The Irish Times was represented by editor Geraldine Kennedy.

MONDAY, 12 JANUARY 2009

Patrick Neary's Departure a Repudiation of Our Approach to Regulation

John McManus

Patrick Neary is the latest casualty of the credit crunch and more specifically the loans to directors controversy at Anglo Irish Bank. There will be others, but Neary's departure is particularly significant as it can be seen as a repudiation of the whole approach to financial regulation adopted by successive administrations here.

Ireland – through Neary and his predecessors both in the Irish Financial Services Regulatory Authority (IFSRA) and the Central Bank proper – has adopted what is known as a principles-based or light-touch approach to regulation. Instead of laying down and then enforcing a vast amount of rules, the regulator has instead set out principles by which it expects the industry to abide.

The idea is to put the focus on encouraging good behaviour by financial institutions rather than simply fostering a culture of compliance. The rationale being, in part, that it's better to have a relatively small amount of rules followed in spirit rather than a raft of legislation that is followed to the letter, with loopholes being routinely sought and exploited.

It was a particularly attractive approach in the context of the concerted effort to build an international financial services industry that has gone on here for the last 30 years. Light-touch regulation is low cost, because the regulator is lean and, ideally, nimble. It is also responsive to industry needs.

It is a sophisticated approach and relies on a great deal of trust and integrity on the part of both the regulator and also the institutions and intermediaries involved, such as accountants and lawyers. It is not without risks. There will of course always be a few bad apples, but if the vast majority of the industry buys into the concept then the regulatory load would be light and everybody would benefit.

Principles-based regulation is for grown-ups and unfortunately completely unsuited to the culture of Irish banking, as exemplified by what happened at Anglo Irish Bank.

How could a principles-based system work in an industry where the chairman of the country's third-largest bank seemed so devoid of basic morals that he was prepared routinely to mislead his shareholders and the regulator about the extent of his indebtedness to the bank?

And he was not some rogue operator. He was facilitated by the second-biggest building society in the State – Irish Nationwide.

Seán FitzPatrick and Anglo Irish Bank behaved in exactly the opposite fashion to how they were supposed to under their part of the light-touch regulatory bargain. FitzPatrick may have been correct when he says that what he did was not illegal but he must take us for fools if he thinks for one minute that anyone believes he was acting in the spirit of the regulations.

Not only was the principles-based approach wrong for the Irish financial services market – and probably for financial services generally – it has also resulted in a regulator that is arguably not fit for purpose.

One of the more extraordinary aspects of the whole Anglo Irish business is that the significance of what FitzPatrick was up to seems to have been

Hannes Louet, from Tralee, windsurfing off Banna strand in Kerry. Photograph: Domnick Walsh/Eye Focus.

lost on the individuals in the regulator who dealt with it.

If there was an issue that merited being brought to the attention of the top management, this was surely it. And it should have been done in a formal manner. Instead it appears that if escalation took place at all, it was by way of some informal channel, although Neary disputes that even this took place. The committee that investigated the affair was not able to reconcile the evidence, but made it clear that in doing so they did not mean to suggest that Neary and his prudential director were told what was going on at Anglo.

What is clear is that a number of things that should have happened did not happen, including informing the bank's own auditors and the Director of Corporate Enforcement about what was going on.

The summary of the committee's report,

published by IFSRA, plays up the pressure that the organisation was under because of the liquidity crisis as a significant factor in why the regulator dropped the ball.

That was no doubt an issue, but the fundamental problem was that the culture engendered in the regulator by its principles-based approach meant that Anglo Irish got a mild telling-off and was made promise to do better next time, when it should have been clear to everyone involved that nothing short of FitzPatrick's resignation would suffice.

The penny appears to have dropped with IFSRA, which noted in its statement last Friday that the principles-based approach was now under review. Nonetheless, it seems still to think the main problem is the global financial crisis rather than the moral ambivalence and greed at the heart of our financial services industry.

It also took a dig at Neary, pointing out that he played a big part in the adoption of the principles-based approach here. It seems a bit gratuitous and comes across as a rather pathetic attempt by IFSRA to distance itself from what has turned out to be a strategic mistake by the whole organisation over several decades.

The Anglo Irish business does not reflect well on anyone, but at least Neary has shown that he for one understands the principles of accountability and responsibility. It is more than can be said for his peers.

SATURDAY, 17 JANUARY 2009

Searching for the Hard-Earned Cash Flushed Down Anglo's Plush Facilities

Miriam Lord

Seán Patrick FitzPatrick's facilities were awesome – a sort of gold-plated executive washroom with an entrepreneurial twist. Each year, he flushed through an enormous amount of money. Now it seems most of it, along with the nest eggs of small shareholders, has gone down the drain.

His facilities cost tens of millions, but the boss of Anglo Irish Bank decided he was worth it and who was going to contradict him? Not him, swashbuckling Seán Fitz of the two Pats, poster boy for The Boom.

The man is on first name terms with the current and previous taoisigh, for God's sake. They both call him 'Seanie'. Anyway, Seanie – we feel we know him well enough at this stage – designed these special facilities for his sole use. Building on a Vision is how he might have described his edifice in some future address to the Irish Management Institute. Were he not now disgraced.

Building on other people's money is how it might be described by the victims of his vanity.

There's a new chairman in Seanie's place now. Donal O'Connor stepped centre stage yesterday. Can't imagine Biffo or Bertie calling him Donie. He is a tall man with swept-back grey hair, wearing a silver grey tie and a dark grey suit. Following the exploits of his high-profile and rather glam predecessor, this time around it's a case of: Grey rather than greed is good. But don't let that signature colour fool you. O'Connor is an accountant.

Donal chaired yesterday's extraordinary general meeting of Anglo Irish Bank, and it was he who brought up the subject of Seanie Pat FitzPat's marvellous facilities. Listen to this. 'Mr FitzPatrick had a revolving facility,' Donal told his quietly seething audience.

The mind boggles. Revolving? Must have been above in the penthouse. Maybe that's why nobody knew about it, including the bank's auditors – both internal and external. They've lost the power of speech with the shock.

But there's more. 'Mr FitzPatrick's facility was clearly very large,' added Donie. (€84 million, at the last count.) His audience, similarly, and, in some cases, prematurely grey, was disgusted. Seanie Pat FitzPat's extremely large facilities were one of the main reasons, according to the Minister for Finance among others, that the bank is being nationalised.

It's a bit like that time when television footage showed the interior of Saddam Hussein's deserted palace, and the whole world marvelled at his bathrooms, with their solid gold fittings. These days, the nation is marvelling at FitzPatrick's facilities, while a large group of people have lost the money they were relying upon to see them through their old age.

You see, Donal O'Connor couldn't really bring himself to use the word 'loan'. So instead he called the astonishing amounts of money borrowed from Anglo by its chairman 'facilities'. Seanie kept these loans a secret. A facility here, a facility there, and the next thing you're looking at €84 million, personal disgrace, national upheaval and heartache for a lot of hardworking people.

There was a board of directors when Chairman FitzPatrick was playing the numbers. Some have resigned, but most remain. They sat on the platform in the Round Room of the Mansion House, a long line of glum faces. Not one of them spoke, not even to each other. They just sat there while the shareholders excoriated them, waxen candidates for an economic chamber of horrors.

'You can come in here and sit like dummies,' protested one angry pensioner. 'And I'm sorry to make a derogatory comment.' The silent suits were lacerated. Apart from the two new appointments – former Fine Gael leader Alan Dukes and former head of the Revenue Commissioners, Frank Daly,

who were ostentatiously exempted by speaker after speaker.

Grey O'Connor apologised again and again for the past mistakes of the bank he has only recently come to serve. He apologised again and again for the deeds of his predecessor. But he gave little new information to the devastated shareholders.

Yet he was courteous and patient. Had he bent any further backwards in his attempts to empathise he would have turned into a croquet hoop. In many ways, Donal O'Connor finds himself in a similar position to Brian Cowen. Not only has he been given a new job, but he has been landed with his charismatic predecessor's mess.

Also like Cowen, O'Connor is loathe to criticise the regime that brought about the debacle. 'I have been enormously impressed by their professionalism

Cartoon by Martyn Turner.

and commitment and work on behalf of the bank,' he said, wringing his hands. This attitude infuriated the mostly elderly shareholders. 'Don't talk rubbish!' came a shout from the hall.

Senator Shane Ross tore strips off the board while his sidekick Eamon Dunphy watched in admiration. Gay Byrne caused a frisson when he arrived. In our time of need, where is Brian Cowen? Never mind, Uncle Gaybo is here. . . He left before the end and was waylaid outside. He said he wasn't a shareholder, but had just popped in for a look because he was in town and his son-in-law happens to be employed by the bank in London.

'The whole thing is bordering on the inexplicable,' declared Gaybo, expounding to the delight of those journalists saddled with the unenviable task of cornering departing pensioners in an effort to find out how much they lost.

And this was the awful part of it. Away from the suits and the platitudes and the polish of the going-forward brigade. The anorak was garment of choice in the hall. Designer shoes and bags were not in evidence. These were not fat cats. Just people who had worked hard and invested their money in the hope it would work for them. At the very least, they had expected appropriate stewardship of their savings.

They didn't get it.

But back to Gay. 'I thought Prionsias De Rossa was absolutely wonderful,' he declared. Which will have come as a surprise to the Labour MEP, who wasn't there. We think Uncle Gay meant Shane Ross.

Most shareholders were resigned to never getting any return on their investments. One lady fixed the board with a steely gaze: 'I'll remember your names, and if I ever have money again to invest and I see you on the board, I'll run the other way.' John O'Leary (85) came up from west Cork. He wanted to know why no Government representative was present, 'as a final courtesy before the final curtain drops'.

A Moment of Utter Integrity

Kathy Sheridan, in Washington

Under a crescent moon, hours before dawn, in sub-freezing temperatures, a tidal wave of humanity poured into the streets of Washington DC to reclaim the US capital for all of the people of America.

From 3.30 a.m., wrapped in layers of clothing, toting folding chairs, picnics, rugs and the most vital accessory – carbon hand and foot warmers – they walked, skipped and sang their way to the National Mall, then bundled up in blankets and, surrounded by architectural symbols of American history, they found a spot near the giant screens and settled down to wait.

The moment came at 11.30 precisely, when the determined face of Barack Obama, his head held high, appeared on the screens and triggered an emotional frenzy of flag-waving, chanting, foot-stomping and wracking sobs in a crowd of millions. Nearby a woman fell to her knees, choking on her tears, thanking God that this moment had not been snatched from them 'by an assassin's bullet', an unspoken but real dread in recent days, particularly among civil rights veterans and visitors from the deep south.

'Thank you, God . . . Thank you, thank you, oh thank you for keeping him safe for this moment.' As the moving, joyful musical interludes, prayers and introductions took their course, a tension of a unique kind was building in the crowd, a crowd bent on nothing as trivial as entertainment or parades. This was an extraordinarily diverse assembly with a single purpose: to see and sense in their souls that moment when power would pass into the hands of a man regarded by many as a Messiah, 'our Jesus, our Moses,' and, by the handful of *Deliverance*-style dissenters around the Mall, as 'a peddler of vile liberal theology'.

As he took the oath of office, it felt like a sacred moment, one of utter integrity. 'He used his middle name, Hussein – that bodes well,' said a (white) doctor as all around him, tears fell and the crowd bowed in solemn meditation, and prayed, and roared soulful alleluias in gospel musicality and raised their arms in ecstasy. 'We heard freedom ring. You heard freedom ring,' exclaimed a woman from Selma, Alabama, feverishly shucking off her two blankets.

Almost from the first sentence of his sombre, forthright inaugural speech, it was evident that they had taken on board the new president's message of unity, when they applauded his tribute to George Bush's 'service to the nation'. It was a sentiment that had been echoed around the Mall from dawn by people of every colour.

His resistance of the 'I' word (used only three times) and clear intent to eschew populism for a 'get on your bike' message about hard graft and sacrifice, left few openings for applause, but this audience was ready for it. They savoured it, not in wild bursts, but carefully, reflectively. They applauded solemnly and fiercely when he talked about the challenges ahead and said: 'They will not be met easily or in a short span of time. But know this, America – they will be met.'

They clung to each other, tears streaming as he talked about 'the God-given promise that all are equal, all are free, and all deserve a chance to pursue their full measure of happiness' and about 'why men and women and children of every race and every faith can join in celebration across this magnificent mall, and why a man whose father less than 60 years ago might not have been served at a local restaurant can now stand before you to take a most sacred oath'.

And they wept anew when he addressed old values, such as sacrifice and the labour of the unsung working people, and the freshly-discovered notion that 'greatness is never a given. It must be

earned . . . It has been the risk-takers, the doers, the makers of things – some celebrated but more often men and women obscure in their labour – who have carried us up the long, rugged path towards prosperity and freedom. For us, they packed up their few worldly possessions and travelled across oceans in search of a new life. For us, they toiled in sweatshops and settled the West; endured the lash of the whip and ploughed the hard earth . . . But our time of standing pat, of protecting narrow interests and putting off unpleasant decisions – that time has surely passed. Starting today, we must pick ourselves up, dust ourselves off, and begin again the work of remaking America.'

The mood was festive, but for the surprising number of families with young children it was a quiet lesson in civics, an event to which hundreds of photographs would bear witness to their presence, a time to retrieve the memory of those who had passed on, but now in a time of pride and triumph.

People who had endured 18-hour bus journeys through dark and ice, shared bunk beds over 100 miles away and walked miles from the drop-off point as early as 3a.m., offered food, footwarmers and positive words to this frozen journalist. They waved strangers ahead of them in the cafe queue. Boy scouts offered high fives, maps and flags. After a mass 'O-ba-ma!' chant, Dr Cliff Andrew, a doctor at Johns Hopkins hospital, began the primal chant synonymous with the Bush 'with us or against us' years: 'U. S. A'. No one joined in. But he did it deliberately, he said. 'I don't want to send the wrong message . . . but we're not going to let Bush take our flag. It's our country . . .' he said mildly.

Denise Roy, a 43-year-old African-American from Selma, Alabama, an iconic location of the civil rights movement, saw a close friend die in what she described as a 'race-related' incident and sees this as 'a new beginning'. She is no Pollyanna, however, identifying problems in her own black community that whites might hesitate to mention. She believes that progress at home has been stalled

Barack Obama is sworn in by US Chief Justice John Roberts as the 44th president of the United States, alongside his wife, Michelle, who holds the inauguration bible used by Abraham Lincoln. The Obamas' two daughters, Malia and Sacha (right), look on. Photographer: Mark Wilson/Bloomberg.

by a lack of that unity of purpose among black residents, who make up well over two-thirds of Selma's population. The soaring hope and pride of these momentous days will be challenged by the stark reality of life back in Selma, a place still carrying the wounds of the past. 'We're too complacent about the little bit we have,' she said, talking of plans for an anti-violence campaign back home.

As the massive screens zoned in on George W. Bush being escorted to a helicopter by President Obama and a shot of a shrunken Dick Cheney in a wheelchair (injured while packing boxes), there was the odd triumphalist roar, little more. Yesterday, America exhaled and began a new era.

FRIDAY, 23 JANUARY 2009

Childcare Teams Working with Scarce Resources

Carl O'Brien

She clasped her trembling hands together, hung her head and stared at the floor. The colour drained from the face of the 40-year-old mother of six as the judge read out the litany of abuse she had forced her children to endure at the family home in Roscommon.

She had admitted to forcing her 13-year-old son to have sex with her; her children weren't properly toilet-trained and had defecated in their underwear at school; she had directed her daughters to tie up their hair to hide their head-lice from teachers.

'These children had no chance from the moment they were born,' Judge Miriam Reynolds said, in a tone which veered into disbelief at times. 'Any chance of a normal and happy life was stolen from them by the woman who calls herself their mother.'

There were hard questions, too, for health authorities and the wider community, who, the judge said, had failed the children. Why were the children only taken into care eight years after they first came to the attention of health authorities? How could social services have failed to notice warning signs of abuse at home? Did teachers fail to spot the obvious signs of neglect among the children? Were State agencies communicating properly with each other?

More than a decade after the public was repulsed by official inaction by authorities involving horrific incidences of abuse such as the Kilkenny incest case, Sophia McColgan and Kelly Fitzgerald, many are asking whether the authorities have learned anything.

The six children, now ranging in age from 10 to 19, are split up and living with foster families. However, they are profoundly damaged and still trying to come to terms with the abuse. Some of the children are suicidal; others have no knowledge of relationships other than one which is violent and abusive.

It is still too early to say why the system failed or why the children were not removed into care

Carolyn Rutherford of the Science Gallery at Trinity College, Dublin, viewing AVIO!, part of the gallery's Lightwave Festival. Photograph: Patrick Bolger.

sooner. It is clear, though, that the State has a positive duty to protect the lives of children at risk where it becomes aware that the risk is one of harm or injury.

The Childcare Act of 2001 – introduced on foot of scandals such as the Kilkenny incest case – gives health boards extra powers to intervene in cases of suspected abuse. It also includes statutory duties to deliver support services. However, despite this, it is clear the system is not working in many places. Most child protection and social work teams work against a backdrop of scarce resources and under-staffing, which only allows them to deal with abuse cases on an emergency basis.

The result is a compromised service that is affecting the quality of support available to vulnerable children and their families, and that flies in the face of official policy, which states that children should be admitted to care as a measure of last resort.

Another issue is that young and inexperienced social workers are too often plunged into the deep end of child protection. They are forced to deal with complex care and welfare issues and required to make life-changing decisions for children and their families.

A review of child and family services shows that some social work teams are forced to place hundreds of cases of suspected abuse and neglect on waiting lists. The reality in many areas is that some of the cases may never be dealt with, unless they escalate into an emergency in the meantime.

Many of those on the front line of child protection are steeling themselves for a wave of criticism following events in Roscommon. Yet they are the ones who have to walk the tightrope between trying to support families in their homes and taking the catastrophic step of taking children into care.

For some time the policy of health authorities has been to shift resources from child protection – which deals with emergency cases – towards prevention in the form of family support services.

There has been little evidence of this in recent years.

Better family support services and a reorganised child protection system are no guarantee that similar cases of system failure may never happen again. However, it would help to ensure that everything possible is being done to intervene in the lives of children earlier and prevent as many children as possible from being needlessly damaged.

SATURDAY, 24 JANUARY 2009

Inside the World's Biggest Prison

Lara Marlowe, in Gaza

There were many ways to die during the Israeli offensive on Gaza. From their hospital beds at Gaza's Shifa Hospital, Atallah Saad, 13, and Yussef Salem, 17, told me how 'zananas' – remotely piloted drones that fire missiles – wounded them and killed Atallah's mother and pregnant sister-in-law, and two of Yussef's school friends.

The drones were given the nickname because they make a loud z-z-z-z-z sound. But the most shocking thing about them is that an Israeli operator watches his target – in these cases, all civilians – through a surveillance camera before launching the missile. Death by remote control.

White phosphorous was another, much publicised means of death. Each M82581 artillery shell, manufactured by General Dynamics in Pine Bluff, Arkansas, bears the initials PB. And each of the 155mm shells contains 116 felt wafers soaked in phosphorus, which ignites on contact with oxygen. The phosphorous makes the white jellyfish-shaped clouds seen on television during the 27 December – 17 January Israeli offensive. It provides cover for advancing troops, but it also burns houses and people. If one of the felt pads lands on your skin, it burns until all the fuel is consumed, creating deep, wide, chemical burns, often to the bone.

Dr Nafiz Abu Shabaan pulls a plastic bag from under his desk. It is filled with white phosphorous, buried in sand. The brown pieces look like dog dirt, and re-ignite if broken open. Mahmoud al Jamal, 18, sits in the doctor's office, his right ear congealed, his fingers and part of his chest eaten away by white phosphorous. The unsightly wounds make him look like a leper.

Al Jamal was walking at dawn when he saw the white jellyfish in the sky. 'Everything was set on fire around me. I felt my body burning. I fell down and I asked the man lying next to me to help me, but he was dead. Then I lost consciousness.' Al Jamal's brother later told him how smoke poured from his body in the ambulance on the way to the hospital.

The Israeli's use of white phosphorous is amply documented. Israel says it is legal, but human-rights groups say its use in civilian areas might constitute a war crime. Dr Abu Shabaan is more concerned by evidence of new, mysterious weapons and appeals for an impartial international investigation into Israel's use of new weapons.

'We've seen many, many cases of amputation – like a cauterised wound, with no bleeding,' he recounts. 'Some have minor chest injuries, but the X-rays show nothing and they die suddenly, without explanation.'

Palestinian and foreign doctors who have treated the war-wounded at Shifa suspect the injuries may be caused by Dense Inert Metal Explosive, also known as Focus Lethality Munition, a weapon invented through Israeli-American cooperation.

'We are guinea pigs to the Americans and Israelis,' says Dr Abu Shabaan. 'The Americans give the Israelis new weapons, and they try them out on us.'

'They are definitely testing weapons on us,' says Dr Sobhi Skaik, a member of the Royal College of Surgeons in Edinburgh and the head of the surgery department at Shifa. 'The amount of damage done by these weapons is not commensurate to the wounds. We found computer chips, magnetic pieces and transistors in wounds. Sometimes there are only minute pin-point punctures to the abdomen and chest, but you see huge damage to internal organs. One patient had his liver burned black, as if it had been grilled. We think there must be something embedded in the human body that is releasing poison and killing.'

Yet for all the high-tech and Frankenstein weaponry, perhaps Israel's most vicious arm against the Palestinians has been 'al-hissar', the siege, imposed on the Gaza Strip 19 months ago when Hamas, after winning a democratic election that the world refused to recognise, seized power from the Fatah Palestinian Authority.

The world turned a blind eye as Gazans languished in the world's biggest prison, unable to travel, import, export or interact with anyone or anything beyond their borders. And the world largely ignored the rockets Hamas fired in anger and frustration from within the siege. As a result of this dual negligence the conflict exploded, killing 13 Israelis and 1,300 Palestinians.

The siege was one reason casualties were so high in the three-week war, says Fred Abrahams of Human Rights Watch. With the Israeli and Egyptian borders closed, 'It wasn't possible for Gazans to escape. The only way to get out was on a stretcher.'

For 19 months, Gaza has endured shortages of fuel, food, medicine and building materials. The Palestinians suffer the additional humiliation of using their tormentors' currency, but two months ago the Israeli government cut the supply of shekels, creating a severe cash shortage. Fayad Salam, the prime minister of the Palestinian Authority in Ramallah, was forced to plead with the Israeli Prime Minister Ehud Olmert.

There were long queues at ATMs in Gaza City this week, but no matter how much they have in salary or savings, cash is rationed and Palestinians

A woman and child in front of a demolished building in Gaza. Photograph: Anja Niedringhaus/AP.

can withdraw only 1,000 Israeli shekels per month. 'If the Israelis could deprive us of air, they would do it,' says a Palestinian doctor.

The siege of Gaza lies at the heart of the conflict. 'If the Israelis want the war to end, they must open all the borders and end the siege,' says Hamas government spokesman Tahir al-Nounou. 'Because the siege is war; the siege is killing our people.'

The only lifeline for Gaza is some 1,300 tunnels beneath the Gaza–Egyptian border. It costs $10,000 (€7,800) to dig a tunnel. The best tunnels are bored with sophisticated machines that compress earthen walls so no give-away sand appears outside. Some have railway tracks and electricity, and the tunnels are a lucrative business for Gazans and Egyptians. Because Hamas is believed to import weapons through the tunnels, Israel carpet-bombed them during the offensive. Yet only an estimated 400 were destroyed, and by mid-week

the tunnels were again open. Huge plastic cubes in metal frames, holding petrol, appeared on the pavements of Gaza City.

But the return to a semblance of normality cannot efface the three-week nightmare. Whole families were wiped out. Abu Mohamed Balousha, who lost five daughters, and the Samounis of Zeitoun, where a four-year-old boy was the only survivor in a family of 30, have become causes célèbres.

Everyone has a worst memory. For ambulance driver Hathem Saleh, it was desperate telephone calls from the wounded. 'When you have been talking to him on the phone and you cannot reach him because the Israeli tank will hit you – it happened to me many times . . . I could hear cries and the Israelis were shooting at us.'

Dr Mahmoud al Khozendar, a chest physician, tells of a colleague whose Russian wife was cut in half when an Israeli missile hit their home. It also

Young Israelis observe the northern Gaza Strip from a hill near the southern town of Sderot during an Israeli air strike on Gaza. Photograph: Nikola Solic/Reuters.

killed their six-month-old child. 'He took the two parts of his wife and put her on the bed with the baby. He escaped with a wounded son and daughter, and asked the Red Crescent to go back for the bodies.'

At Shifa, al Khozendar had a room full of limbs he could not match with bodies, and one body with two heads. 'Most of the bodies were buried without names,' he says.

There were many ways to die during the Israeli offensive on Gaza. Perhaps the greatest number killed were crushed to death when the Israelis fired heavy tank artillery at their houses. Halima Radwan, 60, seemed particularly symbolic to me. Radwan was a young woman when she and her family fled from Israel in the 1967 war. She spent her life as a wandering Palestinian, moving to Gaza, Jordan, Lebanon, Egypt. In 1996, in the glory days when Gaza had an airport and

Palestinians carried passports, she and her husband Ahmad, a PLO official, decided to move back to 'Palestine'. They built a five-bedroom villa in the Abed Rabbo district of Gaza. A month before the offensive, they paid off their debts and celebrated.

Maher Radwan, 36, is Halima and Ahmad's only son and a mechanical engineer with the Palestinian Authority. He, his wife and children lived with his parents. 'Before the ground offensive started, I decided to take my wife and children further from the border,' Maher recounts in front of the ruined villa. 'I begged my parents to come with us, but they said, "No. We are old. The Israelis won't harm us".'

On 6 January, an Israeli tank fired a shell at the Radwans' house. Ahmad was wounded in the head and walked out with a white flag. He begged the Israelis to allow the Red Crescent to rescue his wife Halima, who was buried alive in her kitchen.

The Israelis said no. Halima lived for four days under the debris of her house, which the Israelis then dynamited.

'They knew she was there and they saw her, because they searched the house before they destroyed it,' says Maher. As soon as the ceasefire took effect last Sunday, he went with friends and relatives to dig his mother out. 'I had the tiniest hope she might still be alive.' But Halima's legs, shoulder and head had been crushed by concrete.

Broken porcelain, a framed verse from the Koran and a piece of plaster with Hebrew writing by the Israeli soldiers are scattered in the ruins of the Radwan family home. The pigeons they raised have returned to roost on the broken roof. Maher Radwan's neighbours say there can be no peace with the Israelis who did this. But Maher is more sad than angry. Peace might still be possible, he says, 'if only there were wise Israeli people'.

What the Moneygall Obama Song Really Says about the Irish

Fintan O'Toole

In the second series of *The Sopranos*, Tony's nephew Christopher has a near-death experience after he is shot by two dumb punks. When he comes out of his coma, he tells the family that he has been briefly in Hell. They want to know what Hell is like. It is, Christopher explains, an Irish bar where it is always St Patrick's Day. The Italians have to play cards and the Irish guys always win.

For any African-Americans unfortunate enough to encounter the paddywhackery of Moneygall or

Local woman Nonie O'Beirne talks to Seamus Heaney at the launch of the Yeats Trail in Sligo town hall. Photograph: James Connolly.

the declaration by Hardy Drew and the Nancy Boys that 'There's No One as Irish as Barack Obama,' Christopher's vision of Hell must be familiar. Just when you think you're having a moment in the sun, you find yourself in that eternal Irish bar where the Paddies hold all the cards.

The endless game of claiming everyone as Irish can be fun and even educational – up to a point. That point is the one at which it becomes crass and tasteless. It's the one at which it ceases to be a way of opening up history and showing the complexity of Irish identity and becomes a way of hijacking history and muscling in on other people's identity.

In itself, the attempt to cash in on Obamamania (Fianna Fáil councillors are already demanding 'some sort of heritage centre, museum, some sort of monument' in Moneygall to act as a tourist attraction) has all the charm of a drunken party crasher. What makes it particularly reprehensible, though, is its ignorance of cultural history.

The great black leader Frederick Douglass, whose connections with Ireland and Daniel O'Connell have rightly been recalled this week, had something to say about the 19th-century white performers who put on a black face to entertain their audiences.

He called them 'the filthy scum of white society who have stolen from us a complexion denied to them by nature, in which to make money and pander to the corrupt taste of their white fellow citizens.' The Irish were key participants in this blackface charade. Initially, Irish immigrants were the butt of many of the jokes in the minstrel shows. In a classic example of the phenomenon that Noel Ignatiev summed up in the title of his book *How the Irish Became White*, Irish performers themselves appropriated the form. From the 1850s onwards, Irish and Irish-American performers – Dan Bryant, George Christy, Matt Campbell, Billy Emerson, Edward Harrigan, Edwin Kelly – became the dominant force in blackface minstrelsy. This was precisely the period, either side of the Civil War, in which blackface minstrels moved from a patronis-

ing but nostalgic view of the blacks on the Old Plantation to what Annemarie Bean has described as 'infantilising and demonising the black body like never before; with the possibility of having autonomous free blacks with rights in American society, blackface minstrels set out to prove that they were not worthy of them'. This dominance extended even to the mind-blowing double parody of Irishmen performing as black women. Francis Leon (Patrick Francis Glassey) was one of the world's highest paid performers in the early 1880s, fêted in the US and on tour to Britain and Australia. His speciality was performing as a Creole woman. His only rival was another Irishman, Tony Hart, best known as Harrigan's partner, but also a specialist in female blackface roles.

Blackface minstrelsy was as complex as any other long-lasting cultural phenomenon, and it undoubtedly contained elements of playfulness and subversion. (Its ambiguity carries forward into today's successor, Ali G.) But its essential core was the denigration through parody and burlesque of black music and culture and of black people themselves. It is not unreasonable to expect Irish people to understand that we have this long and largely disgraceful history and to be at least a little self-conscious when we consider the appropriateness of reviving the habit of putting a black face on Irishness.

We might also remember that the constant claims of Irishness have had real effects in making blacks disappear. The most striking recent example of this is the cultural construction of the area of New Orleans called the Irish Channel. It is, as the historian Ann Gernon has pointed out, a 'mythical geographical region'.

It was never an area of particular Irish settlement in the city. But 'this myth can be found traded in the bars of the French Quarter, as each bar vies for tourists and locals alike who want to be Irish'. It is also projected through the hugely popular novels of Ann Rice, who has successfully applied an Irish and Catholic patina to it. But the problem is that the 'Irish Channel' is in fact 68 per cent African-American.

When the levees broke and the area was flooded, that population's cultural invisibility really mattered – they did not exist because the place was 'Irish'. The apparently harmless habit of Irishness trumping blackness fed into the astonishing abandonment of those very real people. It would be, to put it mildly, more seemly for us to celebrate Barack Obama's achievement for what it means for a people emerging from racial oppression than for putting Moneygall on the map. Douglass's words about whites stealing 'from us a complexion denied to them by nature, in which to make money' apply all too directly to the effort to paint Obama as one of us. As we despair of our own political leadership such fantasies may be understandable. But we would honour Obama more by refraining from muscling in on his parade and behaving like the most shameful branch of his family tree.

THURSDAY, 29 JANUARY 2009

Trauma of the Troubles Should Stay in the Past

David Adams

'Just when I thought I was out . . . they pull me back in,' complained Michael Corleone in *The Godfather: Part III.*

The people of Northern Ireland know the feeling only too well. No matter how hard they try to move on from the Troubles, they are forever being dragged back to relive them. The prevailing orthodoxy – driven largely but not entirely by a loose coalition of academic theoreticians, self-interested politicians and their supporters, and various influential well-meaning people – is that we cannot 'move on' without first 'dealing with our past'.

Why this should be so, has never been properly explained. There is occasional mention of the folly of leaving a legacy of bitterness that might someday come back to haunt us. Yet, like so many other inconvenient realities, the certainty that bitterness will be increased by raking over the recent past is ignored.

We are told that genuine reconciliation depends upon a forensic re-examination of the Troubles, and that only in this way can we ensure we do not repeat history. The fact is that the agreed powersharing political arrangements, a panoply of legal safeguards, and a multitude of oversight bodies all make it impossible to repeat past mistakes (even if someone were so inclined), but this seems to be of no consequence. The truth-seekers just plough on regardless, often sounding uncomfortably like big-tent evangelical preachers as they lecture endlessly that only 'the truth' can set us free.

What precisely is the nature of this truth they seek to uncover? It is certainly not the entire truth. Many of those in favour of a forensic trawl through the Troubles are in a prime position to lead the charge if they so desired, but have failed to do so.

Journalists cheerleading for truth-recovery will, for example, argue that professional integrity, if nothing else, demands that they expose whatever they can about the past. Which would be fair enough, but for the fact that the same people have for years been sitting on truths about who did what to whom and at whose behest, and even who ordered certain atrocities. But they have never shown any inclination, professional or otherwise, to share this knowledge with the wider public. Indeed, most would run a mile at the suggestion that they should publish all that they know, even though there is little or no prospect of them being subject to legal proceedings if they did. So much for their commitment to warts-and-all exposure.

Some of the politicians, though not all, who have been most vocal in their support of a 'truth process' are the least truthful about their own history, and probably have more to hide than most. They are not looking to have the entire truth uncovered, but merely a version that will serve

A victims protester holds up a sign behind Sinn Féin's Gerry Adams at the launch of the report of the Consultative Group on the Past. Photograph: Peter Morrison/AP.

their own purpose. That purpose being the rewriting of history so that all blame for the Troubles can be heaped upon the British and the unionists.

It has to be said, some of the well-meaning advocates for a truth process seem to lean in the direction of selective exposure and history rewriting as well. Perhaps they have difficulty in accepting that both communities were equally culpable for what happened in Northern Ireland.

Then there are the 'victims', upon whose behalf everyone claims to be acting, but who are, more often than not, mere pawns in a bigger game. I listened to a radio phone-in programme a few months ago, where a local self-styled 'expert in conflict resolution' was explaining to the presenter the merits, as she saw them, of a truth process in Northern Ireland.

A woman whose policeman son was murdered by the IRA rang in to say that she and her family just wanted to be left in peace with their memories, to get on as best they could with their lives. In the most patronising way imaginable, the expert proceeded to tell the caller that she was totally wrong, that 'closure' could only come through full disclosure of what happened in the past. The views of the victims, it seems, are only important if they coincide with the greater plan, or the grand theory.

A concern for the sensitivities of victims supposedly underpinned the Eames Bradley-led Consultative Group on the Past. Yet by proposing that a payment of £12,000 be made available to the families of everyone killed in the Troubles (or reparation, as republicans are already calling it) including paramilitary members, they stand accused of riding roughshod over the feelings of the vast majority of victims in order to placate a tiny few.

By drawing such equivalence, they have at the very least helped rewrite history. Those, like the Eames Bradley group, who are genuine about trying to encourage reconciliation, must accept that it cannot be forced or contrived. As far as it

can be achieved at all, reconciliation will only come through the gradual maturing and development of the Belfast Agreement.

They should also seriously consider whether by advocating a raking over of the past they are being used to further agendas far removed from their own.

SATURDAY, 31 JANUARY 2009

How An Bord Pleanála Shot Down Dunne Plan and Buried Celtic Tiger

Frank McDonald

This is a huge setback for developer Seán Dunne, for the bankers who so willingly lent him loads of money to buy 'prime sites' in Ballsbridge, and even for those commentators who believed that An Bord Pleanála simply had to rubber-stamp high-rise schemes for the area, to ensure that the banks would survive.

Ireland was a different country in autumn 2005 when Dunne shelled out a total of €379 million for the privilege of acquiring the Jurys and Berkeley Court hotel sites in the heart of Ballsbridge and talked about his ambitious plans to redevelop the combined seven-acre site for a high-rise, high-density scheme.

Ordinary people couldn't believe that any developer would pay staggering sums of €53.7 – €57.5 million per acre for the two hotel sites, although these figures were soon trumped by others in what became a Klondyke-style gold rush rooted in a conviction that values could only go up.

Dunne was also betting that permission would be granted for a complex of buildings up to 32 storeys high, transforming Ballsbridge into 'the new Knightsbridge' (even though that ritzy part of London has hardly any high-rise buildings), with some 600 luxury flats offering a Manhattan-like lifestyle.

Unbelievably, his vision was shared by senior officials of Dublin City Council, including then city architect Jim Barrett.

The Danish architect who designed the development told an An Bord Pleanála hearing that Barrett favoured the 37-storey design over a 32-storey tower originally proposed.

Senior planner Kieran Rose justified it all in his effusive report recommending that permission be granted, despite many objections from mainly well-heeled and articulate local residents. He also endorsed the architects' argument that the proposed high-rise cluster would give a 'sense of place' to Ballsbridge.

Rose's report, which formed the basis of city manager John Tierney's decision to approve the scheme last March, even suggested that many people would find the 'diamond-cut' 37-storey tower 'exciting; in the words of [poet and Nobel laureate] Séamus Heaney, it could "catch the heart off guard and blow it open".'

An Bord Pleanála has taken a different view, refusing permission for the entire scheme on five grounds – although Henning Larsen's design director, Ulrik Raysse, can take some pride in the board's reference to the 'high quality of the architectural treatment of the individual buildings' proposed for the site.

But Dunne's inflated project went down in flames because there was no basis in planning policy for permission to be granted. As An Taisce said in its appeal, not only did it 'materially contravene' the city development plan, it was also 'massively in excess of the plot ratio considered suitable' for Ballsbridge.

The Department of the Environment's heritage division rowed in – with the express approval of Minister for the Environment John Gormley,

Ambassador of Morocco, Anas Khales, inspects the Army's guard of honour after presenting his credentials to President Mary McAleese at Áras an Uachtaráin in Dublin. Photograph: Maxwells.

who is one of the local TDs. It said the scheme would have 'an undue negative impact on the adjacent architectural character and significance of the area . . . a fine Victorian suburb' of Dublin.

After lengthy consideration, An Bord Pleanála agreed. It said the scheme amounted to 'gross over-development' of the site, as well as being 'highly obtrusive' in the context of the visual amenity of the area, 'making a radical change' in its urban form 'at odds with the established character of Ballsbridge'.

Significantly, the board said 'such change is not supported by any local or strategic objective in the [city] development plan.' Nor had Ballsbridge been identified as suitable for high-rise treatment in the policy document *Maximising the City's Potential: A Strategy for Intensification and Height*, published last January.

There were also precedents for the board's ruling. In March 2005, six months before Dunne agreed to purchase the Jurys site, it rejected plans by telecoms tycoon Denis O'Brien for a 26-storey residential tower in Donnybrook on the grounds that its 'excessive height and scale' would have an 'overbearing' impact.

Dunne declared that, unless he got planning permission for his scheme in its entirety, he wouldn't build anything on the two hotel sites. Having racked up over €700 million on the acquisition of property in Ballsbridge, including AIB Bankcentre and Hume House, he is now left nursing huge debts with little to show for them.

With property values in Dublin plummeting, these pieces of real estate are probably worth less than half the huge money paid for them just three years ago. Number-crunchers in the banks with exposure to Dunne's debts – particularly Ulster Bank – must be working overtime to calculate what can be salvaged now.

'What happened in Ballsbridge was planning in a vacuum or, more aptly, a bubble', as colleague Kathy Sheridan and myself wrote in our book *The Builders*. Like everyone else at the height of the boom, Seán Dunne, his bankers and the city planners were all carried away on a tide of hubris.

Ray Grehan, of Glenkerrin Homes, is still awaiting a decision from the appeals board on his plans for the former Veterinary College next door, for which he paid €171.5 million in November 2005. This scheme includes an 18-storey tower, and the board has requested further information on it before it makes a decision.

The huge amounts of money paid by Dunne and other developers for sites in Ballsbridge counted for nothing in the end, because An Bord Pleanála is required to make its decisions on the basis of 'proper planning and sustainable development'.

By refusing permission, the board has officially buried the Celtic Tiger.

MONDAY, 2 FEBRUARY 2009

Shooting Star with World at his Feet

Philip Reid

No longer a boy, Rory McIlroy – just 19 years of age – has the world at his feet. But, then, it has seemed that way for a long time. Yesterday's maiden professional win in the Dubai Desert Classic simply provided affirmation of just how good he is, and how great he might be.

We can all be sages; in the case of McIlroy, however, it was easy to be wise. Anyone who saw him as a lean amateur, whether it was at Rosses Point, where he became the youngest winner of the West of Ireland, or at the European Club, where he became the first player since Joe Carr to retain the Irish Close, or at Royal Portrush, when he conquered the great links with a round of 61, could predict he was more than a little special.

Of course, McIlroy's ability had been obvious to his parents, Gerry and Rosie, earlier than anyone: when he was two, he could hit 40-yard

Rory McIlroy is congratulated by Darren Clarke after his victory in the Dubai Desert Classic. Photograph: Getty Images.

drives; and, as a nine-year-old, he won the World Junior Championship at Doral in Florida.

As a result of that victory, McIlroy was invited on to the Gerry Kelly Show on UTV, where he demonstrated his short-game brilliance by chipping nine out of 10 balls into a washing machine.

As an amateur, he dominated Irish and European golf. By the time he turned professional in September 2007 – signing with Chubby Chandler's International Sports Management company, who include Ernie Els, Darren Clarke, Lee Westwood and Paul McGinley in their stable – McIlroy was a plus-six handicap and had been number one in the world amateur rankings.

'I just want to keep improving,' remarked

McIlroy of his ambitions on moving to the professional ranks. 'Golf is a bit like an exam paper. I like the fact that each day asks different questions of you even though you can be playing the same course.'

McIlroy put the lessons he had learned as an amateur – which included winning the silver medal as top amateur at the 2007 British Open in Carnoustie, as well as claiming the European amateur title – to good use on turning professional. He became the youngest and quickest player to claim a full PGA European Tour card by affiliate membership, finishing third in the 2007 Dunhill Links (just his second tournament as a professional).

But, then, McIlroy has always been destined to succeed. His dad, a scratch player, noticed his son's ability from a very young age – 'I knew there was something there' – and took on three jobs so he could finance the young McIlroy's trips around the world.

And McIlroy's long-time coach, Michael Bannon, once remarked, 'Rory's big advantage is that he has had a golf club in his hands since he was 18 months old . . . for him, swinging a club is like using a knife and fork.'

The expectations that accompanied McIlroy on his move to the professional ranks were matched by a continually upward graph as the player took to the challenge.

Although he had a number of close calls in tournaments last year – losing play-offs in the European Masters (to Jean Francois Lucquin in September) and the Hong Kong Open (to Wen-tang Lin in November) – he became the youngest player to break into the world's top-50 and, in so doing, earned an invitation to the US Masters in April.

McIlroy's win in Dubai – which will see him move to 14th in the world rankings – has brought his prize money in the 16 months since he turned professional to €1.5 million and earns him a place in the field for the European Tour's HSBC Champions event, which traditionally opens the season. He has moved to second place, behind Sergio Garcia, on the Order of Merit with earnings this season of €609,410.

The two-year-old who raised eyebrows when he hit drives of over 40 yards is now averaging 301.9 yards on tour and, according to the statistics, hits 80 per cent of greens in regulation.

In short, he has game.

And the Ulsterman's maiden tour win offers him a springboard for the rest of the season which will see him compete in all four majors – the Masters, US Open, British Open and US PGA.

More immediately, his rise in the rankings will see him compete in the Accenture World Matchplay in Arizona later this month, and at next month's WGC-CA Championship, which will

bring him back to Doral, where a decade ago he was crowned World Junior champion. Much has happened to McIlroy since then; and, yet, there is a sense that the best has yet to come. He just keeps ticking all the right boxes, and has also managed to keep his feet firmly on the ground.

A wise head on young shoulders.

FRIDAY, 6 FEBRUARY 2009

How to Write a Modern Classic in 20 Days

Arminta Wallace

The open road, in one form or another, is a central image in American culture. Representing freedom and boundless horizons, it is such a familiar theme that we scarcely notice it any more, yet it turns up again and again in films, books, ads for Miller beer and song lyrics by anyone from Springsteen to U2.

Jack Kerouac's novel *On the Road*, published in 1957, is the daddy of the form. It expressed the restlessness of a new generation of young Americans who were intent on exploring the vast landscapes of the continent around them, even as they delved into the sometimes murky depths of their personal experience.

But perhaps the most extraordinary thing about *On the Road* was the way it was composed. In 1951, Kerouac, then aged 29, got hold of some architectural tracing paper and cut it into 12-foot lengths, which he then taped together and fed into his typewriter. He started to write, and continued flat out for 20 days until the book was completed. The resulting manuscript is, to say the least, unusual. It will be on display in the Clinton Institute at University College Dublin until the end of this month.

'The scroll is an amazing artefact,' says Liam Kennedy, director of the institute and professor of American Studies at UCD. 'It's probably the most

Jason Connaghton, Digger the dog and Andrea Lowe enjoying the snow at the Sally Gap near Roundwood, Co. Wicklow. Photograph: Garry O'Neill.

iconic manuscript of 20th-century American literature because of the legend that has grown up around it.'

Chapter one of that legend maintains that Kerouac was as high as a kite when he wrote *On the Road*. Scholars now think, however, that his drug of choice was simply coffee.

'He was driven by huge quantities of the stuff,' says Kennedy. He was also a pretty mean typist. 'He could type 100 words a minute because of a job he had in an earlier life – so he was well set up to do this kind of thing. He wrote 127 feet in three weeks, which is pretty good going. And this is also part of the legend, but I think it's actually true: the last seven feet of the scroll were eaten by a dog. So nobody quite knows what was on there.'

What's left of the scroll, however, is pretty fascinating.

'It took six years to get it published,' Kennedy says. 'The rejections are also part of the legend. Apparently Kerouac went to see one famous publisher and gave him the scroll. The publisher just looked at it and said: "You can't publish this – it needs editing."

'And Kerouac said: "There must be no editing of this manuscript. This manuscript was dictated by the Holy Ghost."'

When the book finally did appear in print, the Holy Ghost had been given a couple of coats of white spirit.

'Anybody who knows the book will find that there are huge differences,' says Kennedy. 'The publishers really played down the drugs and sexual references. They soft-pedalled big-time on that. It was the 1950s, after all.'

The names of the protagonists were also altered. The anti-hero of the novel, Dean Moriarty, was actually Neal Cassady, a major figure both of Kerouac's Beat generation and of the psychedelic movement that followed it. Writers William Burroughs and Allen Ginsberg also turn up in the scroll, alias Old Bull Lee and Carlo Marx respectively.

Writing *On the Road* on a single roll of paper was an intrinsic part of Kerouac's modus operandi.

'He had this theory of what he called spontaneous prose – free association, stream of consciousness, just writing with no interruptions. The guy didn't even want to be interrupted long enough to take a piece of paper out of the typewriter and put a new one in.'

Opinions differ as to whether Kerouac really wrote in this way, or whether he did a sneaky bit of rewriting and polishing afterwards. There are also different views on the literary merit of the 'spontaneous' approach. Truman Capote, for one, was famously unimpressed. Spontaneous prose was, he declared, 'not writing, but typing'.

On this subject too, the scroll has a tale to tell.

'There are a lot of annotations,' says Kennedy. 'He went back over the scroll with pencil, scored things out, and changed names and so forth. You can see these changes before your eyes, which is something that scholars would usually have to go to a library or research institute to do. It's great that this can be on display, free of charge, to the public.'

This access is thanks to the scroll's owner, American millionaire Jim Irsay, who bought it in 2001 for just under €2.5 million.

'People were very worried that it would just disappear into a private collection,' says Kennedy. 'But fair dues to the guy, he decided he would do the right thing and send it out so that people could see it. It has been on an anniversary tour of Europe and will go to Maynooth after it has been here in UCD.

'We're also lucky in that our colleagues in Birmingham, where it was on display before it came here, have sent us some other material which they had on display along with it: first editions, other books, posters from the film versions of Kerouac's writing, and so on. So we really have a very full room of Kerouac-related material.'

If you've ever found yourself humming that line from Springsteen's 'Born to Run' – the one about being out on Highway Nine, sprung from a cage and stepping out over the line – or if you enjoy watching travel programmes on TV, or even if you're prone to the occasional touch of cabin fever, you should catch this scroll while you can.

'Kerouac has had a huge influence on American culture in general,' says Kennedy. 'And I suspect that if any of us goes to the US, we succumb to that romance – the excitement generated by the huge open spaces, the cars, the highways. The whole mythology of being on the road. It's very powerful, and it's very much alive in our imagination.'

SATURDAY, 7 FEBRUARY 2009

The Art and Artistry of Tending the Earth

Michael Viney

Awake in our neighbour's house last week was full of fond remembrance and also, as so often in mid-winter, regret at losing another witness to the past. Bridie Ruane, warm and dignified, linked us to the Ireland of *meitheal* gatherings, of *céilídh*ing, of the ever-open door. She was a widow for two decades, surviving a husband, Michael, whose avid interest in life was a byword.

Here are a few of the things he taught me in my early 'alternative' fumbling on the land: how to sharpen a scythe, and not to leave the scythe-stone on the ditch to get wet and useless; how to sow barley evenly on the soil, the grain in a bowl cupped in the crook of the left arm, the right thumb flicking it up from the palm in a golden spray; how to thresh ripe sheaves on a stone; how to winnow the grain on a breezy day; how to lock one's grip, in shouldering a heavy bag, by tucking a pebble or potato in the corner ahead of one's fist; how raking all the stones tidily out of a vegetable patch might be to throw out their store of warmth; how a great rock buried in the ground could be shattered by building a big fire of turf on it, then, after an hour or two, throwing on buckets of cold water.

Some of this was handed on from 'the old people', for Michael had lived through the great change: from horses to tractors, hay to silage, fork-spread manure to machine-scattered 10-10-20, lazy-beds to supermarket potatoes. At this distance from 'the old people', Irish farming history now merits a growing library of scholarly attention. Michael would have relished a new book about the

most basic task of his forebears: building and maintaining the fertility of fields.

To quote first from the book's foreword by Jonathan Bell, the Ulster authority on Ireland's rural culture: 'The revisionist movement in Irish history . . . has done away with insulting stereotypes, which attributed innate laziness, unthinking conservatism, and inefficiency to vast numbers of Irish small farmers. There is now a large, convincing body of evidence that these people were in fact ruthlessly efficient and ready to try any method that could secure a living for themselves and their families.'

The extraordinary range and application of their methods is the subject of *Quickening the Earth: Soil Minding and Mending in Ireland*, a scholarly, exhaustive and lively labour of love by Dr James F. Collins, retired UCD lecturer in soil science. Its 500-odd pages trace the ways and means of enriching and feeding Ireland's soil over many centuries, using every available natural material: clays, gravels,

llustration by Michael Viney.

shell-sands, lake-bottoms, guano, burnt lime, stable manures, green manuring, street-scrapings, composts, old bones, many sorts of seaweed – 'a level of investigation and experimentation that bears comparison with any modern economic or technical project,' as Dr Bell declares.

Despite the limestone bedrock that underlies the centre of Ireland, acid soil was the big problem of a rainy island. Even before burnt lime became the staple treatment of grassland, encouraging its earthworms to burrow deeply, draining and enriching the soil, lime was retrieved in the white marl under bogs and in lake beds and the sands and gravels of glacial eskers and moraines.

Around the coasts, lime came from shell-sand and 'coral' seaweed (or maerl), but seaweed's value as manure, notably for potatoes, has given Dr Collins an exceptionally vivid chapter. Until his book, I had not understood the intensity of local

seaweed-gathering rights, or the extent of seaweed farming – setting out large stones off the shore on which to grow wrack for harvest. A low-tide photograph of such a 'farm' in Mayo's Achill Sound in the early 1900s, almost the size of a football pitch, is one of the book's revelatory illustrations.

Good pictures, past and present, also mark another recent book by Jonathan Bell and Mervyn Watson, both now retired from their care of the Ulster Folk and Transport Museum. *A History of Irish Farming 1750-1950* (Four Courts Press; web price €36) continues their long study of the island's agriculture during the 'Age of Improvement' and how this shaped the rural society and landscape.

Along with chapters on the changing crops and breeds of livestock (the book is supported by Bord Bia), I am pleased to see one on spades, since the back-breaking designs of so many garden-centre spades are one of my hobby-horses. The fact

Cartoon by Martyn Turner.

that, in 1830, a spade mill in Co. Tyrone had 230 different patterns, for different soils and uses, should give one pause.

For my money, forget the short-shafted, broad-bladed spade with stirrup-shaped grip beloved of English gardeners: a plain, long shaft and a narrow blade, dished and flared somewhat at the tip (in a word, the Leenane spade), is your only man.

MONDAY, 9 FEBRUARY 2009

Pete Doherty's Poetry beyond Pat Kenny

Peter Murtagh

There is a great refrain in Bob Dylan's 1968 song 'Ballad of a Thin Man'. In it, Dylan is merciless as he takes apart a hapless journalist, a scribe completely out of his depth and uncomprehending of the scene about which he is trying to write.

The putdown refrain in the song goes: 'Because something is happening here/But you don't know what it is/Do you, Mister Jones?'

It was like that on Friday night watching our own Mr Jones flailing and failing to interview Pete Doherty on *The Late Late Show* to any illuminating effect. There sat Doherty, scruffy strolling minstrel with a foppish fedora-style hat (cigarette stuck in its ribbon), drainpipe jeans, anorexic-like physique, all dirty finger-nails and doe-eyed expression. His face exuded a mixture of wide-eyed innocence and the mien of a rabbit caught in headlights.

And there was Pat, looking like the head of HR, all stiff, formal attire, interviewing the bad boy – or someone he was told was a bad boy, 'cos sure as hell, Pat didn't really know anything about the bloke he was talking to. Eight, nine (or was it 10 or 12?) questions about drugs and Kate Moss. Nothing about Doherty's music, his poetry, his lyrics, what motivates him as an artist, what he's trying to express and why; the influences on his

life, his huge influence on the pop scene through his two bands, The Libertines and Babyshambles. None of that; only accusatory drug questions.

It was relentless, unyielding, toe-curling. At one point – Kenny's breaking a butterfly on a wheel moment – Doherty pulled his hat down over his eyes and made as though to curl up in a foetal position. Trying to make himself small. Trying to get away from it all. And ne'er a question about his music.

'I bet you don't even know the name of any of my songs, do you?' Doherty quipped at one point. Er . . . no, I don't, Kenny seemed to reply.

But Doherty picked up his battered acoustic guitar and sang one, 'The Last of the English Roses', so maybe he does now. It's a lovely lyrical song and it's getting lots of play on YouTube. I wonder if Pat caught the irony of the line 'You charmed the bees' knees off me . . .' Probably not. (You can watch it on YouTube – search under Peter Doherty on Ireland's *Late Late Show*.)

On Saturday and yesterday, the web was humming as debate flared on the tube and on boards.ie and other blog sites. Bloggers tend not to mince their words – embarrassing, painful, uncomfortable, car crash TV, lazy and arrogant – they didn't like what they saw and they weren't, for the most part, referring to Doherty.

My son Patrick bounded into the bedroom some time after midnight on Friday, all energy and excitement. He's still at secondary school but had borrowed a Trinity ID and bluffed his way into the Philosophical Society after queuing for hours to see his hero, Pete Doherty, perform in a more intimate setting before whizzing out to RTÉ. Many queued – hundreds perhaps – but few got in.

'Amazing, incredible, sooooo interesting,' said Patrick. 'He was, like, only about 20 ft from me and he sang loads of his songs.'

'What did he talk about?' I asked, bleary-eyed.

'Yeats and Oscar Wilde,' said Patrick (19). 'Oh and Dad, I've borrowed your book of Yeats poems. They're really good. And did you see Pat

Clara Keoghan of Team Ireland, from Ballsbridge, Dublin, who won two bronze medals at the Special Olympics World Winter Games in Boise, Idaho in the US, hugs her mother, Phil, on her arrival home at Dublin airport. Photograph: Paul Mohan/Sportsfile.

Kenny? (Yes) What an arse; what a complete arse!'

Had Patrick read any Wilde? I asked him. 'No, but I'd like to,' he said. 'I'll get you some,' I said. And we chatted a while about 'The Ballad of Reading Gaol' and other stuff about Wilde and Yeats.

Excited, enthused (and, yes, fully aware of the self-destructive Doherty stuff that is a part, but only a part, of his life) Patrick went to bed thinking of music, and words and poems.

Thank you, Pete Doherty. Thank you for making poetry exciting for a 19-year-old boy learning how to express himself. And lay off the other stuff, eh?

What a complete arse that Mr Jones was. Dylan was so right.

FRIDAY, 20 FEBRUARY 2009

Merrily Meryl

Michael Dwyer

A woman for all seasons, Meryl Streep was a diva in dungarees and a straw hat last summer in the sunny musical *Mamma Mia!* Now she wears a black cape and a forbidding bonnet that encircles her face in the dark drama, *Doubt*, playing Sister Aloysius, a nun as glacial as winter temperatures.

There's a warm glow about Streep herself, who looks radiant when we meet on a chilly Saturday morning in London. Her next stop a few days later is Tokyo for the belated Japanese premiere of

Mamma Mia! 'The Empress has expressed a wish to attend, and she's never gone to a premiere before,' she says.

The ABBA-inspired movie has been a phenomenal success around the world over the past six months. In Ireland, only *Titanic* has proved more lucrative at the box office. 'Oh, I'm very happy to hear that,' says Streep, who has happy memories of working here on *Dancing at Lughnasa*.

'I saw the stage show of *Mamma Mia!* When I was looking for something special for my daughter's birthday,' she says. 'It was about a week after September 11th and the kids were all feeling so low. I took about six 10-year-olds, and the show was an absolute tonic. You just couldn't feel down in the dumps by the end of the show. I felt that there was something there that was really good.'

Did she see the show as a potential movie vehicle for herself? 'Oh, not even remotely,' she says with her distinctive, hearty laugh. 'I thought I was too old to be in the movie then – and that was over seven years ago. Then, when we made the movie, it was such fun that it seemed shameful to be paid for doing it. It was such a great cast. We were on a wonderful location in the northern Aegean. With the food and the company and where we were shooting, we had such a good time that it was more like a holiday.'

Our conversation turns to *Doubt*. Streep is riveting as Sister Aloysius, the intimidating principal of a Bronx school in the mid-1960s. She is so vigilant that when she suspects Fr Flynn (Philip Seymour Hoffman) of sexually abusing a schoolboy, she doggedly pursues the case in a manner that's reminiscent of the way Kenneth Starr went after Bill Clinton.

'Well, I think a lot of that case was fuelled by a great deal of money,' says Streep. 'Her character reminded me more of Javert, the police inspector in *Les Misérables*. They have a feeling about someone, an instinct, almost like a sense of smell. And I'm not sure if she's wrong.

'I have a friend who's in the security business and has dealt with celebrity stalkers. He's a very smart, interesting man and he wrote a book, *The Gift of Fear*. He says that women, in particular, have a kind of sixth sense, and if you feel something's wrong or that something bad could happen, generally there's a reason for it and you should trust that instinct. I think there is some kind of warning mechanism in the pheromones.'

In her characteristically diligent preparation to transform into Sister Aloysius, Streep 'made up a past history for her,' she says. 'It's written nowhere in the play, but for me, it was helpful to know the landscape of her life beforehand. What was her background? What happened to her? I made up for myself a biography that fuelled this kind of hypersensitivity she had, her Javert-like, laser-like certainty about this man.

'And I met some nuns from this dwindling order, women in their seventies, eighties and nineties. I visited them in retirement homes and found them completely fascinating and inspiring. At a very young age, they had given up their families and so much else, so they regarded this group of women with whom they spent their lives as their sisters. And of course they call each other sister. They seemed content and happy. I've been in other old-age homes where that is not the case and the isolation is killing.'

In 1964 when the film is set, Streep was a teenage schoolgirl in her native New Jersey. 'My school experience was upper-middle-class and enlightened,' she says. Although not a Catholic, she often went to Mass, drawn by its rituals. 'I loved going to Mass. I couldn't understand what people were saying because the Mass was still in Latin, and I loved the chant and that thing they swung with the incense. Then everything changed. They started speaking English and they brought in the guitars.'

One sequence in *Doubt* illustrates the sharp contrast between the lifestyles of priests – boisterous, drinking and smoking – and the rigidly ordered lives of the nuns. 'That's the way it was then,' Streep says. 'I remember when I was a

Meryl Streep. Photograph: Brigitte Lacombe.

waitress at the one local upscale restaurant in my home town. The priests came in for lunch every day and they would start by having two Manhattans each. That's a hefty drink for 12.30 in the afternoon. Of course we never saw the nuns there. They stayed in the convent.'

Although Streep continues to act on stage when the opportunity arises in between filming commitments, given her prolific body of work, she hasn't often been tempted by movies based on stage productions. Exceptions have been *Plenty*, *Marvin's Room*, *Angels in America*, *Dancing at Lughnasa*, *Mamma Mia!* and now *Doubt*.

'I think that in adapting a play rather than, say, a novel for the screen, the challenge is for the writer,' she says. 'With *Doubt* we were lucky to have the playwright John Patrick Shanley as our screenwriter and our director. I think that after seeing so many incarnations of his plays with different casts, he wanted to exercise more visually with it and expand it into the school. Looking at the film, I wonder how they could have done the play without these children. They are so eloquent a presence in the film.

'It's a testament to his own imagination, and that he wasn't hidebound or jealous about his ideas, that he was willing to expand the play and look at it from different angles for the film. Of course I was aware of how many of my lines had been cut in the transition between the play and the film, but that was of necessity. There's so much that can be told without words in a movie.'

When Streep had been cast as the nun, director Shanley commented that his options were narrowed in finding an actor to stand up to her as the priest.

She and Philip Seymour Hoffman had played mother and son, Arkadina and Konstantin, in a 2001 Central Park stage production of *The Seagull*.

'I was so happy to work with him,' Streep says. 'I've loved him for so long in film. He really is one of our greatest actors. He's a real shape-shifter, too. You just don't know who's going to come in. I know him well and he's a friend, but you don't know who's going to come in the door when he does a character.'

One of the most effective aspects of the film is the absence of histrionics in the confrontation scenes between Streep and Hoffman. 'The level of restraint, I think, has to do with what's buried and is not apparent to secular audiences,' she says. 'This woman seems like a dragon who's so in charge, but she is inferior to the priest, who's a teacher at her school. She runs the school and he coaches the basketball team, but he's the boss ultimately.

'She reports to him and he can have her dismissed. That power dynamic is what necessitates her care and caution in approaching him. The only way she can get rid of him is by getting him to admit what he has done. It's by dint of her own wit that this will happen, by her ability to cage him and to make him confess — which, of course, is the centre of their religion.'

Streep has already finished shooting her next movie, *Julie & Julia*, in which she and Amy Adams, who plays a young nun in *Doubt*, are cast in the title roles. Streep plays Julia Child, who was a celebrity chef on US TV in the 1960s, long before that term was coined. Is Streep herself an ace in the kitchen? 'No, I'm not, but I'm getting better.' Does her husband, sculptor Don Gummer, get involved? 'No, I'm the cook, but he's tolerant. He's a good support. I like to cook. I didn't used to and it took a while. When you have to cook every night, I think it becomes a task. I certainly couldn't manage it after a day's shooting, when I could be working for 17 hours.'

Before we part, I note that Streep will be 60 in June. 'I'm looking forward to it,' she beams proudly. 'I'm going to have a very big party at my husband's studio, which is the biggest space I can think of, although he doesn't know about it yet.'

SATURDAY, 21 FEBRUARY 2009

My Journey through Anorexia

Fiona McCann

When I was 21, I stopped eating. Not entirely, mind you, but enough to make my hair fall out, my periods stop, my face become hollow and my body shrink to bones and translucent skin. Hunger has a particular resonance in this country where an estimated one million starved to death in the Famine, and where it more recently became a political tool for a group of men led by Bobby Sands. Today, thousands of Irish people — mostly young, mostly female — are starving themselves, and the chances are they won't be registering in the history books.

Which is why I wanted to write this piece: because, as difficult as it is for me to identify now with the gaunt, lank-haired, big-eyed girl whose distorted image peers out at me from the few photos that turn up from that patch of my life, she is part of my history. I had an eating disorder. I know what a terrible, exhausting waste of precious time and energy it is. I know how dangerous it is. And I know too, that it can be overcome.

It wasn't until my final year of college that I even started dieting. Up until then, I had displayed all the habits of a healthy, happy teenager with an appetite for life and always, legendarily in fact, for food. Despite my impressive eating skills, I was never overweight. My family was a loving and stable one, I had never been abused or traumatised, I had a loving and loyal boyfriend who assured me of my attractiveness, and I had never counted calories in my life. Hardly a test case for psychosis. So what went wrong?

As ever, with an eating disorder, it was infinitely more complicated than a simple desire to be thin. After all, in our cornucopian, airbrush-addled western culture, there are few women who have not at some stage either expressed or harboured a desire to lose weight. There is a difference, however, between water-cooler conversations about chunky thighs, and the steely determination with which I approached my first, and only, diet. I was in my final year at university, and suddenly aware that from there on in, it was up to me to shape my future. I started with my body.

I remember the initial thrill at seeing myself so easily shed the curves and layers that at the time were keeping me from what I saw as the ideal. In my defence – in defence, perhaps, of all dieting women – it is hardly surprising that so many strive to embody an underweight ideal. Thinness, after all, is instantly rewarded by compliments, by a greater choice in clothing, by dresses that hang on clothes-hanger collar bones and that glide rather than bunch over curves. Suddenly, for the first time in my adult life, I felt there was nothing I couldn't

Fiona McCann. Photograph: Dara Mac Dónaill.

carry off. Friends who expressed concern at my diminishing size were ignored, at least in the early days: I really believed I was accomplishing what they all wished they could. I was gleeful, and in charge: I felt powerful.

This part was easy. People-pleasing by nature, I was merely taking this to the ultimate degree, carving my shape out to win further approval. Losing weight was a cinch: the difficulty was working out when to stop. Even I knew that there had to be a limit to this, but every pound or kilogram lost, I reasoned, would allow for the inevitable indulgence later. I just kept putting off the later part.

As I continued to deprive myself of food, I stopped thinking about anything else. Even when I fell below whatever ideal weight I had initially set for myself, I became terrified of letting go. Having made meals for so long of apples and diet yoghurts, and measured out my life in coffee spoons and diet drinks, I had lost all sense of the pleasure in food and the relationship between hunger and satiation. I was so in the habit of suppressing appetites that I lost touch with them entirely.

By nature gregarious and sociable to a fault, I became increasingly introspective. A continued and constant focus on food meant I had little left over for the people who loved me, with all my energy required to keep the spring coiled as tightly as I could.

I recall this as a time of strange clarity – never before or since has my vision been so targeted, my focus so fine-tuned. All the rest faded out as I pared down my own physical existence and devoted all my mental and emotional energy to it. My willpower and determination were turned on myself, and my body was the target. But while I was busy avoiding any confrontation on the issue, my body was busy fighting back.

A fine down began to appear on my arms, something I later heard named as lanugo, a telltale sign that a person has lost insulating and necessary layers of fat, and that a body is compensating by growing what is essentially a layer of fur to keep out the cold. I stopped menstruating. My thick, curly and chaotic hair became thin and lank. My face sank into itself, leaving hollowed eyes, a nose out of all proportion, and oversized, equine teeth.

I was 21, the age at which you're meant to enjoy the figure you get to look back on wistfully when gravity later takes over. Yet far from revelling in my youthful body, I was hiding it from view, abetted by a total loss in my budding libido. Even I knew by then that I was too thin, but I couldn't relinquish control, as the very thing I thought I was in command of had begun to command me. All I could think about was food: not just what I ate myself, either, but what other people were eating. I even went to elaborate lengths to prepare food for loved ones that I wouldn't eat myself, in a kind of delirious asceticism.

I saw myself as being fiercely in control, and that was how I wanted it. My study notes, customarily cobbled together on flyaway foolscap pads, became a picture of neatly filed, organisational obsession. My bedroom, traditionally chaotic with exploding drawers and trails of tights and paper, was suddenly, scarily pristine. My financial affairs were not only uncharacteristically in order, but I had developed a control over my limited purse strings that was only matched by that over my caloric intake.

My family, my friends, my boyfriend – all were naturally concerned, but I fobbed them off with talk of exams, feeling no small sense of accomplishment in doing so. I even managed to fool, or so I thought, the doctors they begged me to visit, and then, with a determination that brooked no alternative, I left the country. Being anorexic abroad, specifically in Japan, where I went as soon as my first job came through, was a compounded kind of odd. Even the legendarily petite Japanese students I taught were alarmed at my frame. Osoi – the word for thin – was one of the first I learned. News of my illness travelled fast, and soon I was called in for a rare private audience with my new boss, as he inquired about what was wrong with

A homeless man on Patrick Street in Cork city. Photograph: Daragh Mac Sweeney/Provision.

me. My faltering explanation wasn't enough for a non-English speaker, and he bade me write the name of my illness down so he could have someone look it up. In my distress in so publicly naming my disease, I spelled it wrong.

All that afternoon, an anxious employee could be seen flitting through the university campus where I was teaching, waving a piece of paper with the word 'annorexia' written on it, as he asked all comers to help him decipher the meaning of this mysterious disease. My secret, it appeared, was out.

As if anorexia can ever really be a secret. I recall with embarrassing clarity the moment I confided to one of my new friends abroad that I had – whisper it – an eating disorder. It was a confession I'd worked up to weeks in advance, and I expected surprise, concern, anything but the affectionate laugh that accompanied his reply of: 'No shit, Fiona!' No shit, and yet as clear as my problems

were to everyone else, they were still hidden from me. The slowly dawning awareness that I was caught in something that had to be changed is hard to track now. I can only say that it was part of a subtle and complex process of self-discovery, and that a will to live somehow overcame the death wish that had led me there. Ultimately, the wish to partake in and be wholly present for the adventures and opportunities that were available to me in this unique moment of my life won out over the alternative. Somewhere during that year in Japan, I started loosening my grip.

Recovering was the hardest part. Once I did start to eat, my starving body, so long deprived, refused to be sidetracked any longer and took over in binges of alarming speed and intensity. From eating next to nothing on a daily basis, I went to consuming fridgefulls of food, gorging myself with an abandon I was unable to fight as some reflex kicked in and forced any self-control out of the picture. In those hazy, insatiable moments, I ate almost everything I could lay my hands on. Thankfully, I found that I couldn't vomit on command. This precluded any slide into bulimia, anorexia's stealthily invisible sister. Yet, swinging between starvation and stuffing my face, and fed by a vigilante landlady who took advantage of my Irish politeness to present me with meals and snacks whenever she could, I began to look normal again.

Yet despite my outward appearance, I was far from cured. It turned out that my self-imposed starvation had been helping me to distance myself from what I didn't want to feel or examine. The slow uncoiling made a space for all the repressed emotion to come rushing to the surface and it was hell.

To add to it all, I was embarrassed. I didn't see the logic in my body's behaviour: that binge eating

was a natural defence mechanism kicking in to shore up calories before the next inevitable deprivation. I was ashamed of my lack of control, ashamed of the pain I was causing my family, ashamed of my own chaotic emotions and ashamed of this banal, middle-class, repulsive illness that seemed at once superficial and frivolous, while remaining darkly taboo. Those were my darkest days, and at times I wanted to die, convinced I could never conquer an illness that had taken such a strong hold on me.

Getting through an eating disorder is particularly difficult, given that you have to come face-to-face with the source of your problems every single day. An alcoholic or drug addict can at least remove the source of their addiction from their everyday life. For a person with an eating disorder it's a thrice-daily showdown at mealtimes. I remember

First- and second-year international seminarians play in the snow before attending Mass at the Novitiate of Legionaries of Christ in Leopardstown, Co. Dublin. Photograph: Naoise Culhane/Maxpix.

being hit hard by articles about people who battled with eating disorders all their lives and despaired at ever finding a way out. Would I also have to fight this all my life?

The answer is no, and that makes me lucky and is what I want anyone reading this who is suffering in some similar way to take from this personal exposé. Recovery might be difficult, but it is certainly not impossible, and the sooner it is begun, the better. Get help, seek counselling, talk to eating-disorder specialists and do it as soon as you can, because you will and can get over this and you should do it before causing yourself permanent physical and psychological damage. And take heart: recovering from an eating disorder may even leave you better equipped than your 'normal' peers to avoid the psychological pitfalls of body-conscious-ness that plague the society we live in.

What did I do? I came home. I went to meetings. I sought help. I spoke to a therapist. I read. And this is what helped most in the end: I read my way out of trouble. I read whatever I could find about eating disorders, and this brought me to a book called *Fat is a Feminist Issue* by Susie Orbach (Arrow Books, £9.99), and this brought me to feminism, and for this I am grateful. I read strong women writers, I found angry, intelligent voices, I girded myself with their logic and passion, and I got better.

Fourteen years on, I can even say I am relieved that my emotional disturbances had such a physical manifestation that they had to be addressed, but I still have one regret: dieting.

When I think of all the energy, the willpower, the attention and the youth I put into something so wasteful, so unworthy of my precious time, it makes me angry. Now, when I meet beautiful, charming and healthy young women – and increasingly, young men – clearly doing the same thing, to varying degrees, I am tempted to shake them. 'Are you crazy?' I want to ask them. 'Are you stupid?' But I know the answer. They're not crazy and they're not stupid.

Many people with eating disorders – and they are everywhere, believe me, in all shapes and sizes – are, after all, only responding to a prevalent social soundtrack telling them that to be thin is to be valued. Others use food or abstention from it as a way to dull emotions or battle other demons. But they're fighting the wrong battle. I wish I could call on all that strength, that steel; harness that willpower and personal commitment and direct it against the warped logic that keeps so many people ill and unhappy. Because that force, the fight of all those who are currently battling themselves daily, could really change the world.

MONDAY, 23 FEBRUARY 2009

I Have Known the Bravest, Toughest, Fiercest Man that Ever Lived

Yvonne Nolan

It all begins with words. Words that teem and toss about, that stream and eddy. They're torrential and pressing and insistent. They are lovely to hear inside, they talk to you; they are a delight to hear coming in, hovering, banking, waiting to land – that tree, sitka but call it ever-green, the flowers, 'sweet william', but who is he to be so sweet as to be like raspberry curdling and bleeding into cream? Our place, Corcloon, not a village or a town, but our fields and our neighbour's fields, watched over for miles by the chimneys of a power station, sentinels. The sounds: the ominous scrape and clang of the cemetery gate, the calves bawling for a bucket, the wheedling miaow of the insincere and part-time house cat, the crunch of wheels on gravel, the throaty rasp of Tom Coyne's Volkswagen as he changes gears, the red American kettle that sings on the range, the hum of voltage through an electric clock, the thunk of the hand pump taking water from the well; a deep, dark place – you can't see the bottom.

Your mother and father have words, too many words some say. Where do you get all those fancy words? they say. Why say incinerate for burn? Why say gravity for serious or the earth's pull? Why say boooosum for bosom? To make it extra saucy. The fun of malapropism and mispronunciation – a bollocks is also a ball of wax – no one'll know what you mean. You have to have the lingo – it's a necessity.

The aunties and uncles have words; they have cold air on them coming in the door. They have brown paper bags. Inside, Oxford Lunch, Lucky Numbers, Salad Cream, Swiss Roll, Emerald Toffees. One auntie alights from a bus; she has a bag called a Travel-light, but it's not – it's heavy. JJ has scapulars and miraculous medals. Whelan's dunky, donkey, ass, *asal* brays lonely as the night comes in, the kitchen light yellow, and aunties and uncles have cup after cup of tea. The stories then, red lemonade goes flat with the listening. Tomato sandwiches bleed pinkly and run to slime. From the bedroom you can still hear the voices of the adults talking and laughing in the kitchen. Kit and me, a bed on either side of a small room, the last light of a summer's evening through the curtains that are turquoise with red flowers. Waiting for sleep, listening to words.

Who are our people? We came from people who love words. The Burkes came from a line of doctors. Each Burke baby knew how to be a doctor from the first; they had a way with the suture and syringe. The Flynns knew butchering, sinews and gristle, hanging a hare or bleeding a pig. The Traceys knew wood, dovetailing, morticing, where to drive a nail that it wouldn't split the timber. Grandad knew words. He found them more entrancing than the daggin'-arsed haunches of a Hereford bullock. He was an indifferent farmer. That's why Granny had to cycle the eight miles to Fore to teach, that's why Katy Kane came in to boil the dinner; and he above in the bedroom writing a story. The irrepressible tyranny of the words.

Our people know the mystery and magic of words. It is not recessive; it is a renegade dominant gene. What you say to me, what I say to you, what we both think together. Oh the play and love of it! In the car talking. What kind of cow is that? A simmental. A sentimental cow! She gives milk because she empathises. She cries when she sees a beautiful sunset. She moons over Reilly's bull.

Christy had words. He came into the world with words – resuscitate, revive, critical, damage; a limp blue baby. Later, he's a small boy, bright-eyed, watching, a listening tilt to his head, channelling the torrent of words. The words come, they worm into his head, and he soaks them in, brain like blotting paper. Verbally, he cannot form them; he is not silent but he cannot marshal speech. His eyes, so eloquent, can tell it all, windows to the soul – they move, they gesture, they assent, they disagree, they point, they indicate, they're displeased, they're sad, they're bored, they're happy, they're scornful, they're joking. It's acting for camera; up close, eyes can talk as well as any mouth. But like some infernal punishment from the dankest cellar of hell his body fights his brain with every ounce of its strength. How to live with a body that makes you seem possessed by a medieval demon, a gargoyle? Spasms, automatic muscle contractions contort your face, your arms, your legs. The cold-eyed look on cynically as you grunt and drool, your hands grab and flail without your say-so. You're a freak show. Your body a cruel parody – you're Quasimodo, the Elephant Man, the fool with the secret. Your body is a bitter betrayal. How can you go on? How can you salvage your sanity? Then the words come like balm, like blessings, arrayed like angels, they anoint, they're chrism, they whisper and comfort, they're salvation.

Salvation was writing, finding the means to write kept Christy on this planet for 43 years; he'd have left earlier without the words. And just as he came into the world with words like resuscitate and critical and damage, these too were the words that heralded his departure. We three, my parents

Adam Chytry from Lucan, Co. Dublin, in action at Dublin Institute of Technology in Aungier Street, Dublin, during a breakdance demonstration at the launch of the Institute's breakdance society Skill Masters 2009 competition. Photograph: Frank Miller.

and I, sat by his hospital bed, the ventilator gone, he breathing on, his mutinous body now stilled. Our rational understanding of brain death betrayed by irrational fronds of hope. Then we saw the shadow pass, we saw the words leaving.

I think about war films, about going over the top, about feats of heroism, the all or nothings, the courage to risk all for an idiotic and impossible dream. I think of those sweaty-faced heroes and how manhood is defined in their image. Then I think of Christy broken, twisted, damaged, strapped in a wheelchair; unable to lift a cup or swat a fly but with three books written, letter by slow letter. All this in face of the unbelievers and the ignoramuses, all the hardship and sweat and tears, the setbacks, the physical pain and suffering, and I think that I have known the bravest, toughest, fiercest man that ever lived.

It's 4 a.m. in the morning on the second day after Christy's death. The wheelchair stands empty in the hall. We cough out sighs, we moan, our conversation is punctuated with great heaving groans. My mother and father and I, we sit and cry, helpless. There is only one word for this: bereft.

MONDAY, 23 FEBRUARY 2009 @ 8:48 A.M.

THE IRISH TIMES
irishtimes.com/blogs

U2 *No Line On the Horizon*

On The Record — blog, by Jim Carroll

On The Record readers with an interest in sampling U2's new album should proceed to irishtimes.com/blogs where there are one-minute snippets (yep, 60 seconds) of all the tracks from *No Line On The Horizon* to be heard. Please let us know what you think.

Me? Well, seeing as you asked . . .

The arrival of a new U2 album has a strange effect on seemingly sane people. Many of my fellow critics, for instance, have greeted the new arrival with open arms, ticker-tape parades, unrestrained praise and new shades of purple prose. Such unpoetic arse-licking is to be expected from the band's own golden circle of house-trained scribes, but it's something else entirely when usually reliable bellwethers join the circus. Maybe they're holding out for a 25-minute bull session with The Edge or it's like the banking cowboys exhorting people to put on the green jersey.

A peculiar by-product of this particular release is the chorus of expert voices claiming that this is the album which will save the record business. Save the record business? Such misguided guff — that an album from one of the most marketing-savvy bands in the world will send people back into the shops filling their boots with CDs — makes you wonder when was the last time those experts actually stood in a record store and saw what was really going on out there. Naturally, HMV in Dublin will be opening at midnight on Thursday to provide the obligatory snap of U2 fans standing around on Grafton Street to get their hands on the new album. Have these people not heard of Rapidshare? Joke, OK?

It would be too easy — and, let's face it, far more entertaining — to continue this post in a similarly snarky manner. That would see us going down a road which would lead to an accountant's office in Amsterdam or a room in the White House where Bono is knee-to-knee with George W. Bush. But those are human transgressions. For musical transgressions, you have to head to the new album.

Like every outing since *Achtung Baby*, this album is about trying to go back to that glorious snapshot in time. *Achtung Baby* was where U2 were last at their most thrilling and they know it. Back then, they showed that you could only truly proceed in pop by abandoning everything which had served you well to date. Since then, they've tried valiantly to recapture that high ground, yet have not showed the inclination or bravery required to leave the baggage at the door. Once, it seems, was enough for that.

Like its predecessors, *No Line On The Horizon* doesn't really amount to a hill of beans. It huffs and puffs and throws all the right shapes to make it look like the band are going to the well in search of reinvention and creative salvation. However, it's all show and no substance. There are a flurry of ideas here and the usual retinue of astute helpers are on hand too to turn these ideas into potential gold and platinum, yet there's little to indicate that the band have the mettle to challenge themselves by doing what is not expected of a band in their position. The notion that Brian Eno and Daniel Lanois (and Steve Lillywhite is here too to keep things truly old-school) will always save the day is written large throughout. The fact is, though, that Eno and Lanois are only as good as who and what they're working with and this is where the problems begin.

Actually, no, let's be fair, there are a few positives here, a few turns like 'Magnificent' when U2 fire on all cylinders like it's the most natural thing in the world for four geezers to stand around in a room and make this sort of gut-busting music together. You can hear the cogs turning, the guitars and drums perfectly in synch, the sound of stadiums jumping up and down with glee. You can hear where the album could have gone and how it would have cocked a snook to the notion that such acts as Coldplay, Kings of Leon and The Killers are fit to stand on the same stage as U2. It's the sound of a band not merely applying for their old job back, but actually writing a whole new 'smart boys wanted' advert.

Sadly, such euphoria doesn't last. You listen to 'Unknown Caller,' 'Breathe,' 'Stand Up Comedy' and 'Cedars of Lebanon' and wonder what the hell is going on. It's the comedown after the sugar rush. Like most of the album, each of these four tracks is a bit of a muddle with the band sounding strangely ill-at-ease with each other's contributions and the song itself. It's a strange kind of collective misfit, tracks trying to poke one another into making some semblance of sense together because they sure as hell don't do so on their own.

It would be much too easy to signal out Bono's lyrics for a bit of a lash here, but the truth is that he's just one culprit in this blustery, burpy, over-cooked melodrama. The album's glaring lack of coherence can be attributed to many factors, including a lengthy gestation period and a surplus of chefs at the pass, but such excuses only serve to show up again how a great album needs more than good intentions and ideas. It really needs a bundle of great songs and *No Line On The Horizon* is sorely lacking in this department.

While listening to the album, I kept going back to that careless run of shows in Croker in 2005 when the band went through the motions like a bunch of bored, rich, pre-occupied men, counting their money. But pop fans are always willing to sit around for a second act. Like all romantics, we give our heroes the benefit of the doubt, hence why so many will fire up *No Line On The Horizon* and will it to be great. Just great — no-one is expecting a grime or hip-hop U2 (that was Passengers, wasn't it?) or anything like that.

What we were after was an album to make us forget and overlook the distractions which the band have become about. We wanted an album to remind us that four musicians could stand together and deliver an album which was as honest as the day was long and as true to itself as rock can still sometimes be.

But with every song which doesn't sound quite up to scratch, every groove which sounds too layered and over-analysed, every track which keeps meandering without any direction home and every awful bum lyric which makes you wince with pity for the writer, you're reminded that U2 have other priorities these days and that this is an album created with those priorities in mind. This album will fill stadiums, newspapers, radio stations, web sites, quarterly target spreadsheets, bank balances, pension funds and investment opportunities in the tech sector. But, unlike so many other albums which will be released with far less fuss this year, it won't fill your soul.

WEDNESDAY, 25 FEBRUARY 2009

Working Women almost Certainly Caused the Credit Crunch

Newton Emerson

The answer to all our problems is staring us in the face. It may even be quite literally staring at you, right now, across the breakfast table. So put the paper down, stare back and ask yourself a selfless question.

Does the woman in your life really need a job?

Admittedly, this is not a fashionable question. From Iceland to Australia, men are blamed for causing the credit crunch, while a more feminine approach to finance is proposed as the solution. Of course there will always be a place in the world of business for exceptional women. Women also have an important role to play in jobs that are too demeaning for men, like teaching. But the general employment of women is another matter. Indeed, working women almost certainly caused the credit crunch by bringing a second income into the average household, pushing property prices up to unsustainable levels.

Whether working women actually caused the credit crunch is now a moot point. The point is that removing women from the workforce would mitigate its effects.

Consider the issue of unemployment. There were 221,301 men on the live register last month and just under one million women in work. Surely at least half these women have a partner who is

Archbishop Desmond Tutu shares a joke with Lord Mayor of Dublin Eibhlin Byrne as he signs the visitors' book in the Mansion House yesterday, where a civic reception was held in his honour. Photograph: David Sleator.

earning? Surely at least half would be happier at home? One half of one half is a quarter and one quarter of a million is roughly 221,301. I think we can all see where this argument is going.

It would be ludicrous to suggest that women should be sacked purely to give men their jobs. In many cases, their jobs should be abolished as well.

Women are twice as likely as men to work in the public sector. They account for two-thirds of the Civil Service and three-quarters of all public employees. Yet they are barely represented in the useful public services of fire fighting and arresting people. Encouraging women to leave the workforce would go a long way towards addressing the budget deficit without any downside whatsoever.

Further benefits of sacking women have been uncovered by the Central Gender Mainstreaming Unit at the Department of Justice. According to its research, twice as many women as men travel to work by bus and train, potentially halving the impact of cutbacks in public transport. However, it is probable that three-quarters of the Central Gender Mainstreaming Unit's staff are women, so these figures should be taken with a pinch of salt.

While the economic case for fewer women in the workforce is irrefutable, we should also acknowledge the social advantages. Women make the majority of spending decisions in Irish households and make almost all of the purchases. They are far more likely than men to regard shopping as a leisure activity, far less likely to make savings and investments, and were even almost twice as likely to spend their SSIAs.

In short, women were the driving force behind the greed, consumerism and materialism of the Celtic Tiger years and it was female employment that funded their oestrogen-crazed acquisitiveness.

The time has come to build a more sustainable, equitable and progressive society. Why not make a start by telling your other half to quit her job? She can ask you for the housekeeping on Friday.

(Newton Emerson's satirical column provoked hundreds of emails from outraged feminist readers, almost all of whom either did not get the joke or felt it was a subject unsuitable for mirth-making. The emails came from all over the world, and as late as May, occasional missives continued to arrive from far-off places. To cap it all, in that month, the Polish newspaper Gazeta Wyborcza *published an article about the decline of the Irish economy. The article was spotted by the* Three Monkeys Online *website whose 'Gdansk correspondent' reported the paper's headline 'Women's Spendthriftery Caused the Crisis' and said the article consisted of quotable quotes from people affected by the depression in Ireland … including Newton Emerson.)*

SATURDAY, 28 FEBRUARY 2009

The Secret to a Happy Life? The Keys of a 19-Year-Old Car

Kilian Doyle

I was slouching on my sofa last Saturday plotting global domination, as is my wont, when the doorbell rang. It was my neighbour, a lovely woman altogether.

In a fluster, she revealed she'd just reversed out of her driveway, across the whole width of the road and into my new car. Pretty impressive, eh?

The damage – an axe-wound in a wheel-arch – was minor. I would not normally have been overly miffed. But in this instance, I was. Exceedingly so. For I had, mere minutes earlier, decided to reverse my previous plan to sell Homer, my 19-year-old BMW estate, and flog the Millstone instead. Now I have to fix it first.

I can't explain my decision logically. There is no question that the Millstone – a 2005 BMW 320d Touring – is the better car by far. It has more gadgets and gizmos than Nasa. Homer has none. The turbo-enhanced Millstone is bottom-clenchingly quick. Homer is not. The Millstone

Irma Mali and Karen Fitzpatrick model Basso & Brooke oriental print silk dress designs at the Brown Thomas spring/summer collection launch in the Merrion Hotel, Dublin. Photograph: Matt Kavanagh.

grips like it has claws in lieu of tyres. Homer slides about like a giraffe on roller-skates.

However, fantastic piece of kit though it may be, the Millstone and I have failed to click over the past few weeks on any level other than a utilitarian one.

Were the Millstone human, with its sleek lines and bulges in all the right places, it'd be David Beckham in his underpants, while Homer, a shabby, battle-scarred old banger, would be me in mine.

But then, I'm as beyond fretting about Homer's appearance as I am about my own. How could I not be? Another bit of trim falls off every time I slam his tailgate; his seats are saggy as a sow's udder; and a colony of unidentified organic matter is flourishing in his boot. But these, to me, aren't faults. They're character.

Therein lays the crux of my decision. The Millstone has no character at all. I may as well be driving a fridge. Its sole *raison d'être* is to get me to my destination quickly, safely and with minimum fuss. A job it does impeccably, admittedly.

Whereas with Homer, I never know if I'll get anywhere without him disintegrating en route. And do you know what? That's half the reason I love him. Anyway, where's the fun in knowing a car will always do exactly what you tell it? I like pressing Homer's fog light switch and watching the sun roof open – and I always get a giggle when I yank the handbrake and the bonnet flies up. The Millstone, on the other hand, is too clinical to love.

Take the recent snows, for example. I'd left it in a train station car park that had become a polar bear's back garden by the time I returned. When I tried to drive off, the traction control decided to override me. The car wouldn't budge. A leather-clad Teutonic hand came out of the steering wheel and slapped me across the chops. 'Zis is too danger-ous for dummkopf humans,' a voice snapped.

Homer, on the other hand, was straining at the leash like an excited puppy when I, pushing the recalcitrant Millstone, arrived home. 'Bring me for a spin, willya? Please?'

So I did. And promptly skidded right through a hedge, leaving Homer with bits of branches sticking out of every orifice and me wearing a grin the width of France. The Millstone snorted super-ciliously when we returned.

My experiences with the Millstone have merely served to reinforce my view that I like cars to be like me – a bit mad, decrepit and liable to blow up at any moment. So what if the Millstone attracts stares of slack-jawed admiration while Homer is received with universal contempt? I care not a whit for wealth or prestige. And even less what anyone thinks of me. And that, dear friends, is the secret to a happy life.

MONDAY, 2 MARCH 2009

Young Saudi Women Reinvent the Abaya as a Fashion Statement

Mary Fitzgerald

In Saudi Arabia they say you can tell a lot about a woman from the way she wears her abaya. The cut and fall of the floor-length, long-sleeved black robe she is obliged to wear over her clothes in public from the onset of puberty can be interpreted in several ways.

The kingdom's religious police insist an abaya should be loose, attached to the head, and left to fall to the ground without outlining the contours of the body. The woman who wears her abaya like this, accessorising with a full face veil and black gloves, is deemed to be more conservative. Not so long ago, any deviation from what is known as *abaya sada*, Arabic for plain *abaya*, was considered an act of rebellion. 'Nine years ago I had an abaya subtly dec-orated with little tassels,' remembers one Australian expat. 'It was viewed as positively risqué.'

Today that has changed. The all-enveloping garment designed to comply with Islam's emphasis

Louise Carroll walks with her three-month-old son, Bailey, in the National Gallery of Ireland in Dublin, during a preview of the new exhibition of some 50 works by renowned Irish landscape artist Thomas Roberts. Photograph: Julien Behal/PA.

on modest dress and eliminate any hint of the female form has become something of a fashion statement with many young Saudi women reinventing the abaya as a way of expressing themselves.

In shops, the racks of more traditional shapeless abayas are increasingly ignored by fully-veiled women whose footwear – which can range from Converse trainers to Birkenstocks and ballet flats to the red flash of a Louboutin sole – often provides the only clue to the tastes of the person underneath. Instead they swoon over form-fitting abayas decorated with a swatch of crystals around the wrist, collar or hem; swirls of intricate embroidery and beading; or loud leopard skin and day-glo panels.

I saw one abaya decorated with Japanese characters picked out in blue sequins, and another which featured a large image of a tiger's head rendered in crystals on the back. The variations seem endless, with ribbons, studs, glitter, buttons, lace, leather tassels, and even feathers used to adorn the abayas sold in one shop in Riyadh.

The most daring designs can be found in Jeddah, the port city which is by far Saudi Arabia's most cosmopolitan and one which is considered dangerously 'liberal' by many of those who live in the kingdom's conservative heartland.

A popular style there is the double-layered abaya with dramatic bolts of vividly coloured silk visible underneath sheer black chiffon. Other abayas worn in the city look more like funky kimonos, while some women wear theirs open, often revealing jeans and a T-shirt underneath. At a wedding I attended in Jeddah, strictly segregated as is the custom in Saudi Arabia, the abayas the women scrambled for before the groom entered the banqueting hall with his bride were almost as lavish as the designer gowns they wore underneath.

Sales assistants in Riyadh say they cannot keep

Assistants Alice Kain (left), Eimer Walsh and Rebecca O'Neill, with technical assistant Leona Leonard and curator Matthew Parks, removing some exhibits from the Natural History Museum to be professionally cleaned in the Netherlands. Photograph: Brenda Fitzsimons.

up with the demand for new abaya styles, but the trend has drawn criticism from more conservative Saudis who gripe that a piece of clothing intended to discourage male attention is now becoming a fashion item that risks having the opposite effect.

'Most abayas now need abayas to cover them,' declared a religious pamphlet distributed at shopping malls in Riyadh last year. 'When some girls go out they [look] like prostitutes who invite people to carry out lewd acts.' The religious police have not been slow to respond. Staff at several abaya shops in Riyadh told me their premises had been raided in recent months, with the bearded men tasked with the 'prevention of vice and the promotion of virtue' confiscating all ornamented abayas. 'Most of all they hate anything shiny like crystals or sequins,' said one manager. 'They say

decorations like that draw the eyes of men.' Far from being a mere barometer of fashion, the increasing popularity of stylised abayas, despite the best efforts of the religious police, is a sign of a gradual loosening of rigid social norms in a country where change comes dropping slow. Women are becoming more visible in the workplace and in society generally. Last month the kingdom's first female deputy minister was appointed.

Spend an hour watching the crowds milling around Ladies' Kingdom, the women-only floor of Al Mamlaka shopping mall in Riyadh, and it becomes apparent that a new generation of Saudi women is pushing the boundaries of tradition more than ever before.

Here, away from prying male eyes, women can discard their face veils and open their abayas to show off the much-deliberated-over outfits under-neath. There is much bling and glamour as couture-clad matrons sweep by, heady perfumes trailing in their wake. But there is also the young woman wearing a Sid Vicious T-shirt. Or the posse of girls in baggy skateboarder shorts. One teenager draws stares from passers-by with her nose-ring and hair that has been teased into short, peroxide-tipped spikes. All are Saudis, and all are redefining what it means to be Saudi in their own way.

FRIDAY, 6 MARCH 2009

Surprised to Feel at Home at Equality Authority

John Waters

Although I have been writing about equality for years, I had never, until last Wednesday, been inside the Dublin headquarters of the Equality Authority. To be truthful, I didn't even know it was in Clonmel Street, off Harcourt Street, a short walk from St Stephen's Green. It may be relevant that I have never before been invited. But there was also my sense that the kind of equality the Equality Authority was interested in did not embrace the kinds of things I had increasingly, since the mid-1990s, found myself writing about.

Last week, I was invited to the launch of the authority's *Strategic Plan 2009-2011, Equality for All in a Time of Change*. Curiosity, and a hunch about the new chair of the board, dragged me along. But, still, I half expected the kind of frosty reception I have long been getting in such quarters for pointing out things that have been unpalatable to some of those already ensconced within the equality tent.

I happen to know the recently appointed chair of the authority, Angela Kerins, as a colleague for the past five years on the board of the Broadcasting

Commission of Ireland. For many years Angela has been a towering force in advancing the cause of people with disabilities. She and several members of the authority's staff actually greeted me as though I was not after all in the wrong place. Over the next hour or so, I met several old acquaintances and new friends among those campaigning on behalf of the disabled, the Traveller community and others. I encountered also the long disappeared Peter White, former Fine Gael press secretary, now a member of the authority's board.

For the first time in many years, I felt at home in a place where hitherto I would have found large tracts of carpet opening up around me. But my sense of a change went deeper than the personal. A man sitting beside me drew my attention to page 25 of the new *Strategic Plan*, which outlined under the heading 'Objective 1' that the Equality Authority will henceforth seek to promote 'the status of men as carers, in particular the equal sharing of caring rights and responsibilities between women and men and continuing dialogue with men's organisations on issues of equality for men'. Further down the page was a commitment to respond to 'gender equality issues for men including their impact on health and wellbeing'.

Already I was glad I came.

Addressing the meeting, Prof. John FitzGerald of the ESRI gave an overview of the likely impact of the recession on those already weakened by difference or marginalisation. He highlighted an emerging disparity in the education levels enjoyed by women and men. It seems that an unnoticed by-product of the boom years has been that young men were opting out of education to avail of ready money in, for example, the construction sector.

On a day when newspaper reports were again emphasising discrimination against women, FitzGerald pointed out that whereas almost 60 per cent of women now enter third-level education, the figure for males is 40 per cent. This, he said, will have serious, adverse consequences for men in both the economic and personal contexts, as low

Hundreds of starlings congregate in the skies over Bettystown, Co. Meath. Photograph: Brenda Fitzsimons.

educational attainment is also seriously disadvantageous in relation to marriage prospects.

What I found most remarkable was that FitzGerald spoke as though the outcome for males was as important as the outcome for females. I pinched myself, but found he was still speaking. There were no caveats, no weasel words, no counter-balancing what-aboutery. I have never before, at a public meeting held under the auspices of any State organisation, heard someone say something with the clear implication that the Irish State is as concerned for its sons as for its daughters.

Angela Kerins outlined what, to these ears, sounded like a revolutionary message at a time of seismic change: 'Let there be no doubt that the equality agenda and the work of the Equality Authority is owned by every man, woman, and child in Ireland. We are determined that everyone who has an interest in our work will feel a part of it, and that no one will feel that the authority does not have a real concern about an issue which affects their dignity or their equality.'

It is 13 years since I began to write in this newspaper about the hidden ways in which men are discriminated against in this society – about, for example, how fathers are treated after the personal relationships between them and the mothers of their children have fallen apart. It has been a rough ride. Often, I have felt like a counter-revolutionary, seeking to undo gains achieved in earlier waves of progress and change.

I do not exaggerate when I say that, sitting in the offices of the Equality Authority in Dublin last Wednesday, I felt for the first time the possibility that the day might yet arrive when I will no longer have to annoy myself and everyone else by seeming to be the only one who has noticed what strikes me as the most glaringly obvious things. Before our eyes, the concept of equality in society was beginning to be reintegrated with the dictionary definition.

WEDNESDAY, 11 MARCH 2009

Splintered Republican Dissident Groups Are Difficult to Penetrate

Gerry Moriarty

You can't be lucky always, which in a way accounts for how the Real IRA gunned to death two British soldiers in Antrim on Saturday night and how 48 hours later the Continuity IRA (CIRA) shot dead PSNI Constable Stephen Carroll in Craigavon.

A 48-year-old married man, father and grandfather, he was the first member of the PSNI to be murdered by paramilitaries since loyalists killed RUC officer Frankie O'Reilly 10 years ago.

Terry Spence, head of the North's Police Federation, the PSNI's representative body, in a sense referred to the element of benign providence allied to good policing and security intelligence that has prevented many more members of the police and British army, as well as others, being killed by dissidents in recent years. He said had the dissident republicans succeeded to 'maximum effect' with their gun, bomb, rocket and mortar attacks – note the range of that arsenal – 40 PSNI officers would have been killed by these republican groups.

There was more than luck involved in the Real IRA killings of the unarmed soldiers, Mark Quinsey and Patrick Azimkar. As senior British and Irish security sources acknowledged yesterday, you don't gun down soldiers at the entrance to a British army base in a unionist town such as Antrim without careful planning. The Brownlow area of Craigavon where Constable Carroll was murdered is a disaffected republican place where dissidents would have some level of tolerance if not small pockets of support.

It is suspected that the police were lured into Lismore Manor in Craigavon by means of an act of vandalism on an innocent person's home – and this indicates that the ambush was planned.

But Spence's point still holds. Dissident republicans have been involved in scores of attacks over recent years, much of them against the PSNI with a lesser number directed against the British army. Seven police officers were injured in such incidents. Had the dissidents been 'luckier' several more people undoubtedly would have died.

Most notoriously the Real IRA killed 29 people including a woman pregnant with twin girls in the 1998 Omagh bombing. That prompted them to clear the stage for a while but the organisation later regrouped.

Despite a subsequent split in the organisation, British and Irish security forces and intelligence services continued to regard them as deadly and dangerous, a view they also held about the CIRA.

There is overlapping and co-operation between these two main dissident groups, whom the Independent Monitoring Commission and security and republican representatives suspect are also heavily involved in drugs dealing, smuggling, extortion and other forms of criminality.

The Real IRA's main area of activity tends to be Belfast, parts of Armagh, Derry, Tyrone and areas around Newry. The CIRA mainly operates in Fermanagh and Armagh, but also has a presence in Belfast.

In recent weeks and months MI5 has been reinforcing its resources in the light of the increased threat from the dissidents, something which Jonathan Evans, head of the organisation, alluded to when he gave an unprecedented interview to a number of London newspapers in January. That reinforcement is continuing, according to a British anti-terrorism source.

Security sources appear uncertain about the actual definitive strength of the dissidents. One Dublin intelligence source estimated that the 'hard end' of the dissidents would number perhaps 100 or more, as in people who would directly engage in the shooting and the bombing. A 'limited' number,

Ruby Walsh on Kauto Star, celebrating victory in the Cheltenham Gold Cup on the final day of the Cheltenham Racing Festival. The win was Walsh's seventh, a record for the number of wins at a Cheltenham festival. Photograph: Alan Betson.

perhaps a few hundred, would provide backup in terms of supports such as local intelligence and providing safe houses.

Sources say that membership is from people who have a Provisional IRA track record but who broke away from the organisation because of the political path taken by Gerry Adams and Martin McGuinness. Their secretive leadership structure is understood to be based on the army council make-up of the Provisional IRA, although these groups are more disjointed and smaller.

They would be experienced in planning, training, surveillance and in mounting operations, an experience that they are passing on to younger recruits, some of whom would come from 'purist' republican families. Other disaffected republicans were also susceptible to the lure of such organisations. These groups actively have been seeking younger recruits.

Even going back over the past three years dissidents have been involved in dozens of attacks. In the autumn of 2007 two PSNI officers were seriously wounded in separate gun attacks in Derry and Dungannon, Co. Tyrone. Last May an officer was seriously injured in a booby-trap car bomb attack. These attacks were attributed to the Real IRA.

The CIRA said it carried out a landmine attack near Roslea, Co. Fermanagh, in June last year in which two police officers suffered minor injuries. In August of last year three PSNI officers escaped serious injury in a suspected CIRA bomb attack in Lisnaskea, Co. Fermanagh. That was additionally worrying for the security services in that Semtex was used in the attack, an explosive previously seen as solely in the hands of the Provisional IRA.

Both organisations also have been involved in a number of killings. In March 2007 in a suspected

Cartoon by Martyn Turner.

fall-out among CIRA members, Belfast taxi driver Joey Jones was bludgeoned to death in Ardoyne in north Belfast while on the same day Eddie Burns was shot dead near a GAA club in west Belfast.

Dissident republicans were also blamed for the murder of Andrew Burns from Strabane, Co. Tyrone, whose body was found across the Border in a Donegal churchyard in February of last year. Last month a 38-year-old known drug dealer was murdered in Derry. The Real IRA is believed to be responsible.

Firebomb attacks by the Real IRA in 2006 caused millions of pounds of damage in Newry and Belfast. In January a 300lb bomb was abandoned near Castlewellan, believed destined for the Ballykinlar British army base about eight miles away.

The Real IRA was also viewed as the main suspect in a failed attempt in August 2006 to explode a 70lb bomb at a house undergoing building work in Co. Louth which was owned by leading businessman and former Irish senator Dr Edward Haughey who is titled Lord Ballyedmond. The CIRA has threatened civil servants in Fermanagh.

Dissidents have also targeted senior republicans. They issued death threats against Gerry Adams, Martin McGuinness and Gerry Kelly in 2006 while one year later Mr Adams disclosed at the funeral of former senior IRA figure Martin Meehan that the night before he suffered a fatal heart attack he was searching outside his home for dissident republican bombs.

There are numerous more examples of attacks by dissidents in recent years. That catalogue of violence just proves the accuracy of Spence's view that 40 PSNI officers could have been killed by these groups.

The British and Irish security forces and intelligence services have enjoyed success in combating these groups. There are 80-100 dissidents in prisons in the North and South. Hugh Orde paid tribute to the work of the Garda for saving the lives of his officers from the dissidents. But, as security

sources in Dublin and London acknowledge, every attack can't be thwarted; the PSNI and British army can't be lucky all the time.

As one senior British counter-terrorism expert said: 'One can have good intelligence on the intentions, the plans, the trends of the dissidents. But because of the geographically fragmented nature of these organisations it is quite another thing to be able to say that such and such an attack will happen at such and such a time in such and such a place.'

TUESDAY, 17 MARCH 2009

Fritzl Hides his Face after Years of Brutal Domination

Derek Scally, in St Pölten, Austria

For decades, Josef Fritzl dominated his Austrian family and preyed on his daughter Elisabeth in a secret dungeon under their home. It was a defeated man who shuffled into court yesterday, flanked by three armed guards, to answer to crimes of rape, enslavement and murder.

With a scraggy comb-over and a grey check jacket hanging from his gaunt frame, Fritzl hid his face behind a quivering blue binder. For 15 agonising minutes before proceedings began, he ignored the questions of a crestfallen Austrian television journalist. A final, desperate attempt to bait him: 'If you had your time again, would you do things the same again?'

No answer.

Then 12 jurors, six men and six women, filed into the court. When the cameras left and the binder came down, they saw a wan-faced man, still with insinuating eyebrows and a bushy moustache.

In the wood-panelled Court 119 in St Pölten, 65km (40 miles) from Vienna, Judge Andrea Humer delivered a stern warning to the media gallery. 'This is the trial of an individual,' she said,

Josef Fritzl hides his face behind a file folder before the start of his trial at the provincial courthouse in St Pölten, Austria. Photograph: Robert Jaeger/AP.

behind a crucifix and two unlit candles, 'not the crime of a place or a region.'

Asked by Humer to confirm his personal details, Fritzl gave gruff, one-word replies in a baritone voice more used to giving orders than answering questions.

Then state prosecutor Christiane Burkheiser launched her attack. 'He treated her like a plaything. He came, used her and left,' she said. 'And you know what troubles me the most? He has shown not one sign of regret.'

The rape of Elisabeth Fritzl began on day two of her imprisonment in August 1984, she said. The first baby arrived four years later.

'What kind of birth did she have? Elisabeth had a dirty scissors, unsanitary blankets in which to wrap her baby, and a book on delivering babies given to her two months earlier.'

The monotony of rape continued in front of her growing brood of young children.

Twice the state prosecutor visited the cellar under the Fritzl home in the nearby town of Amstetten. 'It's morbid, creepy and desperately cold; the damp creeps into you within minutes,' said Burkheiser. 'Often it got damp so quickly that water ran down the walls and Elisabeth had to soak it up with towels.'

The closest the jurors will come to the cellar is a cardboard box containing objects from the cellar that Burkheiser passed to them yesterday, asking them to open the lid and smell the damp.

Defence lawyer Rudolf Mayer said he would

The St Patrick's Festival National Lottery Skyfest fireworks display on the river Suir in Waterford. Photograph: Matt Kavanagh.

contest only the murder charge, calling it out of character for Fritzl. 'This is someone who raised a second family,' he said. 'Someone who provided school books and a tree at Christmas.'

When put to him, Fritzl accepted the charges of incest and deprivation of liberty, partially accepted the rape charge and one of two charges of serious coercion.

He pleaded not guilty to the charges of enslavement and murder. Yesterday afternoon, jurors began watching 11 hours of harrowing video testimony from the trial's only witness, Elisabeth Fritzl.

Eight of the 12 jurors – four are reserve members – are expected to return a verdict on Friday.

Outside the courtroom, to the stirring sounds of Bruckner, protesters carried bloodstained dolls and placards reading 'Shame on Austria! Children's rights in the constitution'.

MONDAY, 23 MARCH 2009

Ireland Delivers on a Grand Scale

Gerry Thornley, in Cardiff

Grand Slam champions. Sounds nice, yes? The barbs can be put to one side now and Irish rugby can hold its head higher than ever before. No more references to Ireland being chokers, and there'll never be a mention of 62 years. The golden generation have delivered the greatest day.

First off, this success was about the team. The squad. They're all stars really, but there are no egos. The team adds up to more than the sum of its considerable parts. Modesty forbids of course, for Declan Kidney would detest almost any praise

Ronan O'Gara's drop kick on its way between the posts for what proved the match — and Grand Slam — winning effort against Wales at the Millennium Stadium in Cardiff. Photograph: Getty Images.

being heaped on him. But basking in the glow of a great day for everyone, and one of his mantras is that this is for everybody, he was asked what was the ingredient that pulled Ireland through the tautest of three one-score wins in a row.

You could have guessed the first word out of his mouth. 'Honesty, trust, hard work, willingness to go the extra little bit. It's like what I said earlier, nobody was blaming anybody. We had none of that, no cliques, no nothing. We gave it a go in the best way possible. You cannot overestimate honesty.'

Brian O'Driscoll spoke of Kidney knowing his strengths and delegating, but also admitted he had 'an X factor'. However he helps achieve this honesty amongst the group, be it as a facilitator, organiser, manager or coach, his teams usually have it in spades. That's some trick.

Honesty of effort, an unwavering refusal to let down a team-mate, being able to look each other in the eye and belief in each other. These traits have transcended all five wins of the Grand Slam odyssey.

Critical to that was a squad get-together in Enfield before Christmas. 'That was our opportunity,' he admitted. 'When November was over, we sat down. I have a brilliant bunch of team leaders, Brian, Rog, Paul, Rory. We sat down with Paul (McNaughton) and we had a good, frank discussion.

'We opened it up, asked the players what they think: "Let's put it out on the table, lads." It was nothing hugely scientific. I'm not saying I'm a management consultant or anything, but it was just saying, "Let's be honest with one another now. What are the (wrong) things?" You'd be surprised that by talking about it, and a little bit of slagging, all of a sudden a whole lot of doors were opened, and we just have some *craic* now.'

Having removed a 61-year-old monkey off the back of Irish rugby, Kidney talked about feeding into what it is to wear an Irish jersey, and the honour, sweat and toil that goes into it.

'I'd be a believer that you don't ever own a jersey. You don't ever nail down a jersey. You have it for one afternoon, and that's your chance. You leave your DNA in it, and what way do you leave it? Hopefully the lads today have added their little bit to it, so whoever fills it in our next match in May, they'll feel that onus on them to represent it.'

Kidney was so humble and proud at the same time, and so inclusive, he even mentioned the groundwork done by his predecessor Eddie O'Sullivan as well as the mini-rugby coaches who first gave these players their love of rugby.

Some people want power for themselves; some want it to make a difference. In a country seemingly short of true leaders in recent times, Kidney is a class act. Just what the country needs really.

In many ways Ireland's slightly overdue Grand Slam merely highlighted better than any of the near misses how difficult they are to achieve. O'Driscoll repeatedly talks of the fine lines between winning and losing, the small moments that can decide a game. And this team, this squad, are all about the inches and the small moments. Ronan O'Gara had reminded the players that morning that these chances don't come along very often, especially for the older players. They couldn't regret not giving everything; they would be pushed beyond the pain barrier.

You think of Tommy Bowe and Brian O'Driscoll tackling Simon Danielli and Phil Godman in Murrayfield, and on Saturday of Luke Fitzgerald bravely putting his body in front of Mike Phillips in the 75th minute, thereby halting his momentum, and of Peter Stringer making the

Ronan O'Gara wheels away in delight after scoring the drop goal that won the Grand Slam for Ireland. Photograph: Alan Betson.

Ireland coach Declan Kidney and team captain Brian O'Driscoll hold aloft the Six Nations championship trophy for thousands of cheering rugby enthusiasts, who turned out to greet them outside Dublin's Mansion House on their return from their Grand Slam victory over Wales in Cardiff. Photograph: Bryan O'Brien.

recovery tackle to prevent the Welsh scrumhalf scoring a try which might have put Wales 19-14 in front with less than five minutes to go.

Their honesty, along with O'Connell, Wallace and co. punching the ball, and Marcus Horan, Jerry Flannery, John Hayes, Donncha O'Callaghan, Denis Leamy and Jamie Heaslip working their socks off to recycle the ball, made it possible for O'Gara to land the match-winning drop goal.

'I'd an awful lot of time to think about it,' O'Gara recalled afterwards. 'I was roaring for the ball for 30, 40, 50 seconds, I don't know how long, from 15 metres in. But then Strings showed great composure. I think he knew what he was looking to do. I took about 15 yards from Strings; they obviously got a running start. No way that ref was going to give a penalty; they were well offside. So

I had to concentrate on getting the ball up rather than driving through like a normal drop kick.'

So much for cracking under pressure then, as the Welsh barbs had been suggesting. 'Crack under pressure? I've won two European Cup finals under pressure. No-one of these Welsh fellas have played in a European Cup final. What are they basing this on? They've won Grand Slams maybe. They talked the talk this week but they didn't walk the walk. I'm particularly happy in that regard.'

There was still, of course, the drama of Stephen Jones' 48th minute penalty attempt with the last kick of the game, and O'Gara's sympathy and embrace of Jones gave the lie to the notion that they dislike each other. Not even going to the theatre or the movies can throw up drama on this scale. Only great sporting occasions can do so, and everything about Saturday's finale belongs in the pantheon of great Irish sporting moments. We thought Munster reaching their Holy Grail wouldn't be bettered but it has been.

The sport that unites Catholic, Protestant and dissenter has had its day of days. Pity anybody who can't enjoy it. Some day.

MONDAY, 23 MARCH 2009

Mr Rooney, a Few Tips to Help You Settle In

Ann Marie Hourihane

Dear Ambassador Rooney,
Hope you are well. We are well. Bono is well. The rugby team is tip-top. Only, Ambassador Rooney, the economy isn't too well. Not looking the best, as they say. But you'll see for yourself when you get here.

Congratulations on your appointment! We are absolutely delighted that you are our new ambassador from the United States! And how lucky are you? Think about it, Mr Ambassador, you could have been sent to Paris, or to London, or to Rome, or to any one of those soulless and anonymous cities where they don't know how to enjoy life. We're thrilled for you. We're thrilled for ourselves as well, because we hear that you are a good guy, much respected at home. And also because you're so well got with President Obama, thank God. In our eyes you are virtually a Kennedy.

And we know that you and your family have loved this country for two generations, which is more than we have managed ourselves. Consequently you are pretty well-informed about our complex, internationally recognised and award-winning culture. The literary prize you so kindly donated has worked great, so far.

We also realise that you are a practising Christian millionaire, with a strong record on public service. All of these things might make you

feel a little out of place round here, so we've jotted down a couple of handy hints to help with your move to Ireland.

First of all, Irish Management: Mr Ambassador, we gather that you live quite close to the home of your football team, the Pittsburgh Steelers, and often walk the 10-minute journey to the ground. We have even heard that you do not have a designated parking space at the Steelers' stadium. Can either of these two rumours be true? If so, Mr Ambassador, we can only emphasise that such behaviour will make you very conspicuous here. An Irish executive never walks when he can be driven in a limousine. In the good times he attended most sporting fixtures via helicopter. Over here low-key, democratic management style denotes being a loser.

Dublin: You will be getting one of the very few houses in Dublin which has not fallen in value by roughly 50 per cent. But as you are a foreigner, and also because you do not own that lovely house, we will let you away with it.

Dubliners are an endearingly cranky lot, and always have been. Samuel Beckett, one of our innumerable Nobel Laureates, wrote: 'This tired, abstract anger – inarticulate passive opposition – always the same thing in Dublin.' Mr Ambassador, as a literary man you will recognise that this still pertinent insight comes from Samuel Beckett's recently published collected letters. But you have to understand that most Irish people have simply been too busy to read Beckett's letters, or his novels, or his plays. I gleaned that pertinent insight from last Wednesday's *Irish Daily Mail*. Which brings us to . . .?

The Media: The Irish media is based in Dublin and never leaves it. The Irish media prefers the darker side of the street in all matters, except, until very recently, in the reporting of economic news. Aren't we gas?

Roughly speaking, the newspapers agree on everything, and are kind of hard to tell apart. You can break them down like this: *The Irish Times* contains what people think they should be thinking.

The *Irish Independent* contains what people would be thinking, if they thought about it. The *Irish Examiner* contains what people in the south of the country are thinking – but those people are rather confused.

The *Irish Daily Mail* contains what people are ashamed to be thinking. And the *Evening Herald* has never had a thought in its life; although it does sometimes argue that the whole population should be interned without trial.

The radio stations are indistinguishable from each other. Television stations ditto: they all show American and British drama and comedy series, constantly. People who want to see Ireland on TV have to watch a programme called *Nationwide*.

Shannon: People may approach you from time to time to argue about Shannon. Please don't be concerned. These people will not be objecting to the use of Shannon airport for the transport of US troops to Iraq, or to the way rendition planes refuelled there. No, the people will be arguing about the restoration of the Shannon stop-over, which is never coming back. This is not America's fault.

On the other hand, we gather that in your home country, even before your endorsement of Obama, you were known as a Rino (Republican in Name Only). In which case you will feel right at home here. Surprisingly, Ireland is a bit of a Rino sanctuary.

Immigration: Irish people want the right to live and work and have their children in America, and want those children to be American citizens. Irish people do not want the children born in Ireland to the people who come to live and work here to have Irish citizenship. It's perfectly simple.

Must close now, Ambassador, and sign off with that traditional Celtic greeting – céad míle fáilte. That's one hundred thousand welcomes; if you could bring a job for each one it would be a start.

Kate Stephens from Cardiff pushes Elvis impersonator Daniel Kirwin from Co. Wexford, during the Fr Ted Festival on Inis Mór, the Aran Islands. Photograph: Brenda Fitzsimons.

MONDAY, 30 MARCH 2009

A Grim Tale of Things to Come if Ireland Keeps on Floundering

John McManus

The scene opens. It is early April 2010. We are in the Cabinet Room of Government Buildings for the weekly crisis meeting. Sitting at the table are the Taoiseach, Minister for Finance, various Ministers and the German ambassador.

German ambassador: Good morning everybody! Right . . . Let's get going.

Taoiseach: Hey . . . that's my job. I am in charge.

German ambassador: You think?

Taoiseach: Sorry, forgot.

German ambassador: No problem. It's understandable. These things take getting used to. Right! Minister for Finance?

Minister for Finance: Yes, Herr Ambassador. I am working on the next stability update for Berlin, sorry Brussels. We hope to have the deficit down to 3.5 per cent by 2013, but it's not going to be pretty.

German ambassador: Very good . . .

Taoiseach: Can I just say something at this point?

German ambassador: If you must. I am trying to be understanding, but you must recognise that things have changed.

Liver transplant recipient Lucy Richardson (4) with her father, Conor Richardson, and broadcaster Ryan Tubridy at the national launch of Organ Donor Awareness Week 2009. Photograph: Justin Mac Innes/Mac Innes Photography.

Taoiseach: Understood. It's just I don't think the people are going to wear this much longer.

German ambassador: And why not?

Taoiseach: Well, it's like this. We did what you told us – sorry, we took your advice last year and kept the deficit to 9.5 per cent. We whacked up taxes. Cut the guts out of expenditure . . .

German ambassador: Yah . . . and your point is?

Taoiseach: Well, it has not exactly worked, has it?

German ambassador (with a trace of a smile): That depends on your point of view, my Irish friend.

Taoiseach: Well, from our point of view, it's been a bit of a disaster . . . The economy is even more knackered than when we started. You also said that if we did what you told us then, we would retain the confidence of the bond markets and be able to borrow what we need.

Minister for Finance (jumping in): That's right. And you said we might as well do it to ourselves because if we lost the confidence of the bond markets and had to borrow the money from you instead, you would make us do it anyway. And that would make us look even more useless and you look mean.

Taoiseach: We did everything you wanted and wrecked what was left of the economy. Now the bond markets will not touch us with a barge pole.

German ambassador (trying to contain a grin): Ah so! And you see this as a failure of the plan? You have much to learn about the way of the world, my friends.

Taoiseach: What?

German ambassador: Some other time I will explain. Today, I am here for business. Does the Attorney General have the deeds for west Cork ready yet?

Attorney General: Yes, Herr Ambassador. The Bundesbank lawyers have looked them over and are satisfied as to the title.

German ambassador: Very good . . . shall we proceed?

Attorney General: Taoiseach . . . will you just sign here, please?

Taoiseach (glumly): Okay.

Attorney General: Now, Herr Ambassador, if you could just sign here and hand over the cheque that will be that.

German ambassador: Of course. What did we say again?

Attorney General: It was €20 billion, Herr Ambassador. In return, you get west Cork, including fixtures, fittings and Bushes Bar in Baltimore. But, as requested, we have excluded the county hurling team.

German ambassador (smiling again): Ah, Bushes. So many happy memories. Angela, sorry Chancellor Merkle, is very fond of their toasted special sandwiches. I do hope that they will still be allowed sell them under German licensing laws . . . but that is for another day. Now we move on to your plans for economic recovery. What are you going to do with the money?

Minister for Finance: As I was saying, we hope to be back within the Maastricht guidelines by 2013. And as you want – sorry have suggested – we are really going to go for it this year. If you thought we were harsh last year, wait till you see this year's interim budget.

German ambassador: Very good.

Taoiseach: Look, I am sorry to keep going on like this but what happens if the same thing happens?

German ambassador: I am sorry. What do you mean?

Taoiseach: What if we overdo taxes and cuts and wind up doing more harm to the economy than good? What are we going to do for money then?

German ambassador (grinning broadly): Ah so! Don't worry my not-so-jolly Irish friends. There is always Kerry.

Ah Dingle. Ashes, McCarthys, Fungi the dolphin, so many happy memories.

We would give you at least €25 billion for Kerry.

TUESDAY, 31 MARCH 2009

Will 10% More Protestants Lead to Less Corruption?

Elaine Byrne

'We shall studiously avoid offending the religious susceptibilities of any portion of the community,' stated the inaugural editorial of *The Irish Times* in 1859. My apologies in advance then to Lawrence Edward Knox, the 22-year-old Protestant Englishman who founded this newspaper.

A positive correlation exists between Catholicism and corruption. Political science literature and academic research suggests that the more Protestant the population, the less corrupt the country. Divergent views on sin and loyalty account for this corpulent assertion.

So, with a deep, sacred breath, here we go.

Catholicism is a hierarchical religion. The Catholic Church places emphasis on the inherent weakness and shortcomings of human beings, their inability to escape sin and the consequent need for the church to be forgiving and protecting.

The clergy, as mediators between mankind and God, facilitate, via confession, the possibility to be absolved of guilt. As laid down by the Council of Trent, priests have this authority 'because that our Lord Jesus Christ, when about to ascend from earth to heaven, left priests his own vicars, as presidents and judges . . . in order that, in accordance with the power of the keys, they may pronounce the sentence of forgiveness or retention of sins'.

On the other hand, the egalitarian organisation

Bank workers at a table in the staff restaurant at the AIB Bankcentre in Dublin, on the day the bank announced its annual results. Photograph: Sasko Lazarov/Photocall Ireland.

typical of Protestantism believes that individuals are personally responsible for avoiding sin rather than relying upon the institutional forgiveness of the church. Protestant culture is less understanding when lapses from grace occur.

The institutionalisation of virtue and the compulsion to cast out the wicked is underlined more explicitly.

The implication therefore is that Protestants are less inclined to commit a sin because they do not have the same faculty of achieving pardon as Catholics do.

Diverging attitudes towards loyalty to the state were born when Martin Luther posted his Ninety-Five Theses to the Wittenberg Castle Church door in Germany. The Reformation was initiated in response to growing concerns of corruption regarding the sale of indulgences and church positions by the church hierarchy.

The separation between church and state tends to be further pronounced in Protestant societies which instead promote an autonomous and vivacious civil society.

Research by Robert Putnam, acclaimed author of *Bowling Alone* and key speaker for the 2005 Fianna Fáil annual think-in, has shown that the more civic a society, the greater the degree of trust by citizens in their political institutions. Putnam regards Protestant churches as particularly important for American civic society and characterised a

A portrait of Taoiseach Brian Cowen, which was illegally displayed in the National Gallery of Ireland earlier this month. The identity of the artist is unknown and gardaí are investigating the incident.

A Palestinian police officer participates in an exercise in the West Bank. Photograph: AP Photo.

healthy civic community by its strong sense of civic engagement, political equality, solidarity and social capital.

Detailed academic papers and datasets on the different aspects of this subject are freely available to download from internet search engine results or the personal websites of political theorists – Daniel Treisman, Martin Paldam, Rafael La Porta, AJ Heidenheimer, Donatella della Porta, Seymour Martin Lipset and Gabriel Lenz.

In Treisman's 2000 cross-national study, for example, the University of California professor contends that countries with a Protestant tradition, a history of British rule and a developed economy are less corrupt.

In his comparison between Ireland and Denmark, he suggests that if Ireland had an additional 5-10 per cent Protestant population, our corruption rating would be that of Denmark's, which has consistently been in the top five least corrupt countries in the world since polling began.

Although methodological issues arise regarding the Transparency International Corruption Perception Index, it serves to illustrate this broad point. Take Europe as an example. Over the past 13 years, the least corrupt countries have been our northern European Protestant neighbours, Finland, Sweden, Norway and Denmark. The Catholic countries of southern Europe have wavered in the ranks of the most corrupt in Europe.

Although geographically in the North, Ireland shares many characteristics with the South. Ireland, Italy, Portugal and Spain have traditionally been distinguished by clannish catch-all parties and entrenched centre-periphery politics.

Religion and society share comparable hierarchical predilections. These personages of authority, moulded by absolute deference stretched across a generation, are now crashing down around us – the Michael Fingletons, the Seánie FitzPatricks, the *béal bocht* property developers and the national politicians in their constituency castles.

When I presented these facts at a Belfast University conference a few years ago, I was intercepted by an indignant student immediately afterwards.

I had let down my faith, the men of 1916 and all those going back to 1798, and an act of contrition was at once demanded. I reassured the devotee that the family undertaking background made us quite aware of religious difference and that we were always the very very last to let anybody down, Catholic, Protestant, and Dissenter alike.

Maybe we should cash in on the religious chip on the shoulder and target Treisman's suggestion of 10 per cent extra Protestants?

The Prods aren't always saints all the same, however. Ten years after founding this paper, Lawrence E Knox lost his seat as Sligo MP when unseated by petition for bribery!

WEDNESDAY, 8 APRIL 2009

Tough Budget Went for Tax Hikes and Held Off Attack on Spending

Mark Hennessy

Framing his emergency Budget, Brian Lenihan was haunted by the memory of Ernest Blythe, the finance minister in W.T. Cosgrave's first government in 1923, whose political reputation never survived cutting the old age pension in the 1920s, even if he gave it back.

But Lenihan has made his own history. He has taken decisions that will cost taxpayers billions, and made it clear that even tougher ones are to come in December's Budget and the ones afterwards.

Fianna Fáil TDs cheered Lenihan's Budget to the rafters last October only to find the package blowing up in their faces in the days subsequent after the attempt to curb the over-70s medical card collapsed.

Yesterday, they clapped rather than cheered and studied carefully the details in search of the political time bomb, the simple issue around which public opposition can unite, the issue that could destroy their damaged fortunes. And there are plenty of possibilities.

Perhaps the double Christmas social welfare bonus that will be cut, saving €82 million. Even more, his clear warning that rates could be cut in his next budget just weeks before Christmas threatens political turmoil.

And the middle class – whose members are the most likely to vote, remember – is going to scream loudly, hit as it is by extra income and health levies, cuts in childcare benefits and mortgage interest reliefs.

Landlords have not suffered as much as expected. Their tax reliefs have been cut fractionally, and Lenihan commits to cutting rent supplement next time, but does not say by how much.

Tax exiles were not mentioned, though it is known that the Department of Finance is working on plans that will see the light of day by the time the Budget morphs into the Finance Bill. Politically, it would have been better if these had been ready yesterday.

Equally, the fact that the new toxic bank assets super agency will soak up to €80 billion of bad property loans will be incomprehensible to most of the public, though it, or something like it, is necessary to get credit moving again.

In particular, the decision to include loans offered by Irish banks for foreign properties offers a target a mile wide for the Opposition, and they will make full use of it in coming days.

For weeks, the Cabinet has debated the options in detail, unlike any previous cabinet. Eventually, it decided that it could not cut more than €3.5 billion out of the economy this year, lest it choke what life remains in it – and it had to do it more by tax rises than cuts.

Taoiseach Brian Cowen at a Budget press conference in Government Buildings, Dublin. Photograph: Julien Behal/PA.

But a stimulus package, regardless of the Opposition's demands for one, was not possible: a ship cannot be righted until the crew has first managed to stop new water coming in. And Ireland is still taking water on board.

It's a judgment call on which everything depends. If Lenihan is wrong, the economy will go off a cliff and taxes will collapse. If he is right, Ireland will hit a bottom, and a bad one, but one solid enough from which we can rebuild.

However, he shirked the toughest options. Spending will be the major target next year, he promised. Reform in the public service will happen next year, he promised. These are not easy options: they mean sackings; an increase in school class sizes; the closure of hospital wards; and the spread of potholes on rural roads. This pain will not be shallow or short.

Politically, the Government's figures on this occasion – the fourth attempt since October to get the sums right – have to be correct, since it cannot return to the Dáil if it is to retain any credibility.

However, there is no guarantee that that can be avoided. In the last week, Taoiseach Brian Cowen and Lenihan have repeatedly offered different figures for tax revenues this year.

Last Sunday week, Cowen compared revenues with 2002/2003 statistics: a figure which would offer €32 billion at most. Then the Government said its €34 billion forecast remained. On Monday, Lenihan said €33 billion. Yesterday, he said €34 billion.

Sgt Mandy Gaynor and Garda Regina Carley don high heels in the Jump for Joy Schools Challenge fundraiser for Our Lady's Children's Hospital, Crumlin, Dublin. Photograph: James Connolly.

Now, the Government will have to sit back and wait to see whether the hard decisions will cause people to put a lock on their wallets completely – or whether the catalogue of bad news, however unpleasant, offers a degree of certainty.

PAYE earners will fork out €1.8 billion more this year in extra income taxes, PRSI and doubled levies, while mortgage interest relief will disappear for those owning homes for more than seven years.

The doubling of the health levy was not expected by most, while the increase from €52,000 to €75,000 in the PRSI ceiling was at the far end of expectations. And the lowering of the €100,000 levy threshold will bring tens of thousands in upper middle-class Ireland into the cruel 4 per cent embrace of the supertax.

In a full year, such changes would cost PAYE earners €3 billion; but there is little to indicate that the cost will stop there when Lenihan next stands up in the Dáil with a budget speech in his hand.

The scale of the impositions is stark and shows that it is middle to high earners who will bear the major pain: a middle-class couple with two children will pay €4,000 more in tax and levies, as well as lose mortgage tax relief.

Some of those people will also be employed by the State and already furious about the scourge of the pension levy, and many with children will have seen cuts in their childcare benefits.

And the reductions will be visible before Fianna Fáil and the Greens take to the streets in earnest to campaign for the European and local elections in June. Few in the trade would envy them their task.

One of the juicy fruits of the Celtic Tiger, the €480 million childcare supplement, will be halved in May and ended in January, and replaced by a year of pre-school that will cost some one-third of the bill.

'This is an example of how a programme can be reshaped and made more effective at a lower cost to the taxpayer. We need to see more such initiatives in the public sector,' said Lenihan.

For weeks, State officials have obsessed about the lump-sum worth one and a half years of salary that they receive on retirement, amid fears that the Government would tax it.

Yesterday, Lenihan once again talked about public sector reform but did not deliver upon it – though his deliberately crafted threat to the tax-free nature of the lump sum will make many consider their options. And, make no mistake, it was designed to do so.

For months, the Government has been accused of failing to offer leadership. Yesterday, right, or wrong, it certainly took tough decisions. It can only pray that voters will not savage them for it.

Hearing it for the Poems of Heaney

Arminta Wallace

Ever since the days when the god Apollo wielded his healing lyre over great swathes of the Mediterranean, music and poetry have been intertwined in the European mind. Opera is an obvious meeting point, as are the settings of poems by Goethe and Schiller in the German lieder tradition; but the connection is equally direct in popular culture, with the lyrics of songwriters from Bob Dylan to The Beatles regularly being described as 'poetry'.

When it comes to instrumental music, however, the lines of connectivity are less clear.

As part of its celebrations for Seamus Heaney's 70th birthday, RTÉ commissioned three contemporary Irish composers to write a new piece in which they would each respond to Heaney's poetry. The commission was for string quartet and, if the composer wished, solo voice. Interestingly, all three – Rachel Holstead, Kevin O'Connell and Ian Wilson – eschewed the vocal option. Their pieces will be premiered in the Irish Museum of Modern Art's Baroque Chapel this afternoon, and before each one is played, Seamus Heaney will read the specific poem which inspired it. The poems are 'The Given Note' (Holstead), 'Fosterling' (O'Connell) and 'Horace and the Thunder', also published under the title 'Anything Can Happen' (Wilson).

Seamus Heaney is captured on camera phone by a woman onlooker, during a photocall at the Irish Museum of Modern Art, before celebrations for his 70th birthday. Photograph: Aidan Crawley.

RTÉ presenter Miriam O'Callaghan, reacting to questions from reporters about the possibility of her hosting the **Late Late Show**, *after helping launch the first annual World Meningitis Day at RTÉ, Donnybrook, Dublin. The new host was named subsequently as Ryan Tubridy. Photograph: Frank Miller.*

How did the composers approach the business of making the connection between poetry and music? With delight, says Holstead. 'It was one of those dream commissions – even if you had 10 million trillion other things on, you would have to drop everything and do it. But in a way, one of the biggest challenges of the commission was how to approach it. How do you write music for a poet?'

O'Connell points out that music can't be 'about' a poem. 'If you're setting a poem to music, then you're in league with it,' he says. 'A poem is not just a semantic kind of a thing. It's also rhythmic. It's constructed like a piece of music – at least, a poem by Seamus Heaney is.'

The task for this commission was to use the idea in the poem to suggest something intrinsically musical. For Wilson, the range and freedom of the commission was in itself inspirational. 'It's often useful for a composer to be given something to link to – and very useful not to have the link too specific,' he says. 'By being given the brief to choose your own poem, you're really off and running.'

Even for three Heaney enthusiasts, mind you, choosing a poem isn't necessarily a straightforward business. 'There's one poem in particular – "The Given Note" – which tugs all sorts of strings in me,' says Holstead. 'Partly because it has to do with my home place, the Dingle Peninsula, and with a piece of music, "Port na Púcaí", which is close to me in quite a fundamental way. I've referred to that tune – and even to that poem – in several other pieces. So the very first thing I said to myself

Countess Ann Griffin Bernstorff, the artist who painted the original scenes on which **The Ross Tapestry** *panels are based, with her daughter, Alexis, the project's Director of Embroidery, photographed in front of a tapestry titled* **The Abduction of Devorgilla***. Photograph: Brenda Fitzsimons.*

was: "Right. I'm not having anything to do with that poem. I've been there, done that."

'I was trying to get inside my own head and think: "What is it about Seamus Heaney's poetry that really strikes a chord with me? What is it that gets me every time?" What I came to eventually, and what constantly amazes me about his work, is the process of translation: seeing the world through his eyes, and then seeing how he captures that thing that he sees.

'And once I alighted on this idea, it brought me straight back to "The Given Note", because it's about the process whereby this fiddler on the Blaskets hears this noise – a sound on the wind – and

translates it into music. I thought, that's exactly what Seamus Heaney does.'

For Derry-born composer Kevin O'Connell, inspiration arrived as he was walking along the street one day.

'The line from Heaney's "Fosterling" about waiting until he was nearly 50 to credit marvels just came into my head,' he says. 'I thought: "Well, before that he used to define his poetry as rather earthbound and bog-like; this seems to admit the ethereal dimension coming into it." So you've got an earthy music, which could be dance music – there's an Irish jig in my piece, you know? – and on the other hand a kind of flighty, ethereal music.'

His piece, 'Where Should This Music Be?', takes its title from Ferdinand's question when he hears Ariel's sweet airs in Shakespeare's *The Tempest*: 'Where should this music be – i' th' air or th' earth?'

Ian Wilson says he was looking for 'something striking and strong, in terms of jumping off the page at me. I bought a book a couple of years ago called *Anything Can Happen*. It was a poem that Heaney had written for Art for Amnesty, and it was translated into 16 or 20 different languages, paired by countries or cultures which had been in conflict. So on one page you'd have Serbian and on the other Bosnian – which is essentially the same thing – or German and Yiddish, or whatever.

'The poem itself was one Heaney wrote after the 9/11 attacks, and I suppose I liked the idea of trying to engage with something that stark. I asked RTÉ did it have to be a celebratory piece and they were quite clear in saying, "No, it doesn't." So I said: "Right. Well, then, I'll take the opportunity to react to this very striking poem – which I think is actually a reworking of an ode by Horace. It's very powerful, and it has very clear links to what happened in New York, and I just liked the idea of trying to react to that musically."'

The title of Wilson's piece, 'Across A Clear Blue Sky', pays tribute to the poet's ability to 'always respond to diverse aspects of the human experience with insight and dignity'.

Speaking on his way to the first rehearsal with the Vanbrugh Quartet, Wilson adds: 'This is the first proper quartet I've written for about eight years. I've done a couple of others, but they were transcriptions of other pieces of mine. I wanted to do something different, so I have a big bag of drumming toys and analogue radios. I've written into the score that at certain points the players have to tune these radios to get a bit of white noise – and at the end, the idea is that they all wind up these little drumming toys and just let them wind down. A kind of ironic nod towards the whole art of war. But today is the first time to get together to see if this works or not. If it

doesn't, then there'll be no drumming toys.'

For O'Connell, the commission offered an artistic double whammy. 'I love writing for string quartet, and I love Seamus Heaney's poetry – I've been a fan since my teens,' he says. 'So it sort of pulls together two strands of my life as an artist.'

Holstead, on the other hand, found the musical medium somewhat daunting. 'I've only ever written one string quartet before, and at that time it freaked me out entirely,' she says. 'I spent months fighting with it, trying to come to terms with all the baggage that comes with the string quartet repertoire. But a few weeks before the call came through for this commission I had said to a friend: "You know, I'd really love to write another string quartet." You put the idea out into the world, and something comes back.'

Can she describe her piece? 'It's probably best to leave it to be heard. It's a very tiny piece – a fragment, in some ways. I didn't set out to write a weighty piece of music. It's a small birthday offering for the poet. That's what it is.'

TUESDAY, 14 APRIL 2009

Keeping a Full Life in Sight

Ronan McGreevy

Three years ago Senator David Norris went to his optician looking for a change of prescription. Things were becoming a little more blurred. Reading was a little harder and he often found himself dazzled at night by headlights.

His optician suspected it was something more than just a new prescription that he needed, and referred him to a specialist who diagnosed him with age-related macular degeneration (AMD).

AMD affects about one in 10 people over 55 to varying extents. There are two types of AMD – wet and dry. The dry version is caused by solid

Senator David Norris outside Leinster House. Photograph: Frank Miller.

deposits called drusen in the macula, which is in the centre of the retina. The macula is a tiny spot which helps clarity of vision and acts as a natural sunglass. The dry version accounts for about 85 per cent of all people with AMD.

Senator Norris has the wet version or, as he describes it, the 'nasty' version, which is caused by new blood vessels growing behind the retina causing bleeding and scarring which leads to sight loss. Wet AMD can occur a lot faster than dry AMD and can lead to deterioration of sight, especially central vision, and even blindness.

'He [the consultant] quoted a lot of Latin terminology at me and he said that it looked like I had AMD,' Norris recalls. 'When you translate it, it means that basically I have a condition that is progressive, can lead to blindness and there is nothing that can be done about it.

'I asked the doctor "Is that a proper summary?" and he said yes. "In that case," I said, "let's not waste any more time. Give me the bill and I'm going."'

Since the diagnosis, Norris has been overwhelmed, by his own admission, by well-wishers and those sending him cards and cures. 'I released a most wonderful wave of sympathy and affection which I didn't feel I deserve because I don't consider this condition to be serious. I've had people calling me from all over the country telling me about all kinds of cures. Some of those cures are superstition, but it was all terribly well meant,' he says.

Fortunately, the disease has not progressed to any great extent yet and, aside from giving up night driving, it has not affected his life or his essentially sunny disposition.

'I said it three years ago when I was diagnosed and I'm saying it now that I am 65 years old. Things wear out, get rusty and fall off. When enough of these things happen, people dig a hygienic hole in the ground, put you in a box, say goodbye and that's it. It's part of the life cycle.'

One 'constant thread' in the advice he received was from people urging him to take Lutein, a carotenoid, or organic pigment essential to good vision, which is found in green vegetables such as spinach or cabbage.

On the advice of the Waterford Institute of Technology (WIT), which is a world-leader in AMD research, Norris has been taking the supplement MacuShield which has shown promising early results.

MacuShield contains three dietary compounds, lutein, zeaxanthin and meso-zeaxanthin, which are also found in the macula. MacuShield may have a role in either preventing the disease or slowing its progress. In a number of cases, patients who took it claim that it reversed it, a process that was not thought possible before. Trials of the supplement are taking place at WIT.

In any case, the redoubtable Senator has decided to raise awareness of the condition on behalf of Fighting Blindness and the National Council for the Blind of Ireland (NCBI). 'I have the "wet" one which is irreversible, but most people have the "dry" one which can be halted or diverted. I'm prepared to make a song and dance about it and use my profile to help to save people's eyesight,' he says.

Although there is not yet conclusive proof, there is some evidence that taking dietary supplements can help control dry AMD and reduce the risk that it will change or progress to wet AMD. He also hopes to raise awareness of the work being done by WIT and the support groups for those with AMD.

Norris's intervention is greatly appreciated by the NCBI, given that there is hardly a more eminently quotable or, indeed, colourful character in the whole country to raise the profile of the illness. NCBI Chief Executive Des Kenny says: 'David started by going on one of our fundraising events before the detection of his impairment. He has volunteered his services to us.

'He's aware that he has wet AMD, but it is under control. It has not beset him in the same way as people who are less au fait with it.

'It is great that he has put what I call his "artistic and political toolbox of goodness" at our disposal. David is an upbeat man about everything. Because of the amount of material that he has to read, he would be palpably aware of what others might suffer and that's why he is so keenly interested in helping.'

For his own part, Norris says his arthritis and prostate problems cause him much more irritation and he is determined to carry on with that lust for life which informs everything he does and says.

'I tire out people half my age. I had Lucy Kennedy [TV presenter] staying with me for her *Living With Lucy* series and she had to go to bed for a week afterwards,' he admits.

'I'm having a wonderful life and I have been so lucky to have 65 wonderful years with love, romance and laughter. I have had a dose of everything. When you think there are people who are lucky to get to 25 and have to endure misery, poverty and slime, I've been exceptionally lucky.'

All the same, though, he has taken an even keener interest in the beauty of the world around him. 'I can see plenty, there is plenty around to still see. It has had a rather interesting effect on me,' he says.

'I've always enjoyed the senses and the beauty of nature, animals and birds, seas and landscapes, skies and clouds especially at this time of year. I've made more of a conscious effort to savour them, just in case.'

The newest resident at the White House, Bo, a six-month-old male Portuguese water dog, runs down a corridor with his master, US president Barack Obama. Bo was a gift to the Obama children, Malia and Sasha, from Massachusetts Senator Ted Kennedy and his wife Victoria. Photograph: Pete Souza/Reuters.

WEDNESDAY, 15 APRIL 2009

Woof Introduction to a Dog's Life at the White House

Diary of a First Dog

Monday

Alo! I am Bo, the Portuguese Water Dog of Senhor Kennedy. Or at least I was until this morning, when he drove me to a big white house to meet my new master, Senhor Obama. I had my head out of the window the whole way over. That is always a good idea with Senhor Kennedy.

Tuesday

Today I was house-trained, or 'house-broken', as the Americans say. El Senhor put me outside to spend a penny, or 'spend a trillion dollars', as the Americans now also say. Then he gave me a bath which I did not like because the shampoo stung my eyes. I do not think shampoo should hurt the First Dog. Still, I suppose that is the audacity of soap.

Wednesday

I have finally been introduced to the rest of El Senhor's pack. There was some concern that I would make them itch or give them a rash. However, so far it is only El Senhor who is itching to be rash.

Afterwards we all went out to the South Lawn where a lot of journalists asked about my pedigree. I couldn't quite put my claw on it, but something about this felt a little awkward.

Thursday
Took a dump in the Roosevelt Room. El Senhor was not impressed. 'Rules must be binding,' he said. 'Violations must be punished. Words must mean something.' *Ai meu Deus*! I'll go in the Rose Garden from now on. Nobody minds if you dump on the bushes.

Friday
The vet arrived to 'give me some shots', which seemed to upset El Senhor. He said I would 'need to be neutered shortly', which also seemed to upset El Senhor. Then he asked if I had insurance, which was when El Senhor totally lost it.

Saturday
Overheard El Senhor shouting 'Sit! Beg! Roll over! Good boy!' For a moment I thought he had got another dog but it was just the Prime Minister of Great Britain and Northern Ireland. Later, I heard El Senhor say, 'He's barking', although I had not been barking at all. Very strange.

Sunday
There is definitely another dog on the way. El Senhor was shouting down the phone about 'the Afghans', who he thinks are 'all shitzus'. Then he asked for 'some pointers' and hung up because he was 'getting a little husky'.

Monday
It sounds like the new dog will be female. All day I heard people whisper 'the bitch is coming', but then Senhorita Clinton arrived so everyone was too busy to mention it again.

I considered giving the Senhorita an over-friendly welcome but changed my mind. Apparently, if you get a stain on her dress, she goes *loco*.

Tuesday
My afternoon nap in the Oval Office was rudely interrupted by El Senhor and Senhorita Clinton. 'We need to give the North Koreans something,' she was screaming. 'What in God's name do they want?' he was screaming back. 'Just a gesture to begin with, like a culturally sensitive gift,' she replied.

'Some kind of Korean delicacy, perhaps?' he asked.

Then they both turned and gave me the strangest look. I don't like this, *mes amigos*. I don't like this at all.

As told to Newton Emerson

THURSDAY, 16 APRIL 2009

Why Was Italy so Unprepared?

Paddy Agnew, in L'Aquila

It was about 7.30 p.m. on Monday when the earth started to move under our feet in L'Aquila – again. It was now 16 hours since the major earthquake which had claimed some 280 lives in and around L'Aquila that morning.

Nerves, however, were understandably still very raw. Even though we were outside the town, sheltering from the rain under the plastic awning of a filling-station bar, people panicked and rushed out into the street to get away from the building. Some people – those who had been there for the big one and lived to tell the tale – started to scream and cry.

To be fair, though, not everyone panicked. Many people – including the journalists and the curious who had flocked to L'Aquila – at first did not even realise that the slow, grinding, shuddering shake that came from the ground was actually a minor tremor. If you did not know any better, you might just think it was the sort of shudder that hits your window when a very heavy lorry drives past. But then, this was just an after-tremor.

Next morning, in a fourth-floor hotel room in Castel del Monte, high up on the Gran Sasso mountain, about 40 km from L'Aquila, I had another minor taste of life with earthquakes. I was on the phone, doing a live radio piece, when the room began to shake. It did not last long but because I was on the fourth floor, the shaking and the swaying were disturbingly vivid.

This particular aftershock measured 5.1 on the Richter scale, which is serious enough and explains just why, notwithstanding our 40 km distance from the earthquake's epicentre and the fact that, as the night porter assured me, the hotel was built on a very solid rock foundation, you could still feel it. Which left me wondering about the truly terrifying experience that 30,000 or so Abruzzo inhabitants went through at 3.32 a.m. on Monday. If these are just earthquake 'afterthoughts', then most of us would be more than happy to skip the main dish.

Italy has a long history of earthquakes. Put simply, this is a country where the earth moves – regularly and sickeningly. From 1693, when an estimated 153,000 people were killed in Sicily and Naples, through to 2002, when 29 people, including 26 small children, were killed in a schoolhouse collapse in San Giuliano di Puglia, Italian earthquakes have regularly made the wrong sort of headlines.

Firefighter Roberto Contu inspects the damaged Duomo church in L'Aquila. At least four Romanesque and Renaissance churches and a 16th-century castle were partially destroyed by the quake. Photograph: Alessandro Garofalo/Reuters.

Seismologists claim that, since 1693, there have been at least 20 major earthquakes in Italy, not to mention hundreds of thousands of minor tremors. If you look at the website of the Italian Institute of Geophysics and Vulcanology (*www.ingv.it*), you will find that their experts list more than 70 seismic tremors in the L'Aquila region since 1 April.

On occasion, earthquakes have done horrifying damage in Italy – 86,000 dead in Sicily and Calabria in 1908, 32,000 dead at Avezzano (not far from L'Aquila) in 1915, and 2,735 dead in Campania (Naples) and Irpinia in 1980.

Geologists have no difficulty explaining just why Italy is so earthquake prone. It is all related to the overall movement of tectonic plates and the fact that European and African plates have long been on a collision course. Add to that some well defined fault lines and you end up with a lot of seismic activity. Not for nothing, Italy still has two active volcanoes – Vesuvius, near Naples; and Etna, in Sicily – which also have a nasty habit of grabbing world headlines.

So, with all this underground activity around, how come Italy seems unable either to predict or prevent tragedies of this scale? Well, of course, here we are immediately into major polemics. One of the most controversial developments of this week concerned 62-year-old seismologist Gioacchino Giampaolo Giuliani, the L'Aquila-based expert who pointed out that his warnings of an imminent earthquake not only went unheeded but earned him a *denuncia* (judicial complaint) from the Mayor of nearby Sulmona for having 'alarmed the population'. (Giuliani's prediction had been that the earthquake would strike not in L'Aquila but rather in Sulmona, about 70 km away.) Giuliani claims

Aerial view of some of the destruction of L'Aquila – Italy's deadliest earthquake in nearly three decades. Photograph: AP/Guardia Forestale.

that he has over the years developed a system that can predict earthquakes. Basically, he measures the amount of radon gas coming up through the earth. The more gas coming up, he argues, the more movement down below. Based on nine years of studies, he claims that if the radon gas levels suddenly shoot up, an earthquake will follow between six and 24 hours later.

For example, he claims that just prior to the San Giuliano quake in 2002, radon levels rose 100 times. Diagrams he released to news media this week show the levels rising dramatically at about 6 p.m. on Sunday. Giuliani lives in Coppito, just outside L'Aquila. In tears on television this week, he said that he knew it was going to happen but he could do nothing to lessen the impact of the disaster. No one would listen. So, he moved out his family and saved them. His daughter opted to pass on his warnings, sending the following text to friends on Sunday: 'Papa advises us not to sleep in L'Aquila tonight. Don't ask me why . . . just trust him.'

Even the institute for which Giuliani works, the Nuclear Physics Institute of Gran Sasso, issued a statement a few days ago distancing itself from his 'predictions' by saying that they were the fruit of his own 'personal research' and nothing to do with the institute.

So was Giuliani just lucky? A majority of seismologists would say so, arguing that an early-warning system in relation to earthquakes is just about impossible. Alessandro Amato of the Institute of Geophysics and Vulcanology pointed out this week that extensive seismic activity (called foreshocks) does not necessarily mean that a 'big one' is on the way: 'Those sort of messages are practically useless. A swarm of small tremors are simply not enough to announce that a big quake is on the way. We record tremors all the time that lead to nothing. There is about a one-in-10,000 chance of being right.'

Enzo Boschi, head of the Institute of Geophysics and Vulcanology, put it even more

succinctly this week when asked, for the umpteenth time, if this earthquake could have been predicted. 'Every time there is an earthquake, there is always someone who claims to have predicted it. As far as I know, no one predicted this one with precision. It is simply not possible to predict earthquakes,' he said.

Of course, there is always the exception that proves the rule. In 1975, authorities in Haicheng, China, ordered the evacuation of more than one million people after scientists had detected excessive seismic activity. The move was well timed. On 4 February, a massive earthquake, registering 7.3

Orlando Duque diving at the Serpent's Lair on Inis Mór, off the Galway and Clare coasts, to publicise the Cliff-Diving Series event at La Rochelle in France in May. This image was taken by Ray Demski using a multiple-exposure camera.

on the Richter scale, hit the area. It was estimated that as many as 150,000 people would have lost their lives had they not been evacuated.

Yet, just when seismologists and geologists were ready to hail a vital breakthrough in the art of earthquake prediction, Mother Nature struck back with a cruel vengeance. One year later, in 1976, a massive quake just about wiped out the city of Tangshan, killing 250,000 people. The same scientists and the same technology that had predicted the Haicheng quake had failed totally to predict an even stronger one in Tangshan.

It would seem, then, that for the time being, and with all due respect to Giuliani, earthquake prediction remains a very inexact science. Which switches the onus of a country's readiness from prediction to prevention. In other words, if you know that huge tracts of the national territory (perhaps more than 50 per cent) are potentially 'seismic', then the only thing to do is ensure that all houses are built to withstand earthquakes.

This is clearly not the case in Italy, where at least 70 per cent of houses were built long before the 1974 legislation regarding anti-seismic standards and where many modern constructions have, for reasons of economy, not respected those requirements anyway. Even by spending as little as €20,000-€30,000, an existing house can be rendered, if not 100 per cent earthquake proof, at least a lot safer.

The measures in question concern the use of reinforced concrete (only 10 per cent of the buildings that collapse are made in reinforced concrete), rather than just bricks, and the 'binding' of the house with a *cordolo* or ring of reinforced concrete that goes right around the house, below the roof and over every floor. Other measures include giant, hidden wall-to-wall 'clamps', as well as X-shaped braces for internal walls. An important tip is to strengthen a wall where a window or door might have been blocked off. Obviously, foundations too could ideally be reinforced and rendered 'elastic' but that is a much more complicated, expensive, not to say dangerous, operation with an old house.

Buildings where such measures are not introduced are death traps in the case of an earthquake. If there is no binding *cordolo*, the quake moves the building walls outwards, causing the whole construction to implode. The roof falls in on you.

Standing on Via XX Settembre on Monday evening, one rescue worker pointed out something that can be seen all over L'Aquila. Namely, two small apartment blocks side by side where one stands shaken but steady and where the other is flat as a pancake, with the dead buried somewhere in the rubble. Clearly, one builder has taken some form of basic anti-seismic precautions and the other has not.

In a country where building without proper planning permission is commonplace, the devastating impact of the L'Aquila earthquake comes as no surprise. Alessandro Martelli, who teaches construction in seismic areas at the University of Ferrara, puts it emphatically: 'In Japan, an earthquake like that which hit L'Aquila wouldn't even have made the papers.'

He and other experts argue that where a grade-seven earthquake would probably kill 50 in Japan, it might kill 5,000-11,000 in the Italian Apennines. Regional legislation for safe houses in seismic zones has long been in place in most of Italy, but the problem, as always, is enforcing the application of those building norms.

Clearly, Italy will long remain at risk of desperate tragedies such as that which struck L'Aquila this week. Only one comforting thought emerges from this tragedy, namely the nationwide expression of solidarity that became so intense that the prime minister, Silvio Berlusconi, was obliged, on Wednesday, to ask people to stop sending food and clothes to Abruzzo. Italians know all about natural disasters and to many it seems only normal that you either go to help (an 8,500-strong volunteer rescue army has functioned all week) or you send food and clothing.

Alan Healy and Bebhinn O'Keeffe at their wedding on 6 April 2009, minutes after meeting for the first time as a result of the radio station Beat 102-103's Two Strangers and a Wedding competition. They broke up a week later, after their 'honeymoon'. Photograph: Dylan Vaughan.

THURSDAY, 16 APRIL 2009

THE IRISH TIMES
irishtimes.com/blogs

Foreign Workers

outsidein

Bryan Mukandi

Not too long ago, someone asked me if there had been a perceptible change in the way migrants are treated in Ireland since the onset of the recession. I live in Galway, one of the friendliest and most accommodating parts of the country and I haven't noticed a significant shift in attitudes.

That's not to say that there are no problems. But, as far as I can tell, nothing has escalated with the worsening economic environment.

There is some anecdotal evidence that in other parts of the country there may be growing hostility or resentment towards immigrants. Frankly, that doesn't surprise me. Human nature is such that the only thing worse than enduring hardship is watching someone else benefit at what you perceive as being your expense. In the recent past, only those in the lower income bracket felt threatened, rightly or wrongly, by migrant workers. What happens when formerly well-paid professionals begin to lose their jobs?

Yesterday, the government announced that it

was tightening the requirements for foreign work-ers to get work permits. Very reasonably, the Tánaiste said, Ireland has benefited greatly from immigration, particularly so over the past decade. Our immigrant population have and continue to make a significant contribution to our economy and to society as a whole here in Ireland. We need to ensure however that for our flexible migration policies to remain as a successful tool of Irish eco-nomic policy, that they are adapted on an ongoing basis to reflect the changing realities of the Irish labour market. Those realities have altered dramat-ically over recent months. As a result, it is essential that we now take steps to ensure that every possi-ble effort is made by employers to find a suitably skilled employee from within the existing labour market.

I'm torn. On the one hand, I respect the need for the government to protect its citizens from unemployment. That said, work permit holders only make up 1.5 per cent of the workforce. In addition, the hoops one has to jump through in order to get that permit are so high, frustratingly complicated and numerous that the existing rules were probably adequate deterrents. The fact that the number of work permit applications has been in free fall is testimony to that.

Worst of all, making it harder for the spouse and dependants of a work permit holder to work means that those who are married and/or have children are much less likely to apply for the per-mit in the first place. That may seem to some as a good thing, but isn't there an inescapable contra-diction between an open economy on the one hand, and a closed labour market on the other?

All of which begs the question, are these changes really about protecting the work force from foreign workers? If they are, whoever decided that refusing to grant non-EU midwives Irish work permits would protect Irish midwives needs to have a chat with members of the immigrant com-munity and hospital administrators. By the time a non-EU professional gets a job offer, more often

than not a suitable EU candidate could not be found.

Bryan Mukandi was born and grew up in Zimbabwe. He lives in Galway.

FRIDAY, 17 APRIL 2009

Verdict from All Sides of 'Job Well Done': a Fair Testimony to Sir Hugh's Record

Gerry Moriarty

It says a lot for the standing of Sir Hugh Orde that the general verdict – from unionists, loy-alists, nationalists and republicans alike – was that he did a good job in his seven years in Northern Ireland.

The 50-year-old Surrey native took on a huge brief when he was appointed by the fledgling policing board in 2002 as chief constable of the PSNI. He had key ambitions, to implement most of the remainder of the Patten policing reforms that flowed from the Belfast Agreement, to entice Sinn Féin to support the police, and to establish a state-of-the-art police college in Northern Ireland.

As he acknowledged at a press conference at police HQ in Belfast yesterday, we're still a dis-tance from seeing the first sod turned at the college. But most of Patten is in place, and most impor-tantly, Sinn Féin supports the PSNI.

Sir Hugh was appointed president of the British Association of Chief Police Officers by his peers but is not due to take up the post until September, after the marching season. Therefore, he is unlikely to witness the formal devolution of policing and justice powers to the Northern Executive expected later in the autumn, barring unforeseen problems.

Mary Lou MacDonald of Sinn Féin reading some of the names of the victims of violence in Northern Ireland at the Good Friday service, in the Unitarian Church on St Stephen's Green, in Dublin. Ms MacDonald subsequently lost her seat in the European parliament. Photograph: David Sleator.

He will, however, have played a significant part in that anticipated achievement. Gaining wide public backing for policing was almost as important as power-sharing politics. If Sinn Féin supported the PSNI, then the IRA war was over. In fact, Sinn Féin's historic decision to endorse the PSNI early in 2007 paved the way for Ian Paisley and Gerry Adams to work together in March that year. You couldn't have had one without the other.

Sir Hugh Orde was one of a number of pivotal figures in facilitating that policing and political transformation. He was a 'cop's cop' who was prepared to speak in a very straight way to politicians and members of the policing board. But he was also a political policeman.

In the early days of his tenure he went on patrol with his frontline officers in republican west Belfast and in loyalist areas too. He walked the tricky line between maintaining operational independence and demonstrating to politicians, particularly Sinn Féin, that he was leading an impartial police force that welcomed nationalists as much as unionists. Now, more than one in four police officers are Catholics.

The PSNI is on target to reach the 30 per cent Catholic representation target by 2011, when 50:50 Catholic/Protestant recruitment is to end. The only possible block is if dissident republicans succeed in terrorising Catholics away from seeking jobs in the PSNI. Sir Hugh said yesterday that not one nationalist or unionist recruit had resigned despite the recent dissident killings and other activities, while scores of people were continuing to apply for posts.

Besides the big successes, there were failures too. No one was convicted for the Omagh bombing, the Northern Bank £26.5 million robbery, or the murder of Robert McCartney. He acknowledged how Omagh was a particular disappointment, but referred to how he was working with 'second-hand goods': meaning his was a reinvestigation of the original inquiry which took place when Sir Ronnie Flanagan was in charge – a comment that sounded like implicit criticism of his predecessor.

The next chief will not come from the PSNI because none of his assistant chiefs is eligible to apply, while his deputy Paul Leighton is retiring at the end of next month.

Sir Hugh believed a serving chief constable from Britain was likely to take over as PSNI chief. Despite the difficulties, it is a plum posting. 'I don't think a rookie will take over. It will be a highly experienced and professional police officer.'

Whoever succeeds him will face a demanding task to thwart the ambitions of the dissident republicans. He described his seven years as a 'rough and

challenging ride' in which the conditions were created to 'allow politics to move on'. That's a neat and accurate summary, and in terms of what he faced when he stepped into the post seven years ago, it ranks as a job well done.

SATURDAY, 18 APRIL 2009

Countdown to C-Day

Róisín Ingle

It's not like we didn't prepare for a natural birth. First off we reclined on beanbags for a two-day-long, eye-opening birthing workshop in Dublin's Elbow Room. Empowered by green tea and group sessions, I came straight home and lectured my mother on the new, enlightened birthing methods we'd just learnt.

Buzzing with knowledge, I gave her the lowdown on visualisation techniques. The kind where you picture the cervix as a flower about to open its petals. I may also, in my zeal, have mentioned the

Christine Lockhart, Lisa Cummins, Matt the Hat and Bobby Lost pose for photographs at Tripod night club in Dublin, where the first 47 music acts for the 2009 Electric Picnic festival were announced. Photograph: Niall Carson/PA.

benefits of perineal massage. I certainly told her of my plan to squat on the floor for the whole thing if I fancied it, no matter what the midwives said. I certainly wasn't going to be forced next nor near anything as old-fashioned as a hospital bed.

When she tried to give me her take – 'the midwives are the most amazing people you could meet, they do everything they can to help the mother, you can trust them to be on your side and do what is right for you' – I was deeply sceptical.

I mean, she'd only done this giving birth lark eight times and that was in the dark days when they whipped the baby out of your arms to be baptised in the nearest church. I, on the other hand, had attended a two-day class complete with inflatable birthing balls.

Another week, another ante-natal demonstration. We watched closely as the highly entertaining Margaret in Holles Street, a woman with one-liners sharper than Graham Norton's, squeezed two 'babies' through a 'pelvis' while fielding increasingly hysterical questions from first timers, one of whom may have been me.

'The only side effect from a Tens machine is the pain of paying to rent them,' quipped Margaret, who also suggested *Please Release Me, Let Me Go* as appropriate birthing music.

In other preparation, my boyfriend has been reading Adam Brophy's wickedly funny *Bad Dad's Survival Guide*, which he says is essential reading, especially if the father-to-be role has left you feeling a bit surplus to requirements.

I, meanwhile, dutifully ploughed through *The Irish Pregnancy Book* and *What to Expect When You're Expecting*, and scanned endless internet accounts of twin births until my head spun. Regarding the latter, can I reiterate for people just starting on this adventure that when it comes to pregnancy, Google Is Not Your Friend. I plan to have a load of maternity T-shirts made.

Now it turns out that all this knowledge, the recipe for a herbal drink called 'labouraid', the visualisation techniques, the breathing exercises,

are going to count for nothing when in a few days' time a deep incision is made across my belly and two babies are pulled out of me while I lie behind a tent screaming blue murder or staring into my beloved's face chanting Sanskrit, depending on which way I eventually face the procedure.

YouTube Is Not Your Friend either in these matters, by the way. You might think watching Caesarean operations would be a healthy way to acquaint yourself with the ordeal ahead but having watched three I wouldn't recommend this approach. There are things one just doesn't need to see, video footage the proud dads might better have left on the cutting room floor. I'm talking about what looked to me like intestines.

'Whoo-wee, this one's a real hoss,' declared a surgeon in one of the videos I watched as he pulled a giant baby out of some bewildered-looking woman's abdomen. Nice.

At this point I will recap on my own situation with apologies to those with zero interest in pregnancy/childbirth/major abdominal surgery:

At first Baby A was breech and the lovely scan man in the twins clinic said a C-section was the only way. A couple of weeks later Baby A had somersaulted, so it looked as though the head was engaged ready for a 'natural' delivery. In the last few weeks, the little one turned again and adopted the bottom-stuck-in-pelvis position, which it has inhabited ever since.

All this time Baby B has lain transverse across my middle, waiting patiently, happy with its lot. (I'm thinking that one is going to be more like its Daddy.)

At my last hospital appointment the scan man lays it on the line. There's no more room in that uterus. They are not moving anywhere now. So he sets the date. Shows me roughly where the incision will be. Tells me to fast from midnight and come in to the hospital at 8 a.m. It's like we are talking about a dental appointment instead of a procedure where I am going to be CUT WIDE OPEN ACROSS THE BELLY WITH A KNIFE.

Oh, and if labour starts before then, I am to come straight into the hospital – don't bother ringing first – where an emergency C-section will be performed.

All that preparation down the swanny. Now I know it's all about mental acceptance, trust and equanimity. It's about believing my mother's counsel, that the men and women in the hospital are on my side. I read the supportive e-mails from women who have been through it. I laugh again courtesy of the woman who says 'on the upside, a C-section means you stay honeymoon fresh'. I also reread the e-mails from women who have done it the natural way and not for the first time am moved by what a leveller pregnancy and childbirth appear to be.

I talk to my friend, she of the lowest pain threshold on the planet, who had a Caesarean three years ago and lived to tell the tale. Apparently when the KNIFE is going through you, it only feels like a biro is being dragged gently across your stomach, thanks to the epidural. There is some comfort there.

And anyway, says absolutely everyone, at the end of it there will be two babies placed in your arms and everything else, even the KNIFE and the FIVE LAYERS OF STITCHES, will pale into insignificance. I know they are right but still, I don't mind telling you that by the time you read this, a few days before C-Day, I am still more than a little bit terrified.

Thanks for all the good wishes over the past six months. See you on the other side.

TUESDAY, 21 APRIL 2009

A Country still in Thrall to the Likes of Lowry

Fintan O'Toole

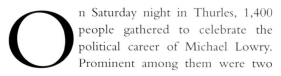On Saturday night in Thurles, 1,400 people gathered to celebrate the political career of Michael Lowry. Prominent among them were two important public figures. Ivan Yates, a former minister for agriculture and a successful businessman, is about to become a national broadcaster with Newstalk radio. Seán Kelly, a highly distinguished former president of the GAA, is a Fine Gael candidate for Ireland South in the European elections. Both are people of substance, with legitimate aspirations to influence public opinion and to help set the tone of public life in Ireland. That such men believe that there is anything worth celebrating in Michael Lowry's political career tells us something quite simple. Nothing has been learned.

Michael Lowry is a cheat and a liar. He entered public life and rose to the highest level of public trust as a member of the cabinet but showed utter contempt both for the law and for his social obligations. Over a decade ago now, Mr Justice Brian McCracken pointed out the appalling damage done by 'the public perception that a person in the position of a government minister and member of cabinet was able to ignore, and indeed cynically evade, both the taxation and exchange control laws of the State with impunity'.

Lowry wasn't a casual cheat.

His evasion of taxes was complex and organised and large-scale. His company Garuda under-declared both VAT and PAYE, and eventually had to cough up €1.2 million after a Revenue audit. He also diddled his personal taxes, and settled for almost €200,000. A key part of his business arrangement with Dunnes Stores was described in the McCracken report as 'a sham'.

Lowry's lies are legion.

He lied to the Revenue when he availed of the 1993 tax amnesty without declaring all his hidden income. He misled the Dáil in December 1996 by failing to mention a series of large payments from Dunnes. He told the Dáil that if he had been trying to hide money, he would have 'put it in an offshore account', creating the impression that he had no such account. In fact, he had at least four: one in the Bank of Ireland in the Isle of Man; one in an Allied Irish Banks subsidiary in Jersey; another Isle

Dawn Leaden Bolger fixes her shoe, watched by her mother, Bernie, on day one of the Punchestown Racing Festival.
Photograph: Niall Carson/PA.

of Man account held through a company called Badgeworth; and an Irish Nationwide Isle of Man account.

Only the first two of these accounts were disclosed to the McCracken tribunal – the existence of the other two emerged at the Moriarty tribunal. He indignantly denied in the Dáil that 'my house in Carysfort, Blackrock, was somehow financed in an irregular way'. In fact the house was bought in trust for Lowry by a developer and the money for its extensive refurbishment was routed through the Isle of Man Nationwide account and came from a loan to him from the Smurfit executive David Austin.

Lowry, moreover, has shown no real remorse. He has never apologised. He regards himself, as he told the *Sunday Independent* as 'a victim of my own success', whose only fault was to 'stick my head too high above the parapet'. He sees himself as a target

of 'State oppression', who was 'only judged by the hob-nobs'.

And why not? The impunity that Mr Justice McCracken highlighted has remained in place – Lowry has never been prosecuted. The good people of Tipperary North have repeatedly re-elected him, and he is a much-cosseted supporter of the current Government, which is happy to have him on board.

But why is a man like Seán Kelly, who has given every impression of being principled and courageous as well as intelligent and able, sucking up to Lowry? What exactly does he find worthy of celebration in Lowry's career of contempt for the law, of brazen mendacity and of unrepentant self-pity? Has he no conception at all of the degree to which Lowry embodies the values that have brought this country to its knees?

Judge McCracken got to the heart of the wider meaning of Lowry's career when he wrote: 'If such a person can behave in this way without serious sanctions being imposed, it becomes very difficult to condemn others who similarly flout the law.' The culture of corruption in Irish politics set the public standards for the greed, cynicism, dishonesty and downright fraud in the banks and the property market for which all of us must pay such a heavy price.

If Lowry's low standards make him not a pariah, but a respected public representative to be celebrated and honoured, nothing has changed. We're still stuck with the culture that has corroded public faith in politics, encouraged cute-hoorism in business and finance and turned regulation into a game of nods and winks. We're still in thrall to the self-pity and self-righteousness, the lethal cocktail of victimhood and entitlement, which turn basic notions of right and wrong into a sentimental mush.

When, either from misplaced notions of friendship or in blind pursuit of votes, media and political players bend the knee at the altar of Michael Lowry's career, they are shaming, not just themselves, but a public realm that would be far better off without the likes of Lowry.

SATURDAY, 25 APRIL 2009

The Life and Death of Michael Dwyer

Tom Hennigan, in Santa Cruz, Bolivia

In the early hours of 16 April, Michael Dwyer's young life came to a brutal end, machine-gunned to death in room 457 of the Hotel Las Americas, in Santa Cruz, Bolivia.

It was 4 a.m. when around 30 members of an elite police squad swarmed into the hotel, cut the phone line, and demanded that night staff tell them where the Irishman and his four travelling companions were staying.

They were the only guests on the fourth floor, in a row of five rooms. Having located their quarry, police silently made their way upstairs. The next thing the two staff members on duty heard was a huge explosion which shook the building, followed by 10 to 15 minutes of intense gunfire, 'a rain of bullets' in the words of the night manager.

Today, as Dwyer's remains are due to make their final journey to his home in Ballinderry, Co. Tipperary, almost every aspect of the raid is sunk in controversy. The only undisputed facts are that by the end of it, the 24-year-old lay dead in his room, as did the occupants of the rooms on either side of his.

The two other men in the group — a Hungarian and a Bolivian of Croatian origin — were arrested at the scene. The only witnesses, apart from the officers involved, are now being held in isolation cells in a maximum security prison in the capital La Paz, more than 900 km away.

Dwyer's body still lay in room 457 when Bolivia's vice-president gave a press conference in the capital saying police had broken up a cell of 'mercenary terrorists' who planned to assassinate Evo Morales, the country's left-wing president. Since then, the government has claimed the group was linked to right-wing separatists in Santa Cruz who want independence for eastern Bolivia.

The Dwyer family have dismissed the accusations about their son as preposterous. In Santa Cruz, a ramshackle boomtown on Bolivia's tropical eastern plains which is the motor of the country's economy, many believe the men were summarily executed, victims of a dangerous escalation in the struggle between Santa Cruz and La Paz over the destiny of South America's poorest nation.

Family and friends of the former bouncer and security guard understood that Dwyer went to Bolivia last November to take part in a bodyguard training course. But one source described it as a 'course that never was'. On realising this, several of Dwyer's travelling companions reportedly left Bolivia but he decided to stay on. It was around this time that he met a 49-year-old Bolivian of Hungarian descent named Eduardo Rózsa Flores, the man killed in room 458 and named by the authorities as the group's leader.

Flores came from a well-known family in Santa Cruz. His father was a Hungarian communist émigré and painter. The family fled one of Bolivia's numerous military dictatorships and went to Chile. When Pinochet staged his coup, they moved to Europe.

A communist in his youth, Flores later fought with the Croatians in the Balkans conflict, and was awarded Croat citizenship. After the war, he worked as a documentary filmmaker and wrote poetry. He later converted to Islam and supported a wide and often contradictory range of causes, many on the right-wing fringe.

One was a group that advocated autonomy for ethnic Hungarians in Romania. Sources say that other members of this group worked in security in Ireland and may well have introduced Dwyer to Flores. By early January, Dwyer, Flores and four other men – two Hungarians, an ethnic Hungarian travelling on a Romanian passport, and a Bolivian with a Croat passport – checked into the four-star Asturias hotel in Santa Cruz, where they stayed until 3 April. One of these four – the Romanian Arpad Magyarosi – was killed in room 456 in the Hotel Las Americas.

One staff member at the hotel remembers Dwyer clearly. 'He was lovely. He did not speak Spanish but he was a good person. We remember him playing around by the pool, singing. He didn't seem at all like what they say he is now.' The Asturias's owner, Maria Diez, says the group seemed close and Dwyer was an integral part of it. 'The Irishman was very well behaved, always polite,' remembers Diez. 'He had his own room

Shell to Sea protester Willie Corduff peers from under a truck that had been delivering material to the Glengad site of the Corrib gas pipeline project, during protests against the resumption of work. Photograph: Peter Wilcock.

The parade of stallions at the launch of the studbook from the Miniature Horse and Pony Society of Ireland, at Kilbeggan racecourse in Co. Westmeath. From left, Toby is led by Brendan Flynn, Bedwbach McPorran by Denis Halpenny and Glen Kee Brack by Greg McGovern. Photograph: Dara Mac Dónaill.

but was very friendly with the others. They break-fasted together and in the evenings were around the pool together. We never saw them with any-one else and they never said what they were doing in Bolivia. But they were good guests, never drink-ing excessively or anything like that.'

Little is known about what the group did during their weeks in the Asturias. Staff said they did not seem to have a regular routine that implied they were working.

The Irish Times has seen evidence that during this time Dwyer and his companions made at least one excursion into the countryside around Santa Cruz. It has also seen evidence that the group enjoyed a social life in Santa Cruz and had several nights out with locals. They visited the city's bowling alley and Dwyer went with local friends to at least one

football game. They had evenings out in the city's bars and an area where young people gather in cars and in Santa Cruz's ubiquitous 4x4s for parties. There is also evidence that Dwyer had a girlfriend.

During the group's stay in the Asturias, *The Irish Times* has learned that Flores was in the com-pany of local separatist extremists and that at one such encounter in February, Dwyer was present. But given that Dwyer's Spanish extended little beyond 'gracias', it is uncertain that he would have understood whatever conversations Flores had at this time.

It is also unknown how much Dwyer knew about the tense political situation in Santa Cruz, especially in the months leading up to his arrival, when the unrest threatened to spill over into open violence between the country's east and west.

The funeral of drowned fishermen Féichín Mulkerrin and Tony Coohill, from Claddaghduff in Co. Galway, making its way across the strand to Omey Island for burial. The pair were checking lobster pots when their motorised currach was overturned by a freak wave. Photograph: Keith Heneghan/Phocus.

On 3 April the group moved to the five-star Hotel Santa Cruz, closer to the central plaza. As at the Asturias, staff here remember always seeing the group together but in no way drawing attention to themselves or seeming out of the ordinary. 'We get a lot of business groups here. I just thought they were foreigners in Santa Cruz to buy land,' says one employee.

The city's major theatre festival had booked up the Hotel Santa Cruz from 14 April, so the group had to move again. This time they went to the four-star Hotel Las Americas. Less of a holiday resort than the Asturias, and less plush than the Hotel Santa Cruz, it is a functional business hotel on the grittier side of the central plaza. At night on blocks nearby, prostitutes tout for business.

The group checked in and Dwyer did not leave the hotel again, according to staff. After a busy Easter week, business was slow and the group had the fourth floor to themselves. They told the maids not to bother making up their rooms, which staff did not enter after they arrived. The group had their own food with them and ate in their rooms, according to Hernan Rossell, the hotel's manager. The only time Dwyer was again seen by staff was when he appeared in the lobby looking for a stronger Wi-Fi signal on Wednesday, 15 April, says Rossell. Apart from the other members of the group, it seems the next people to see him were those who killed him.

These are the facts known about Dwyer's sojourn in Bolivia and they raise more questions than they answer. Was there an armed confrontation between police and the five guests on the fourth floor of the Hotel Las Americas, or were Dwyer and his two colleagues summarily executed, as many in Santa Cruz believe? Were there guns in the rooms and is the group linked to an arms cache found in the city shortly after the police raid, as the authorities say? How come three of the five died from multiple gunshot wounds to the chest – with not a single head, leg or arm wound between them – while their two companions were taken prisoner almost unscathed? How was it that the 30 or so officers involved did not suffer a single wound between them in what they say was a half-hour shoot-out? Why, as reported by the hotel's manager, are all the bullet holes in the walls of the fourth floor inside the bedrooms, with none appearing to be the result of gunfire fired from inside the rooms towards attackers in the corridor?

If the five men were under surveillance for weeks, as the government claims, how did they then supposedly manage to plant a small bomb that partially destroyed the front gate of the house of Santa Cruz's cardinal the night before the raid on their hotel, as the police claim? And if the group was as armed and dangerous as the government says, why was this attack so inept, blowing just a small hole in the wooden gate at a time when the cardinal was not even at home? And why did Flores, a former war veteran, not practise even the most basic of security precautions if his group had just carried out a terrorist act? They were caught like rats in a trap – found holed up on the fourth floor of a hotel with little possibility of escape should they be discovered, in the centre of the city where they had allegedly just placed a bomb.

There are also many unanswered questions about what led the group to the Hotel Las Americas. In a video recording with a Hungarian journalist that Flores asked be released in the event of his death, Flores claimed he had returned to the town at the request of the Council of Santa Cruz in order to organise self-defence groups to take on what he called pro-government elements. But this video was the first time anyone had heard of the Council of Santa Cruz.

What is it and who bankrolled the group's six-month stay in the city? Having supposedly gone to do a bodyguard training course that fell through, did Dwyer instead accept an unspecified security job from Flores? Did Flores lead him to believe that this was in some way official work linked to the opposition-controlled regional government? Dwyer's actions in the months leading up to his death do not hint at someone who thought he was involved in clandestine activities. But on his Bebo page, since taken down, he would only vaguely say that he was 'travellin, workin, doin a bit a dis and a bit a dat'.

The official investigation now under way will supposedly attempt to answer some of these questions. But it is already being undermined by a government intent to use the events of the last 10 days to attack the opposition. Its work is being prejudged by officials, led by the vice-president, who have made their own charges against Dwyer and the others without providing evidence.

Two high-ranking Bolivian legal officials have told *The Irish Times* that the investigation breaks all standard legal procedures. 'It is ugly. The legal process is already totally contaminated; they are breaking the law with impunity,' says one official.

The Irish, Croatian and Hungarian governments have called for an international inquiry. Bolivia's government has vacillated on whether to agree to this outside scrutiny.

Such an inquiry, even at a remove from the events, might be able to solve many of these riddles. But it is unlikely to be able to answer the two questions at the heart of the brutal death of Michael Dwyer in room 457.

Did he ever fully understand what Flores – a charismatic advocate of obscure causes and whose posthumously-released video hints at something of a martyr complex – was up to in Bolivia? And just what exactly did he think he was doing in Bolivia during his six-month stay?

Stick to Rashers and Sausages – Fish Plays Tricks on the Heart

Displaced in Mullingar, Michael Harding

There's a new fish shop in Mullingar selling fresh fish, so last week I decided to give up meat. I ate tuna, and haddock, and cod, and mackerel and shellfish, all week. And I felt lighter. Which was good, because I had to appear in public on Friday evening.

I had a minor involvement with *Moby Dick*, a theatre adaptation of the book, which was playing in the Pavilion in Dún Laoghaire. When the show was over, the director and some friends were going to party, but I was tired so I went off to my room in the Royal Marine Hotel.

I asked at reception whether there was any possibility of getting supper, but I was disappointed. Not even a sandwich was available, the receptionist explained, because the dining room was closed and the night porter was not yet on duty.

I went up the street in the lashing rain, passing two young police officers, who were sheltering at the entrance of the shopping centre. They were deep in conversation as I crossed over to Burger King, which was still open.

I was sitting at a plastic table, munching a big burger, when a woman came in, drenched to the skin, and sat down beside me.

Ipswich football club manager Roy Keane, a long-standing supporter of Irish Guide Dogs for the Blind, with trainee guide dog Ella at the launch of the IGDB/Specsavers Shades 2009 campaign. Photograph: Alan Betson.

'Well, I don't believe it,' she exclaimed. 'What are you doing here?' As if people from Mullingar shouldn't be in Dún Laoghaire.

I knew her years ago. She used to be a painter. She had a big room overlooking the sea, and she never had any money. But now she was wrapped in gold and silk so I presumed she was no longer an out-of-work artist.

'Have you given up painting?' I asked.

'Yes,' she said. 'I am married to a solicitor and we have two children and a house in Wicklow.'

I said: 'Lucky you!'

'What are you at?' she wondered.

I said: 'I was at *Moby Dick*. In fact, I was in Moby Dick, this evening, in the Pavilion.'

There was a pause.

'How is your mother?' I inquired.

'She has a new hip.' 'That's great.' 'Yeah, she would be in a wheelchair if it wasn't for the new hip.' 'What age is she now?'

'Eighty-seven.'

'Good God,' I exclaimed, 'so you were the shakings of an old bag.' She looked annoyed.

'It's just a metaphor,' I explained. 'I don't mean that your mother is an old bag.' 'Good.' 'Do you know that there is a statue of Joe Dolan in Mullingar?' I asked.

'No.'

I said: 'It's a literal replica of him holding a microphone. But it doesn't work because there is no metaphor. Art requires metaphors. You should know that; you used to be an artist. And good conversation is peppered with metaphors.'

She asked me had I been drinking.

I said: 'No. But I've been eating fish all week.' She said: 'You're eating a burger.' I said: 'That's an exception. Because I couldn't get a sandwich in the hotel.'

Clearly, she was getting uneasy.

I said: 'You are a beautiful woman.'

Her brow was furrowed, as if she was thinking of phoning her husband to come immediately and rescue her.

'Text me your number,' I suggested, 'so I can meet you sometime, when I'm up from Mullingar again.' She said: 'Okay.'

In bed that night I dreamed a giant cat was chasing me. And then I was awake in a great sweat and I couldn't find the light switch. And then I slept again and dreamed that I was in charge of a zoo and the animals were going crazy.

The next morning I woke up feeling very fragile, so I sent a text to a friend to cheer myself up.

'How-r-u? Me-in-Dublin. Met-woman-last-night.' The text went on to outline my opinion of her marriage to a solicitor and how sad it was that she could abandon the artistic life, and the degree to which I desired her and was lusting for her body.

And at the very moment I sent it, I realised that she had already sent me her number by text overnight, and that she was now perhaps choking on her strawberries, or just lying speechless on her pillows, as she read the text that had just gone to her in error.

So, for breakfast, I decided to have two rashers, two sausages and lashings of black pudding. There's only so much fish any man can handle.

SATURDAY, 2 MAY 2009

Time for Fall Guys to Stand Up and Be Counted

Keith Duggan

The good people of Connacht and Ulster have become refugees in the hurricane caused by this rugby game. The forgotten provinces need guidance. Big Ian, take to the pulpit! And where are you gone, Pee Flynn? A province turns its lonely eyes to you. Munster versus Leinster has become inescapable and has been deemed more than just a rugby match; it is a clash of two cultures and if you are not on one side, then you must be on the other.

Bella, a Jack Russell terrier, joins motorcyclists at Cathal Brugha Barracks, in Dublin, where Defence Force troopers announced they would take part in the Annual Across Ireland Motorcycle Run. Photograph: Julien Behal/PA.

Those belonging to the other two quarters of Ireland can shut up and listen – but then there is nothing new there. Ireland is about Two Tribes and today is their day of days. And to those of us who are impartial in all of this, it seems as if the Leinster crowd ought to be feeling pretty unhappy about their role in this national rivalry.

On the face of it, Munster versus Leinster is a potentially thrilling rugby game that should settle the argument about the supreme force in Irish rugby this season. But what will happen on the field is merely a sporting metaphor for the perpetual struggle between two ways of Irish life. Munster versus Leinster is not just – or perhaps not even – about rugby.

It is about choices and values and about Who You Are: Country or City, West or East, Wranglers or Levis, Copper Face Jacks or Lily's Bordello, shirt tucked in or hanging loose, red meat lover or vegetarian, Jackie Healy Rae or David Norris, porridge or muesli, cute hoor or cute guy, Doc Marten's or Italian loafers, heart or head, hard or soft.

At least those are the messages that have been coming across in the profusion of coverage of the game on the Irish airwaves and television over the past couple of days. Munster rugby has been as successful as the Barack Obama machine at subliminally spreading its message among its people.

Quite how or when the citizens of Kerry, Cork, Tipperary, Clare and Waterford began to believe in the cult of Munster is probably impossible to pinpoint. The attraction was made easy by the fact that Munster could offer them a strong and charismatic team with a flair for producing thrilling victories. But it was more than that. The fabled days when George Hook and Tom McGurk would stand on the gantry overlooking a misty Thomond Park contributed to the Munster mythology.

It was always January and always Saturday and always freezing, the lights were just beginning to twinkle over Limerick city, the sky was West-of-Ireland epic and Hookie would hold us spellbound with his Munster incantations, raising his hands aloft and delivering streams of consciousness that were half rugby-analysis and half prayers of thanks to his people. It was a bit like watching Chief Sitting Bull in the midst of a rain dance.

Or maybe not. But Munster fans were always pretty clear about how they liked their rugby. They liked it raw and loud and medieval. They enjoyed clocking up what rugby men insist on calling 'the hard yards'.

They liked their victories to resemble 80-minute brawls, with the rugby ball on view about once every 15 minutes, except when Ronan O'Gara sent a penalty over from a quarter of a mile downfield. They tolerated flashy tries, but preferred the kind that involved someone like Peter Clohessy or the 'Bull' John Hayes ploughing through a perfumed French fullback from three yards out and belly-flopping over the line, seconds before the entire red pack landed on him.

A few stitches and head wounds acquired in the heat of battle were obligatory. They liked it when the boys trooped off the field in a cloud of steam, muddied from head to toe and invincible to the last. Soon, a profile of the Munster fans was developed. They were cheerful, good-natured types, strong as oxes, carelessly handsome and not at all vain.

They liked to travel in numbers of 15,000 or more, bringing good cheer, irreverent wit, plenty of spending power and a frightening store of Irish ballads, which they would sing en masse in over-populated hotel lobbies until dawn broke over places like Toulouse, London, Perpignan, Cardiff and Gloucester.

They were generous, upstanding, went to Mass on Sunday, but were utterly unscrupulous and ingenious in the practice of securing tickets for big games. They had the sense that they were born lucky, and Munster winning epic, nerve-wracking cup matches became a matter of manifest destiny.

They would celebrate their heroes with the kind of monster meetings that reminded old men of the days of Daniel O'Connell and by writing plays and other memoirs. After the team won the European Cup in 2006 and again last year, it was clear that Munster had won a special place in the hearts of the nation. Munster had become rugby's representatives of the better qualities of the Irish nature.

And all this was very well if you happened to be from anywhere but Leinster. Because everything Munster stood for was, by inference, everything that Leinster did not. Somehow, Leinster have become the fall guys in this story. And more than that, the blame has been placed not so much on the team as on the crowd that follows them.

The Leinster identity is more delicate and complex than that of Munster. Part of the problem was that, for a couple of seasons, the only tries Leinster seemed capable of scoring were, in the words of Derek Zoolander, really, really good looking. They involved incredibly fast and intricate passes and stunning solo runs which facilitated great slow-motion replays, gritted teeth, flowing locks and moans of genuine ecstasy from match commentators Ryle Nugent and Tony Ward.

The best Leinster tries were glorious feats that seemed to marry the highest triumphs of mathematics, rugby and Vidal Sassoon. It didn't seem right that Leinster's tries were worth a mere seven points: the ice-skating scoring system, where judges could hold up cards for perfect tens, would have been fairer.

And perhaps that was why Munster folks came to believe the joke was on Leinster. No matter how beautifully they played it, they could always be cudgelled and caught. And their fans would always be out-shouted. The word on the street is the Leinster fan is by now a cowed fellow; a suave mover to Kanye West perhaps, but in matters rugby meek and polite and, deep down, kind of scared of his hearty cousin from Munster.

Today the Munster Nation will swagger into the capital like they own the place. They have probably earned that privilege. They will be confident and good-humoured and will go berserk for the duration of the game. They will expect their Leinster rivals to look stylish, smile a lot, enjoy the day out and accept the result when they are beaten.

That has been the way of things down the years. Sooner or later, the Leinster guys are going to crack. There's only so much Munster Mania they can take.

The rebellion could begin today.

In the words of a favourite Munster ballad: *You Gotta Fight For Your Right To Party.*

THURSDAY, 7 MAY 2009

Bob Dylan: O2, Dublin

Tony Clayton-Lea

Here's a potentially interesting question: what other bona-fide pop-culture icon would treat his audience the way Bob Dylan does? Not a word is said to the capacity crowd between songs; apart from a few dainty steps and hand movements, his stage presence is non-existent; his voice now approximates a series of growls; and some of his best-known songs are altered almost beyond

Queen Elizabeth greets Ronan O'Gara and other Irish rugby internationals at a reception in Hillsborough Castle, Co. Down, to mark Ireland's Grand Slam season, as Brian O'Driscoll, Tom Court, Stephen Ferris and Jamie Heaslip look on. O'Gara's hands in pockets drew critical comment from readers. Photograph: Frank Miller.

recognition. Perhaps more to the point, why does a Bob Dylan audience accept this kind of treatment?

The answer to the latter is that they're Bob Dylan fans and they know the score (although aren't they getting ever so slightly weary of it by now?). The answer to the former. Well, as the man himself sings it, the answer, my friend, is blowin' in the wind. In other words, go figure.

That Dylan continues to evolve as an artist isn't in question. Over the past 12 years he has released a series of albums that has even further cemented his position as the pre-eminent figure-head of rock music. Yes, there is filler between the good stuff, but Dylan's reputation as an artist is copper-fastened, his back catalogue comprises an unequalled number of truly great songs and classics – it's just a shame, to these ears and eyes at least, that he regards his live performances with such a dismaying lack of engagement.

There are – as per usual for us Dylan fans who traipse along to his gigs pretty much every time he visits – moments of unadulterated pleasure. His version of 'Just Like A Woman' (one of three songs he played from *Blonde on Blonde* – the others were the gig opener, 'Leopard-Skin Pill-Box Hat' and 'Stuck Inside of Mobile with the Memphis Blues Again') was amazing, while the rendition of 'All Along the Watchtower' snatched it from the hands of Jimi Hendrix and refused point-blank to give it back.

And, as per usual, there were moments of bewilderment and banality: the totally askew version of 'Blowin' in the Wind', the croaking, complacent version of 'Masters of War', too much time given over to bar-band blues chugging.

But, you know, with a Dylan show, what you come for doesn't exactly correlate with what you get. A few notes from Block D, Row 21, Seat 104: slivers of brilliance, but not really entertaining, not genuinely exciting. More an exercise, perhaps, in how to keep moving – creatively, frustratingly – from one place to the next. Where he's bound? Who can tell?

THURSDAY, 14 MAY 2009

Happy Days as Beckett Bridge Tests Attention Span

Ruadhán Mac Cormaic

ACT ONE. Eastlink Bridge. Afternoon. Mother and Boy.

Boy: I can't see it.

Mother: You can.

Boy: Where's the bridge?

Mother: Just look at it.

Boy: That boat there?

Mother: No, the other boat.

Boy: Are we on the bridge?

Mother: No. This is the Eastlink.

Boy: I can't see the bridge.

Mother: That's it, in front of us.

Boy: Where?

Mother: There.

Boy: Why's it not coming faster?

Mother: Just look at it.

Boy: How did they stick the bridge on?

Mother: Nuts and bolts.

Boy: I want to go.

[They Go]

Act Two. The tug has begun its approach. Two men. Shay Tarpey and Liam Hendley. From Dublin.

Shay: Just came to see it going through.

Liam: That's all.

Shay: Give us a bit of a lift. With all the doom. The doom and gloom.

Onlooker: If it gets through.

Shay: Don't say that. Nah, it's fantastic. Good to see improvements down here in the docklands. The bridges and that.

Liam: Hope the rain holds off.

The Samuel Beckett Bridge arrives at Dublin Port, after the €60 million structure was floated from Rotterdam, and delayed by strong winds. The 120-metre bridge, spanning the Liffey between Guild Street on the northside and Sir John Rogerson's Quay on the southside, was designed by Spanish architect Santiago Calatrava, who also designed the James Joyce Bridge near Heuston Station. Photograph: Peter Dorney/Digital Post Production.

Act Three. Two journalists. Sodden notebooks. Little going.

J1: Are you sure it was here?

J2: That's what they said.

J1: Where?

J2: Here.

J1: How will we know?

J2: 120 metres long, 48 metres high. A giant white harp, sideways.

J1: Two o'clock?

J2: They've been wrong before.

J1(forlorn): What's the delay?

J2: High winds. Low tide.

J1: And if not today?

J2: Tomorrow.

J1: Will there be much in it?

J2: Much in it?

J1: The Beckett. When it comes.

Act Four. Two tourists. The bridge inches closer, ropes taut, creaking and crunching. Crowds now line the quayside. Overhead, a helicopter.

T1: We are just walking this way. We are from Denmark.

T2: We didn't know this. What is happening?

From the crowd: We're waitin'. For the bridge.

T1: The bridge?

From the crowd: The bridge.

T1: We thought there was an accident or something. The police came.

T2: And the ambulance.
T1: We'll wait to see.
[They wait]

Act Five. An hour has passed, and now the bridge passes gracefully through the Eastlink. Phones aloft! Camera shutters. Otherwise silence. Shay and Liam. Again.
Shay: Absolutely fantastic. Something to be proud of.
Liam: It's good to be able to say you were here, in fairness.
Shay: Well? We head?
Liam: Let's head.

WEDNESDAY, 20 MAY 2009

All New Car Buyers to Recite Five Decades of the Rosary

Emissions, by Kilian Doyle

I was on the train the other day, unashamedly eavesdropping on two youngwans opposite me. They were blathering about all manner of girlie guff and giving me great silent gigglage.

Eventually, one turned to the other and announced, in all seriousness, that she wouldn't buy a new car in the current economic climate because of the 'stigmata'.

My eyebrows lifted. For a second there, I half thought manufacturers of new cars had started embedding their steering wheels with nails. Why wasn't I told? No wonder nobody's buying them.

'Don't be bleedin' ridiculous,' said her mate, obviously the brains of the operation. 'If ye've gorrit, flaunt it, dat's what I say.'

Then it dawned on me that she obviously meant stigma. An easy mistake to make. My apologies for ever doubting you, Lil' Miss Zeitgeist, for you are right on the button.

It's a sad truth for the motor industry that there really are lots of consciences being wracked these days among Ireland's limited pool of potential car buyers. The dismal sales figures, down by more than two-thirds on last year, would suggest many are putting off buying as a result of their soul-searching.

But why should this be? Presumably, many think it would be vulgar to drive a brand new car, when all around are losing their jobs. This is just silly. The streets are still full of SUVs. How vulgar would your new hatchback have to be to stand out in that sea of tawdry boorishness?

Still, I can understand why people don't want to be seen to be rubbing their prosperity in the noses of the less fortunate. But did they never think that their stance, however noble it may be, could actually be making things worse?

Let's look at the economics. This grand little country is up to its oxters in financial trouble. There are a lot of reasons for this, not least the plummeting levels of consumer confidence.

The whole joint is riddled with fear. Even people with little or nothing to be afraid of financially, who are probably far better off than they were six months ago due to falling interest rates and prices, are terrified to spend a bent penny.

We in the media have to hold our hands up and take some responsibility for this. Good news doesn't sell newspapers. It's the doom and gloom that shifts shedloads.

And what happens when people won't spend? The whole system grinds to a halt. Businesses go to the wire and people get laid off. Even before their lost income taxes are taken into account, each extra person on the dole costs the State the guts of €20,000 a year. To be able to afford to pay this, the Government has to cut services and raise taxes on everyone else who still has a job.

Therefore, by not spending, you are in effect costing yourself the money that you think you're saving. And thousands of people get to experience the misery and indignity of a life lived on handouts.

Labour leader Eamon Gilmore launching the party's local government election manifesto in Dublin. Photograph:
Matt Kavanagh.

Now, I know real economists are scoffing condescendingly into their cappuccinos while reading this simplistic view. I don't care. I'm the first to admit my grasp of high finance isn't the tightest – which goes a long way towards explaining why I'll never be in a position to buy a new car myself.

But I don't begrudge anyone who is. I reckon the logical thing if you have the money and want to buy a new car is to go and do it. Now. You'll be doing the country a favour. Rather than pointing and scowling, the rest of us should be cheering you on.

But don't go pulling up in it outside the local dole office and flinging wads of fivers out the window. For then you'd definitely deserve the stigmata. Indeed, I'd come and drive the spikes through your hands myself.

WEDNESDAY, 20 MAY 2009

Bitter Harvest for Lost Afghan Youth

Mary Fitzgerald

Like ghosts they move in and out of the shadows, shrunken, emaciated figures with stooped shoulders and dead eyes. Shuffling and stumbling their way through rubble splashed with excrement and vomit, they pass under a crumbling mural of Lenin illuminated by shafts of sunlight that fall through the collapsed roof.

In one corner Hamid, a former soldier, staggers away with pinhead eyes after taking one of his first hits of the day. He has been using heroin for 23 of his 45 years. A dirty jacket hangs open over his bare concave chest, revealing a tattoo of a coiled cobra along with the names of two friends, now dead. 'Without you life means nothing', it reads in Pashtu.

Nearby, a young Afghan with a faded gash across his cheek pulls the skin of a fellow addict taut as he injects him in the leg, while another man with glazed eyes leans back in a stupor. Others sit with their heads in their hands, rocking back and forth.

These are the denizens of what was once one of the most impressive buildings in Kabul, known then and now as the Russian Cultural Centre.

Kabulis remember when the sprawling, modernist complex hosted recitals and opera performances, and showed films celebrating Mother Russia. During the years of civil war that followed

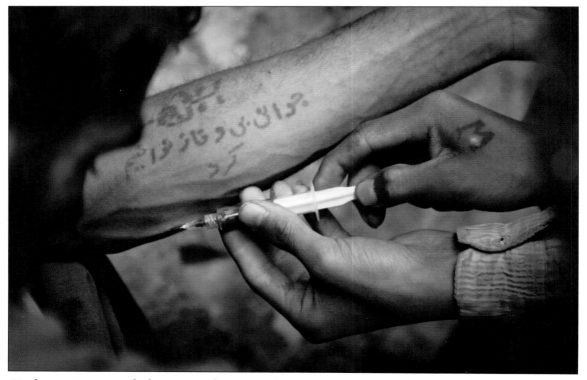

'Youth is not forever' reads the tattoo on the arm of a heroin addict injecting amid the ruins of Kabul's Russian Cultural Centre. Photograph: Brenda Fitzsimons.

the Soviet withdrawal in 1989 the centre was pum-
melled by shells and mortars as the surrounding city
tore itself apart.

Today the abandoned warren of bullet-pocked
walls, dank rooms and ruined stairways is home to
more than 600 destitute Afghans who have fallen
prey to their country's biggest export – opium.

One man, also called Hamid, clutches a pink
towel to his face against the stench that rises from
the gloom, a mix of human waste and the distinctive stale odour of heated heroin. Earlier that
morning he watched a friend die amidst the filth
and decay.

Hamid is 22 and lives in another part of Kabul
with his wife and baby. His face, smooth and handsome, and his clean clothes contrast with the wild
and desperate appearance of those who slump
around him, but Hamid too is an addict. He, along

with thousands of others, comes here every day to
feed a habit he began three years ago.

'I wanted to get treatment,' Hamid explains
almost apologetically. 'But when I went to the
hospital they told me they had no room for me.
There were already too many like me.'

Those who run the handful of drug treatment
clinics in Kabul say their limited facilities are overwhelmed by the scale of addiction in the city and
its environs. They talk of waiting lists that stretch
into thousands. They talk of Afghanistan's drug
problem finally coming home to roost, with devastating consequences.

The opium grown in vast poppy fields across
Afghanistan was once smuggled abroad for refining
before it appeared as heroin on the streets of
Europe and the US. In recent years, however,
Afghan drug barons have begun processing the raw

*Young men relaxing after taking heroin in the ruins of Kabul's Russian Cultural Centre, home to around 600 des-
titute Afghans who have fallen victim to their country's biggest export – opium. Photograph: Brenda Fitzsimons.*

opium in the country to achieve greater profit margins.

They have also discovered a ready domestic market in the legions of returned refugees who became addicted to heroin and opium while living in exile in neighbouring Iran and Pakistan.

A United Nations survey carried out four years ago calculated that despite the stigma attached to drug use in this deeply conservative country, addiction rates in Afghanistan have risen sharply since 2003, with an estimated 200,000 opium and heroin addicts in an overall population of around 33 million.

Tens of thousands of Afghan women and children use drugs, although this aspect of the problem remains for the most part behind closed doors due to the segregated nature of Afghan society.

Afghanistan produces more than 90 per cent of the world's opium and profits from narcotics are estimated to make up more than half of the country's gross domestic product. Bumper harvests in recent years have driven down the price of heroin sold on the streets of Kabul – one hit now costs around 50 afghanis, or $1.

Last year's opium crop, despite falling slightly due to efforts to persuade farmers to switch to alternatives, proved the second biggest on record, according to the UN's International Narcotics Control Board (INCB).

While the area under cultivation was reduced by a fifth, better yields meant opium production dropped only 6 per cent to 7,700 tonnes, after a record 8,200 tonnes in 2007, the agency said in its annual report. It noted, however, that a further five of the country's 34 provinces had ended opium production last year, bringing the total number of 'opium-free' provinces to 18.

Most of Afghanistan's opium is now farmed in the southern provinces where NATO-led troops are locked in a stalemate with an increasingly assertive Taliban. Its production powers the insurgency to the tune of $200-300 million each year, the UN says, sums gathered from taxes levied on opium farmers by the Taliban.

'Insecurity and drug production and trafficking . . . are very much inter-related,' INCB president Hamid Ghodse said earlier this year. 'It is very difficult to say which is the cause and which is the effect.'

Aside from poor security, rampant corruption is one of the biggest obstacles in the battle against Afghanistan's drugs trade, the INCB report notes. It accuses Afghan officials of allowing drug traffickers operate with impunity, and says those who do try to tackle the problem risk their lives. Last year, 78 officials working to eradicate opium crops were killed, six times the number in 2007.

'Corruption among officials at almost every level of the government is a major factor of the drug problem,' Ghodse adds.

When asked about their journey to addiction, many of those living in the shell of the Russian Cultural Centre tell similar stories to that of Abdulrahim Rahman. He first tried heroin nine years ago after fleeing Taliban-controlled Afghanistan to work in Iran.

'I had never heard of heroin before, but I saw people using it there and I wanted to try it for myself,' he recalls.

Abdulrahim, though still an addict, works for international aid agency Medecins du Monde, combing the ruins of the cultural centre daily for discarded syringes. 'I collect between 100 and 150 syringes every day,' he says, his gloved hands holding a yellow plastic bucket full of bloodied needles. 'And I see many who are close to death.'

The crowded and squalid conditions – dozens of men huddle together in fetid rooms, and many share needles – mean the spectre of Aids and other diseases such as hepatitis is never far away. International agencies estimate the number of HIV cases in Afghanistan runs to thousands. One addict says at least two people die at the centre every day, but the cause of death is rarely ascertained.

Close to the entrance, a tall man with matted hair and unkempt beard emerges from behind a ragged curtain pinned over a doorway. His name is

Khan Agha and this has been his home for three years.

He began taking heroin 10 years ago. 'You see my life,' he asks plaintively, gesturing around him. 'This is not a life. We are outside everything. No one accepts us, not our families, not this society. We are better off dead.'

THURSDAY, 21 MAY 2009

The Savage Reality of Our Darkest Days

Editorial

The Report of the Commission to Inquire into Child Abuse is the map of an Irish hell. It defines the contours of a dark hinterland of the State, a parallel country whose existence we have long known but never fully acknowledged. It is a land of pain and shame, of savage cruelty and callous indifference.

The instinct to turn away from it, repelled by its profoundly unsettling ugliness, is almost irresistible. We owe it, though, to those who have suffered there to acknowledge from now on that it is an inescapable part of Irish reality. We have to deal with the now-established fact that, alongside the warmth and intimacy, the kindness and generosity of Irish life, there was, for most of the history of the State, a deliberately maintained structure of vile and vicious abuse.

Mr Justice Ryan's report does not suggest that this abuse was as bad as most of us suspected. It shows that it was worse. It may indeed have been even worse than the report actually finds – there are indications that 'the level of sexual abuse in boys' institutions was much higher than was revealed by the records or could be discovered by this investigation'.

With a calm but relentless accumulation of facts, the report blows away all the denials and

Cartoon by Martyn Turner.

obfuscations, all the moral equivocations and evasions which we have heard from some of the religious orders and their apologists. The sheer scale and longevity of the torment inflicted on defenceless children – over 800 known abusers in over 200 institutions during a period of 35 years – should alone make it clear that it was not accidental or opportunistic but systematic.

Violence and neglect were not the result of underfunding – the large institutions, where the worst abuse was inflicted, were 'well-resourced'. The failure of the religious orders to stop these crimes did not result from ignorance. The recidivist nature of child sexual abusers was understood by the Brothers, who nonetheless continued deliberately to place known offenders in charge of children, both in industrial schools and in ordinary primary schools. At best, this represented what the report calls 'a callous disregard for the safety of children'. At worst, it was an active protection of, and thus collusion with, the perpetrators of appalling crimes.

Nor did the abuse continue because of secrecy. Again, the very scale of the violence made it impossible to keep it sealed off from either officialdom or society at large. Contemporary complaints were made to the Garda, to the Department of Education, to health boards, to priests and to members of the public. The department, 'deferential and submissive' to the religious congregations, did not shout stop. Neither did anyone else. Indeed, perhaps the most shocking finding of the commission is that industrial school inmates were often sexually exploited by those outside the closed world of the congregations, by 'volunteer workers, visitors, work placement employees, foster parents' and by those who took them out for holidays or to work.

The key to understanding these attitudes is surely to realise that abuse was not a failure of the system. It was the system. Terror was both the point of these institutions and their standard operating procedure. Their function in Irish society was to impose social control, particularly on the poor,

by acting as a threat. Without the horror of an institution like Letterfrack, it could not fulfil that function. Within the institutions, terror was systematic and deliberate. It was a methodology handed down through 'successive generations of Brothers, priests and nuns'.

There is a nightmarish quality to this systemic malice, reminiscent of authoritarian regimes. We read of children 'flogged, kicked . . . scalded, burned and held under water'. We read of deliberate psychological torment inflicted through humiliation, expressions of contempt and the practice of incorrectly telling children that their parents were dead. We read of returned absconders having their heads shaved and of 'ritualised' floggings in one institution.

We have to call this kind of abuse by its proper name – torture. We must also call the organised exploitation of unpaid child labour – young girls placed in charge of babies 'on a 24-hour basis' or working under conditions of 'great suffering' in the rosary bead industry; young boys doing work that gave them no training but made money for the religious orders – by its proper name: slavery. It demands a very painful adjustment of our notions of the nature of the State to accept that it helped to inflict torture and slavery on tens of thousands of children. In the light of the commission's report, however, we can no longer take comfort in evasions.

Almost unbearable though it may be it is important that everyone who can do so should read and absorb this report. We owe that especially to those victims who first broke the silence on the RTÉ documentaries *Dear Daughter* and *States of Fear* and to those who came forward to tell their stories to the commission. It is to be hoped that, in spite of the failure of the religious congregations to take full responsibility for what happened, those who have suffered have found some comfort in that process and in a report of such unflinching lucidity.

Most importantly, though, we owe it to all who are vulnerable in today's Irish society. For their sakes, we need to know what happens when institutions acquire absolute power over defence-less people and when the State and society come to believe that it is better to collude in crimes than to challenge cherished beliefs. Mr Justice Ryan suggests the erection of a monument to the victims of abuse with the words of the State's 1999 apology inscribed on it. That should happen, but the real monument will be that we inscribe on our collective consciousness as a society the two words 'Never again'.

Defiant Leinster the Nearly Men No Longer

Gerry Thornley, in Edinburgh

Leinster. European champions. Saturday, 24 May, at Murrayfield just capped it off. The last piece of an unbelievable year-and-a-half in which Irish rugby retained the Heineken Cup, retained the Magners League and made off with the Grand Slam. And now, last but by no means least, the nearly men are no more.

Hugely deserved, and won the hard way too. The heroic defiance in Harlequins, the clinical dissection of the reigning European champions and then the gritty comeback against the English standard-bearers brooks no argument and counts as a huge character endorsement.

As with the other stupendous Irish days, it came down to tiny margins, and there were a myriad of factors to the win. Leinster enjoyed a three-to-one ratio in travelling support, perhaps helped by neutrals joining their cause, but the final count for the Blue Army may have been 40,000. It mattered hugely, as Brian O'Driscoll stressed, and he thanked the marketing team for getting all those blue flags into the ground.

It was an unstinting effort from first minute to last across the board. It had to be.

Leinster slipped off defensively and conceded 13 points while Stan Wright was yellow carded

Leinster players celebrate as the final whistle has given the side their first Heineken Cup victory, after beating the Leicester Tigers 19-16 at Murrayfield, in Edinburgh. Photograph: Gareth Copley/PA.

Jamie Heaslip stretches and scores a try, which Jonathan Sexton converted during Leinster's Heineken Cup win over Leicester in Edinburgh. Photograph: Dara Mac Dónaill.

either side of half-time, but they realigned their 'up and out' defensive system, and worked harder to have fewer tight forwards in the belly of their defence.

Taking five early Leicester throws hadn't been scripted, but the counter-rucking and turnovers at the breakdown is a new string to Leinster's bow, and the ball wrestled away by Chris Whitaker and Wright was the catalyst for the eight-phase attack that led to the winning penalty.

The scrum was immense too; Wright paid his dues and Cian Healy came of age. So too, of course, did Jonathan Sexton. On a career-defining day his was a career-defining performance. While he couldn't sleep for two nights before the game, he still brought an infectious self-confidence to the game.

'Our belief,' Malcolm O'Kelly cited as the winning factor, before revealing: 'Jonny Sexton

said to me, and it stuck in my head throughout the match, "There's nothing we can do about it, we are actually going to win this match. It's written."

'That unerring belief certainly helped him kick that drop goal. Every kick I was thinking, "I wonder what he's thinking now or how he's going to kick this over?", but it was out of his hands almost because he knew it was going to go over, that we were going to win the game.'

Along with the savvy and leadership of Leo Cullen and Shane Jennings, in their time of need Jamie Heaslip came up with another massive second half and a killer try.

Then there was Rocky Elsom and Brian O'Driscoll. Elsom seemed like one of those over-age ringers in a schools match, rumbling through Alesana Tuilagi to draw the initial line in the sand, stealing lineouts, putting in monster tackles and galloping and slaloming through all-comers.

'Let's put it this way, we wouldn't have won the Heineken Cup without Rocky Elsom,' said O'Driscoll with a huge grin and deliberately massive understatement. 'The guy – as Will Greenwood rightly put it during the week – irrespective of what happened today, Rocky Elsom was the player of the Heineken Cup before the final. You saw the display he put in today.'

'He's a remarkable player. I'd say he's probably the best player I've ever played with and I've played with some very good players. He doesn't make that many errors, he has a massive work-rate and his ball-carrying is frightening.'

Coach Michael Cheika expressed guarded optimism Elsom might stay another season, although arguably there's less reason now for him to hang around. It won't be a question of money.

Other things might keep him here though. Asked if his name had ever been serenaded quite like that at home, Elsom sheepishly admitted: 'No, it hasn't.'

Long after the trophy celebration and the lap of honour, the blue hordes were still chanting his name and, for the last time, that of a suited Felipe Contepomi as he was lifted shoulder-high by Stephen Keogh to hold the trophy aloft.

The players' decision to have Chris Whitaker lift the trophy with Leo Cullen was a mark of their respect for him and what he has contributed over three years.

'I tried to avoid it,' Whitaker admitted. 'I tried to go up there earlier. I said, "Mate stop, it's not my day. There's guys here who are here a lot longer than I am." I was really upset. I don't think I really warranted it.'

That said, it showed they cared though? 'Aw yeah, it means a lot to me that they would even think about doing that.' Whitaker maintained his elation was not tinged with sadness at this being his last game, although it must have been.

As for O'Kelly, when asked if he was considering bowing out, he smiled and said: 'Are you kidding, lads? There's a recession on.'

Later, Bernard Jackman brought the cup back to Kielys in Donnybrook. While the only sadness on the day was that Denis Hickie and co. missed out, among those to kiss the cup was Chris Pim, as defiantly tough, hard and uncompromising a player as any the province has produced. Saturday was a heritage thing too.

Leinster may have silenced their detractors for now and by rights once and for all. But while acknowledging that, there's no doubt an element of bitterness remains, as O'Driscoll admitted.

'Yeah, we have. We haven't forgotten the things that were said about us in December by certain quarters of the media. I could list off a name, a number of names, but I'm not going to do so. You don't forget that. We've gone and proved those people particularly wrong. There were some very distasteful things said.

'But today it's sweet, we'll enjoy it amongst ourselves, just ourselves. The real diehard support, we know who they are and we'll enjoy this victory with them because they have been there through the thick and thin.

'There'll be a few people jumping on the bandwagon, as there always are; they can enjoy the ride as well, but the diehards are the ones we really respect and cherish.'

TUESDAY, 26 MAY 2009

Irish Society Shot Through with Debased Authority

Elaine Byrne

A passage from the *Book of Proverbs* reads: 'When the righteous are in authority, the people rejoice: but when the wicked beareth rule, the people mourn.'

The Report of the Commission to Inquire into Child Abuse reveals an uncomfortable history of Ireland in its five volumes. It is a history of how power was defined since the foundation of the State. The absolute authority of the Catholic Church rested on the assumption that it was above reproach, without question and beyond criticism.

Sr Carmella, teacher and principal from the Mercy order at St Joseph's Industrial School in Clifden, 'just did what the Reverend Mother told me to do' because she 'was that kind of person that her word was law, she was in authority and that was it'. Part of this authority included beating children whose crime it was that lice had infested their heads.

The Christian Brothers at St Joseph's in Artane 'were obliged by their vows of obedience to carry out instructions without question'. Such instructions consisted of 'frequent and severe punishment' where sexual abuse 'was a chronic problem'.

The Sisters of Mercy at St Vincent's in Goldenbridge numbered among them 'very powerless people' who had 'enormous and immediate power over troubled and troublesome children. The abuse of the power and powerlessness was almost inevitable. Almost any kind of abusive incidents could have occurred'.

And they did.

Hunger forced children to fight for scraps thrown into the playground. Thirst coerced children to drink from toilet bowls.

This was an infallible divine authority based on a premise of respectability and hierarchy. Buttressed by a culture of secrecy, this righteous and wicked authority brutally punished poverty. This was an entrenched yet anonymous authority more powerful than the supposed accountable authority of the State.

RTÉ's former **Late Late Show** *host Pat Kenny at the studios in Donnybrook talking to reporters about presenting his last show after 10 years. Photograph: Brenda Fitzsimons.*

The Ryan report found that the Department of Education 'had considerable powers, but it lacked the initiative and authority to do anything more than maintain the status quo'. The intense trust and 'deferential and submissive attitude' by the department toward the religious orders endorsed a culture that rejected complaints and vilified complainants as 'troublemakers'.

A deliberately contradictory mindset became normalised through blind loyalty and apathetic conformity. John Banville described this choice in last week's *New York Times* as one where 'we knew, and did not know'.

This was an Ireland hypnotised by a superficial veneer of values – the Ireland of James Joyce's *Dubliners* characterised by spiritual paralysis, where Irishness was expressed through the prisms of suf-focating nationalism and oppressive Catholicism.

One by one, the traditional pillars that have held our institutional life together have been torn down. Our generation is bearing intimate witness to a painful process of self-scrutiny.

For example, the final instalment of the Morris tribunal report on Garda corruption was published this time last year. The Moriarty and Mahon reports into political corruption are due shortly. The most popular and successful taoiseach of the modern era, Bertie Ahern, resigned last year following allegations of impropriety.

Last week's resignation of the Bank of Ireland governor, Richard Burrows, now means that only two of the 12 chief executives and chairmen in situ since the September Government guarantee of the six main financial institutions remain.

Financial Regulator Patrick Neary resigned in January. The Office of the Director of Corporate Enforcement, the Garda fraud squad and the Irish Stock Exchange are among the bodies investigating irregularities at Anglo Irish Bank. The director general of Fás, Rody Molloy, resigned in November following allegations of excessive expenses incurred by the semi-state body.

And the list goes on.

Ireland had preached ethical self-regulation since independence and it has failed. Instead we gave birth to a morally corrupted definition of authority, complemented by accomplices in our Civil Service and judicial system. Our individual indifference embraced the luxury of believing in what we were told by authority. We ignored our responsibility to constructively challenge such orthodoxies.

But is there something particular to Ireland which facilitates a hierarchical ethos? Where the philosophy of authority is moulded by absolute deference to those with monarchical tendencies? A divine right to clandestine privileges from golden circles?

Have we been pretending to live in a Republic? This place where we pay lip service to the memory of men who stood on the steps of the GPO proclaiming that all children of the nation should be cherished equally?

The traditional character of authority in Ireland had consequences – 2,600 ugly pages of it.

'The beast which I saw was like unto a leop-ard, and his feet were as the feet of a bear, and his mouth as the mouth of a lion: and the dragon gave him his power, and his seat, and great authority.' This is how the Book of Revelations in the New Testament depicts debased authority.

An epiphany of malevolence.

WEDNESDAY, 3 JUNE 2009

Order Denied Abuse Five Days before Report

Patsy McGarry

Just five days before publication of the Ryan report last month, Br Kevin Mullan of the Christian Brothers insisted in writing that the only form of corporal punishment allowed by the congregation was 'moderate slapping on the palms of the hands with the approved leather strap . . .'

He also said the congregation 'totally rejects any allegations of systemic abuse . . . or that boys were inadequately fed or clothed . . . and vehemently repudiates all unsubstantiated allegations of sexual abuse . . . or that sexual activity or emotional or physical abuse amongst the boys was facilitated by lack of vigilance on the part of the staff'.

In a letter to the Residential Institutions Redress Board, dated 15 May 2009, the Christian Brothers' province leader, Br Mullan, was responding to allegations made by a former resident of the O'Brien Institute in Dublin. It was managed by the Christian Brothers and is one of the institutions covered by the State redress scheme for former residents.

It is usual for the Redress Board to contact a relevant congregation on foot of such allegations. There is no onus on the congregation to reply,

though it is believed the Christian Brothers have done so generally, and in a similar fashion.

The Ryan report, published on 20 May, concluded of the institutions it investigated, including those for boys run by the Christian Brothers, that 'a climate of fear, created by pervasive, excessive and arbitrary punishment, permeated most of the institutions and all those run for boys. Children lived with the daily terror of not knowing where the next beating was coming from'.

It found that 'children were frequently hungry and food was inadequate, inedible and badly prepared in many schools' and that 'clothing was a particular problem in boys' schools where children often worked for long hours on farms'.

It said educational standards were 'consistently poorer than in outside schools' and that 'academic education was not seen as a priority for industrial school children'.

It found that 'in reality, the industrial training

Members of freestyle BMX group Xtreme Action from the UK performing stunts at the launch of National Bike Week in the Phoenix Park in Dublin. Photograph: Aidan Crawley.

afforded by all schools was of a nature that served the needs of the institution rather than the needs of the child'.

It concluded that 'sexual abuse was endemic in boys' institutions' and that 'older boys sexually abused younger boys and the system did not offer protection from bullying of this kind'.

In his 15 May reply to the Redress Board, Br Mullan wrote that 'the only form of corporal punishment allowed by the congregation was moderate slapping on the palms of the hands with an approved leather strap (some 12 ins long approx. – *including* [his italics] shaped 'handle' – and without metal inclusions).'

He continued, 'No other form of corporal punishment could be condoned by the school authorities, nor could such punishment be administered without sufficient reason.' He said 'the congregation totally rejects any allegations of systemic abuse having taken place in the above-mentioned institution, or that boys were inadequately fed or clothed or denied proper medical attention or an appropriate education'.

He continued that the congregation 'vehemently repudiates all unsubstantiated allegations of sexual abuse there of pupils by staff members, or that sexual activity or emotional or physical abuse amongst the boys was facilitated by lack of vigilance on the part of the staff'.

In a similar letter to the Redress Board, dated 20 November last, Br Mullan responded similarly to allegations made by a former resident at the Artane industrial school that 'the only form of corporal punishment allowed by the congregation was moderate slapping . . .', as above.

He added, however, in this instance that 'the congregation does not accept that an overly repressive regime obtained in the institution (Artane), as the applicant alleges'. He also said the congregation 'totally rejects any allegations of systemic abuse having taken place in the above mentioned institution . . .'. He denied there were the people on the staff at Artane named by the

former resident. It later transpired the names of the staff members alluded to had not been spelled correctly.

Where Glin industrial school in Limerick was concerned and St Joseph's industrial school in Tralee, Br Mullan used the same formula in rejecting all allegations made by former residents. Where Glin industrial school was concerned, he did so in a letter dated 7 November 2008, and where St Joseph's in Tralee was concerned, on 18 July 2008.

Br Mullan was a member of the team which, along with then CORI secretary general Sr Elizabeth Maxwell and Sr Helena O'Donoghue of the Mercy Sisters, negotiated the 2002 redress agreement with the Government.

A similar stance to all allegations made to the Redress Board was taken by the Oblates of Mary Immaculate who managed St Conleth's reformatory at Daingean, Co. Offaly. An example, seen by *The Irish Times*, was a short letter by Fr Michael Hughes on 14 February last, in response to allegations by a former resident.

MONDAY, 8 JUNE 2009

Electorate Rounds on Fianna Fáil and Greens

Stephen Collins

Fianna Fáil has suffered the worst defeat in its history, and Irish politics will never be the same again. How a Government that has taken such a drubbing can continue to govern and take the decisions necessary to restore the economy to health is now the critical issue facing the political system.

The decision of Fine Gael to table a motion of no confidence in the Government was the obvious move, given its historic breakthrough as the biggest party in the country. More importantly, it is an attempt to focus minds on the profound implications of the election results.

Cartoon by Martyn Turner.

Probably the most striking symbol of the reversal suffered by Fianna Fáil was the fate of Maurice Ahern, brother of the former taoiseach, who was beaten into a humiliating fifth place in the Dublin Central by-election with just 12 per cent of the first preference vote.

Just two years after Bertie Ahern led Fianna Fáil to an amazing three-in-a-row general election victory, his inability to deliver even a modestly respectable vote for his brother showed how the mighty have fallen. To rub salt into the wound, Maurice Ahern lost his city council seat to party colleague Mary Fitzpatrick, who had been so cruelly stitched up by the Ahern machine two years ago.

What the scale of Ahern's defeat illustrated more clearly than anything else is that Fianna Fáil is being held responsible by the electorate for the nature of the economic disaster being suffered by the country. Everybody knows there is an international recession, but the 'crony capitalist' connections with builders and certain bankers, symbolised by the Galway tent, have provoked a fierce backlash against the party following the bursting of the property bubble.

Brian Cowen and his ministerial colleagues, including the two Green Ministers, are now suffering for the sins of the Ahern era. Unfair as that may be, Cowen cannot avoid accepting a share of responsibility for what went wrong. During his period as minister for finance, he failed to act to stop the bubble getting bigger and, in his first six months as Taoiseach, he was consistently behind the curve in responding to events.

Paradoxically, the Government is now broadly on the right track, having got to grips with the scale of the economic disaster which has derailed the public finances. The problem is that the Fianna

Taoiseach Brian Cowen leaving the Tullamore Court Hotel, Co. Offaly, at the weekend, aware of his party's poor showing in the local and European elections. Photograph: James Flynn/APX.

Fáil–Green Party coalition has no mandate for the kind of decisions that were required, and will continue to be required, to get the public finances in order.

Minister for Transport Noel Dempsey, with characteristic honesty, conceded yesterday that it was 'a very, very bad result' for the party, as he accepted the scale of the defeat. He rightly pointed out that it was the negative reaction to the 'very difficult but necessary decisions' taken by the Government in recent months that had provoked such a disaster.

Backbench Fianna Fáil TDs who complain that Ministers are out of touch with the impact of their decisions miss the point entirely. Tough decisions are required to get the country back on track and there is no way that pain can be avoided. What the public appears to be saying, though, is that it won't accept that pain from Fianna Fáil.

The substantial cuts in income suffered by workers who have been lucky to keep their jobs, never mind the pain inflicted on those who have lost them, is something that people are simply not willing to accept from this Government. The Opposition's claims that bankers are bailed out while ordinary people suffer may be a trite simplification, but it clearly resonates with the electorate.

The spectacular triumph of George Lee in Dublin-South illustrates the public mood, particularly in middle-class Dublin.

The majority of voters have simply lost all faith in the Government's ability to do the job and it is hard to see how that mood will turn around while the coalition continues in office. The problem is that as long as the mood remains, the ability of the Government to do its job will be severely hampered.

The election result exposed the fallacy of the dictum that all politics is local. Real politics is

Green Party leader John Gormley arriving at the count of the Dublin Central and Dublin South by-elections, at the RDS in Dublin. Photograph: Niall Carson/PA Wire.

national, particularly in times of crisis. While some politicians can buck the trend, due to local popularity, the national mood swept away many councillors who had actually worked very hard for their constituents over the past five years.

The anti-Government trend was most pronounced in the large urban areas, but it rippled all across the country in a wave that has made Fine Gael the biggest party in the country for the first time, that gave the Labour Party its best local election result to date and that left Fianna Fáil nursing its worst result since the party was founded in 1926.

The impact on the Greens has been even more severe. The party has had the bad fortune to be in the wrong place at the wrong time. It has suffered a near total wipe-out in the local elections, and a dismal European election result. Every single one

of its Dáil seats would be under threat in an early general election, and the party has some real soul-searching to do in the weeks and months ahead.

The Fine Gael decision to table a motion of no confidence means that pressure on the Government will continue this week and there will be no respite until the Dáil summer recess next month. The pressure on the coalition will remain intense for as long as it survives.

Next week the Taoiseach will attend the critical EU summit in Brussels, which is due to finalise the legal guarantees to enable a rerun of the Lisbon Treaty in the autumn. Over the summer, reports from 'An Bord Snip Nua' on reform of the public service and the Commission on Taxation on reform of the tax system will have to be digested by the Government, and decisions made on what measures to adopt.

There have to be serious doubts about the ability of such a badly wounded Government to take decisive action on such important issues, deliver a Yes vote to Lisbon and then formulate another swingeing budget.

THURSDAY, 11 JUNE 2009

Lee's Speech Is a Wake-up Call for Sleepy Ministers

Miriam Lord

A man stood up yesterday and made a speech. A proper speech. It was measured and thoughtful. From the heart and delivered without recourse to a script. It was very good, but the most unusual thing about this speech was that it was delivered on the floor of the Dáil by a TD.

Seldom is wonderful. If George Lee keeps up this high standard, he might succeed in bringing a bit of credibility back to a chamber where deputies routinely troop in with their allotted pages and read them into the record.

To be fair, not all TDs are products of the regurgitation school of public speaking. Nonetheless, when one of their number comes in and delivers an address worth listening to, it is a standout moment.

The new deputy for South Dublin had a lot to live up to, arriving in the Dáil for his maiden speech at the end of the longest fanfare in Irish political history. He rose to speak just after midday. The Fine Gael benches filled up rapidly behind him.

Minister for Europe Dick Roche held the fort across the way on the Government side. He smiled across indulgently at George – not because he was the new boy, but because that is what Dick does.

Unusually for the time of day, the press gallery was packed. Down in the members' bar, the place hushed when George rose to bowl his maiden over

and the volume was turned up on the television. There was a lot riding on this speech. What followed was a powerful presentation from a skilled communicator. His colleagues were impressed and relieved.

With a broadcaster's ear for a soundbite, Lee honed in on a jocose remark by party colleague Charlie Flanagan when the Taoiseach opened the two-day confidence debate on Tuesday.

'It's so bad, even three of your Ministers are asleep!' spluttered Charlie, as the drowsy Cabinet members blinked at his affrontery. The tired trio who appeared to be grabbing 40 winks were later identified as Snoozy O'Cuív, Martin Manzzzzergh and Sleepy Cullen.

However, all three would insist that they were merely thinking deep thoughts. Deputy Lee hasn't

Fine Gael leader Enda Kenny and party TDs welcome to Leinster House the party's newly elected TD for Dublin South, George Lee. Photograph: Matt Kavanagh.

Cartoon by Martyn Turner.

been very impressed by what he described as the 'antics' he has seen in the chamber.

'While I was here yesterday there were three Ministers over there asleep,' he said, shooting a glacial stare across the floor. Rather pointless, given that it was absorbed by Dick Roche's smirk. 'It's just not good enough, in my view, that people in this House can take that kind of attitude to the difficulty that people are suffering out there.'

To put it in context, he noted that in the short space of time when those Ministers were in the land of nod, 'that would have been another 152 people on the dole.' Aghast at the idea that somebody might think TDs occasionally fall asleep in the chamber, Leas Cheann Comhairle Noel O'Flynn rushed to mark George's cards.

'Members here may be in meditation, they may have their eyes closed or their heads down. They're meditating, they're contemplating, but I have never seen a member from any side of the house deep in sleep.' His serious point of information was somewhat marred by guffaws from his fellow ruminators.

Noel mustn't have been looking very hard. Over the years, we've seen quite a few of Dáil Éireann's finest snoring their brains out. There is one Fianna Fáil deputy who does a very good imitation of the leaning tower of Pisa, listing in his chair as his eyelids dust the desk.

But back to Fine Gael's star signing, who delivered his address from a berth on the front bench. Is this a sign of things to come? (By the way, an FG staffer tells us that the party has already received over 800 CVs from eager young West Wing types who want to become a parliamentary assistant to George.) In another novel parliamentary departure, the new deputy was very fair in his treatment of the Government and had words of praise for Taoiseach Cowen and his Ministers.

But then he got stuck in, highlighting in particular what he called 'the human consequence of economic collapse'. Brevity is not George's strong point. 'Your time is up,' said the Leas Cheann Comhairle. 'For today.' The gallant Michael Ring stepped into the breach. 'I don't mind givin' way to talent,' he roared.

Because of his selfless gesture, Michael was left with 'only two minutes and 20 seconds' to make his contribution. It's amazing how much roaring a man can manage in 140 seconds.

George's maiden outing went down a storm with his own party, but not so well with Government speakers, who began taking their first tentative steps towards tearing strips off the new arrival. The celebrity sheen is beginning to wear off, although not with junior minister John Moloney,

who extended a warm welcome to new deputies O'Sullivan and Lee. 'I was not present in the chamber when the deputies received an official welcome, although I met Deputy Lee in a corridor.'

With the numbers on their side, the Coalition was never going to lose its motion of confidence in itself. Again, George wasn't impressed. The administration is only in power because it did little sweetheart deals with Independents. Running a country 'isn't all about roads and bridges and drains', he argued.

It is when your name is Jackie Healy-Rae, who is reportedly doing very nicely out of the Government's difficulties.

To the delight of his colleagues, Lee finished with another good soundbite. He directed it at the 30th government of Ireland.

World and European champion athlete Sonia O'Sullivan in University College Cork, where she was conferred with an honorary doctorate of arts. Photograph: Michael Mac Sweeney/Provision.

Historian and biographer of W.B. Yeats Roy Foster and actress Fiona Shaw, at the National Library in Dublin for a talk which was part of the library's Summer's Wreath series, marking the 60th anniversary of the poet's death. Photograph: Alan Betson.

'I've got a message – Come in number 30, your time is up!' And Dick Roche beamed indulgently.

SATURDAY, 20 JUNE 2009

On her Canine Friend, Lola

Upfront, by Fiona McCann

In a column a few weeks back I made passing reference to my flatulent dog. That she is prone to deadly, gaseous emissions which could fell a grown man – or woman – at 50 paces is not in dispute. Yet her sulking since the appearance of said column is a daily reminder that to characterise her thusly is to give a one-dimensional representation of my three-dimensional, four-legged friend.

For Lola is more than the sum of her windy parts, and it is only fair that if gombeen dogs like Marley have entire books and films in their honour, Lola should get more than an afterthought about her odorous releases. Consider this my attempt to make amends, my Marley Me but without the dead dog at the end.

Lola L. Lolerson, to give her full name – a seven-year-old, medium-sized, gravy-eyed mutt whose breed is described on her veterinary certificates as 'brown' – is the only dog in my life, though truth be told, she's not the first. Knowing that she probably won't get round to perusing this piece herself, I can admit to loving other dogs before her. My first were two frisky Scottish Terriers of delightful temperament, whose only drawback as dogs go was the fact that they were invisible to everyone but me.

Having beseeched an unresponsive Santa Claus for years for some canine company, I finally accepted the beardy lad was not going to cough up, so I took matters into my own hands. The result was two adorable, if imaginary, dogs – a black and a white Yorkshire Terrier called Paddy Black and White Whiskey – no prizes for guessing the inspiration. My parents were initially amused until I began walking the dogs to Mass and tying them up outside the church, the whole parish watching as I patted the air.

Shortly thereafter, Santa caved in and Bruno arrived, a small brown Jack Russell who spent most of his all-too-short life waiting for a crack in the front door so he could make one of his desperate bids for freedom. After Bruno left us for a place where the door is always open, along came Toby, a squat ball of fur with the charm of a Kennedy, who could persuade a death row prisoner to give up his last meal with just a whimper.

When Toby died, my parents called it a day on dogs, and it wasn't until Beyoncé and I became acquainted that another four-legged friend, the all-important subject of this column, trotted into my life. When she and I were introduced, I knew that if I didn't win her heart, his would be out of the question.

Thankfully, I had one major advantage: my gender. Lola has a weakness for women, and while she will treat most males with ill-concealed disdain, she's fierce fond of a bit of skirt. In the end, all it took was a limitless supply of surreptitious dog treats for her to become my number one fan, so devoted that any separation, even a trip to the bathroom, left her whimpering in my wake. So we moved in together, and life ever since has been hairier, smellier, noisier, wetter – she likes a good, slimy face-lick, does Lola – and improved in just about every way.

Just one look at her tiny, upturned head that's a little too small for her body can instantly transform my mood. She tries to disguise this imperfection by sitting in such a manner as to maximise the effects of foreshortening, folding her corpulence behind two skinny, sandy legs as she hops from one to another in undisguised excitement. Her own moods are changeable, too: she can sulk like a woman scorned when, for example, you make public her flatulence, and comes over all the grand dame, stretching her jowly neck when affronted and refusing to be won over by anything other than food.

For Lola, impeccably mannered in all other respects, food is her one vice: she will, in fact, steal candy from a baby should the opportunity present itself. Her life revolves around eating – oh, the slavering joy of it! – and walking, which she does with equal joy, tail wagging, ears flapping, though usually without expending too much energy, and definitely not when it's raining. Never a fan of excess effort, she draws the line entirely at running, and watches me bolt out the door in disbelief, following me for 30 seconds before insisting that I slow the pace to something more along the lines of a manageable amble which allows her to investigate every empty crisp packet on the way.

Sleeping is more her thing, as Lola likes to conserve the bulk of her energy for eating and barking at the doorbell. Then there is the aforementioned flatulence, carried off with affected nonchalance, her expression unchanging as she unleashes toxic fumes on unsuspecting visitors who have been taken in by her doe-eyed gaze.

But oh, when she wakes in the morning and tries to scratch her face, sandy paws wiggling at her eyes; when she snuggles her warm furry body against me and plonks her head in my lap; when I open the door after one of those days and am greeted by a bounding ball of delight at my return – all this is why I will now scoop up a mess twice daily. All this for the sight of her wet snout hanging out of the car window, taking the air.

Coast Guard crew rescue Eibhlín Ní Dhochartaigh and her daughter Jean (2) from the upstairs window of her flower shop after a flash flood in Derrybeg, Gweedore, Co. Donegal. Photograph: Eoin McGarvey.

Lola L. Lolerson may never make it Marley Me big, but she is the sweetest, calmest dog I've ever known and the sight of her furry ears is a bulwark against all the ills that life throws at me. The fact that she's not a figment of my imagination is one bonus. The fact that she comes with such a good-looking master is another.

SATURDAY, 20 JUNE 2009

Lost Competitiveness Did its Damage Long Before Credit Crunch

Garret FitzGerald

Twice recently I've tripped on a couple of steps at home, banging my head on the same wall each time! I feel that this is a metaphor for the fact that since early 2004 I have been banging my head against a wall of political and media indifference to the disastrous national loss of our cost competitiveness.

Checking back on my contributions to this column I find that in the period of five years from early 2004 to the end of last year 2008 I raised this issue here no less than 16 times.

The point I was making is a simple one: by the spring of 2001 we had reached full employment, which, of course, brings severe inflationary pressures, as employers compete with each other for workers. In such a situation the first duty of a government is to seek to ensure that full employment is not undermined through an excessive growth of current public spending – for that would overheat the economy.

In the early years of this decade, prudent public spending became an absolute economic imperative – because at that very moment, for good reasons, we were about to lock ourselves into the euro. This eliminated any possibility of offsetting a

USA Breakdancers perform their prize-winning routine during the Street Performance World Championship in Merrion Square, Dublin. Photograph: Dara Mac Dónaill.

higher inflation rate than that of our euro zone partners by means of a currency devaluation.

The maintenance of moderate spending growth should not have been politically difficult, for it would merely have involved continuing the prudent policy of preceding governments, which, throughout the previous five years from 1992 to 1997, had held the growth of current spending to a modest 7 per cent a year.

Unhappily, at the very start of the new decade, our then minister for finance Charlie McCreevy instead chose to reverse the prudent spending practices of his predecessors, boosting the growth rate of current public spending to 11 per cent in 2000, to 12 per cent in 2001 and then, in 2002, to a phenomenal 14 per cent. Because of that spending spree, by the end of 2002 our annual current spending was (and has since remained) more than €8 billion above what it would have been had the

current expenditure growth rate of the period 1992 to 1997 been maintained.

While it was McCreevy who initiated this dangerously inflationary policy, then taoiseach Bertie Ahern and the cabinet of that period (five of which, including Brian Cowen, are members of Government) share collective responsibility for its immediate consequences.

These consequences were that in the first half of this decade our prices and pay rates rose twice as fast as in other euro zone countries, and by 2005 were – and still are – 15 to 20 per cent above those of our European competitors.

On what was that extra €8 billion a year spent? A fair share of it went on two benchmarking exercises to boost the pay of public servants, whose pay was already higher than that of equivalent private sector workers. And more of it went on increasing the actual numbers of civil servants – which today are higher by 22 per cent than in 1999 – and of local government employees, up by 27 per cent.

Moreover, the number of workers in the health service has since then increased by over half! This includes an additional 1,900 administrators, on top of the surplus of such workers that the HSE had inherited from the over-staffed health boards.

Largely because our pay costs rose so far above such costs elsewhere in western Europe, after 2002 the remarkable export boom of the Celtic Tiger years came to a sudden end. Since then, the annual growth rate of the volume of goods exports has been reduced by nine-tenths, and 30,000 jobs have been lost in manufacturing. When combined with a drop in export prices, the virtual stagnation in the volume of Irish goods exports consequent on our loss of competitiveness has reduced our export earnings from this source by 10 per cent.

Let's be quite clear about it: all this happened well before the housing bubble burst, and well before the credit crunch. And before the 2007 general election. Yet in that election, the fact that reckless government budgetary policies had pushed our prices and pay costs up far beyond those of our European competitors was almost totally ignored by all the political parties, as well as by most of the media, then and since.

This competitiveness crisis was effectively swept under the carpet by all concerned, despite the fact that it left our economy hugely vulnerable to the housing bubble, which we might otherwise have been able to survive without too much damage. Even if the housing crisis resolves itself – as it will eventually – and even if we also survive the banking crisis, the fundamental labour-cost problem created by indefensible budgetary policies remains to be dealt with.

Unfortunately, while the housing bubble and the banking crisis are the subject of endless debate, there is little or no discussion of the competitiveness crisis, the resolution of which is possible only by pay adjustments that have begun in the private sector. We will not know until later this year how large these adjustments are likely to be.

In these circumstances there must be serious concern about what Jim O'Leary in yesterday's *Irish Times* described as 'rash and foolish' guarantees reported to be on offer by the Government to the public sector unions, 'handcuffing pay and pensions' in that sector. Depending on the scale of the current reductions in private sector pay rates, this could have the undesirable effect of opening a fresh gulf between pay levels in these two sectors.

PS: I would like to repeat a suggestion I made some time ago on radio. Now that Ministers have accepted a cut in their salaries, why is a similar cut not being imposed on the pensions of former ministers, like myself?

In the past, every time that ministers' pay has gone up, my pension has been increased correspondingly. Surely the same principle should apply when ministers' pay is cut.

FRIDAY, 26 JUNE 2009

Moving Encounter with Master Storyteller

Eileen Battersby

In its long, glorious history has the elegant Examination Hall of Trinity College Dublin ever seemed quite as relaxed a place as it was yesterday morning? The great Canadian writer Alice Munro arrived for a press conference marking her victory over an impressive shortlist of major novelists. It proved unexpectedly moving probably because the small, ladylike, white-haired Munro is direct, quick-witted and businesslike.

She doesn't deal in mystery, there was no artistic torment and she gives the impression of being able, within minutes, of describing everyone in the room. Looking at her were admirers who could smile at each other and claim to have read all of her stories. She is that kind of writer. Read one Munro story and you will continue to read them.

Alice Munro, winner of the International Man Booker Prize, at Trinity College Dublin. Photograph: Alan Betson.

She also belongs to one of the most gifted literary tribes in the world; while their US counterparts can look to eastern Europe, many of Canada's writers, including Munro, draw on a different heritage – that of Scotland and Ireland. When Munro mentioned that being praised in Canada often led to uneasy sensations of doubt, Irish members of the audience sighed in sympathy.

Writing about the ordinary brings its problems, particularly if it happens to be in your own town. Munro made it quite clear that instead of being overly popular at home, she knew what it was like to anger people through her stories.

Lives, her own and others, are her material.

Previously won by the Albanian Ismail Kadare and Nigeria's Chinua Achebe, the International Man Booker Prize, worth £60,000, is based on a body of work. Munro's Canadian editor famously said on hearing the news that Alice Munro didn't need to win it. She doesn't – Munro has one of the most loyal followings enjoyed by any writer. Fellow writers also revere her.

As early as the late 1980s, Munro's name was mentioned by critics alongside masters of the short story such as Cheever, Updike, Pritchett and Trevor. The truth is a great short story can say far more than a novel.

No interviews were being granted; in fact it was not even possible to greet her personally, which is a shame as Munro's genius lies in bringing a reader into the world of her fiction, so her admirers responded by asking a question, framed within offering congratulations on the prize. 'I write stories', she said, 'to find out what happens to the characters placed in human, real life situations.'

She likes connections and seeing where a story will go; there are no tricks. She grew up in a small rural community. On marrying at 20 she had become a mother within a year. Suddenly she was living in a suburb in British Columbia, in Vancouver. Reading was important to her and she read Flannery O'Connor, Eudora Welty and Carson McCullers, all Americans.

The photographers worked on, taking pictures from all different angles, the sunlight shone in the long windows and Munro, who will be 78 on 10 July, listened to the questions, often replying with an anecdote. She remembered one headline announcing 'Housewife finds time to write story', and paused to add, 'I wonder were they asking if I was a good housewife?'

She has won many prizes and has also judged many prizes. Since her International Man Booker win was announced – and this award is really a salute to a life's work – observers have consistently praised Munro. It is as if the prize is really an excuse for discussing her work.

The real victor is the short story form. Munro yesterday admitted to the difficulty of pursuing a proposed novel beyond 'page 30'. Of her one novel to date, *Lives of Girls and Women*, which was published in 1971 and followed her debut collection *Dance of the Happy Shades*, winner of the Governor General's Award, she said, 'If you look at that novel it is really a series of stories.'

Her stories are long, but never too long. Yet somehow she always seems to say more than most novelists writing at 10 times the length. It is about art and wisdom, the life experience, as Munro pointed out: 'I look back on stories I wrote a long time ago and I know I'm not the person I was then.' Sometimes they go wrong.

Munro recalled that a story she wrote while

Playwright Brian Friel trades words with Seamus Heaney, after being presented with University College Dublin's highest award, the Ulysses medal, at a Bloomsday ceremony at the campus. Photograph: Julien Behal/PA.

staying in Ireland for four or five months, some 15 years ago, went very wrong. She threw it out. It all comes back to place. And place is vital to Munro. Her first marriage ended after 20 years and she returned to her native Ontario. It is the place she knows and has watched over the years.

Munro is interested in the layers that make up a life. Describing her new book as the bleakest stories she has ever written, Munro seemed pleased. For all the perfection of her art she has often experimented.

Munro, who has made a study of the lives of women, has above all, in her adroitly apolitical way, proved herself to be consummately political.

Later, novelist Colm Tóibín pressed the panel for why it had chosen Alice Munro. The discussion, dominated by US novelist Jane Smiley, took reading as a theme. Smiley spoke about how the initial list was reached and how it slowly became smaller.

Referring to herself and her fellow judges, Indian novelist Amit Chaudhuri and Russian satirist Andrey Kurkov as 'writers and readers, not critics and scholars' – overlooking perhaps that Chaudhuri is an outstanding critic – the stage was set for a wonderful discussion as to how Alice Munro was chosen from a field that included James Kelman and Antonio Tabucchi. Chaudhuri, who has explored the several literatures of India, referred to how writers on the edge tend to come to the centre. He has many interesting things to say, but didn't get the chance.

It soon became evident that the real story was how this panel ever reached an agreement. Tóibín looked on with gentle resignation.

Audible gasps met the panel's agreement that the short story is an endangered form. No chance, not as long as Alice Munro's stories are read.

In her long citation Jane Smiley praised Munro, the writer whose engagement with the private is also universal.

Trinity College choristers singing 'Palestrina', part of a Hassler Mass and *Gaudeamus Igitur*, an early 18th-century celebratory song in Latin, escorted Alice Munro into a banquet worthy of a winner.

SATURDAY, 27 JUNE 2009

Fallen Idol

Brian Boyd

The child star deprived of a childhood has become the adult deprived of adulthood. The tragic irony of Michael Jackson's untimely demise at the age of 50 is that in three weeks he was supposed to have been launching a spectacular comeback with a

Michael Jackson fan Terri Pines signs a large poster at the Staples Center in Los Angeles, site for the late pop star's memorial service on Tuesday. Photograph: Chris Carlson/AP.

Fans cast shadows on a makeshift memorial for the late pop star Michael Jackson, outside the Jackson family home in the Encino section of Los Angeles after the announcement of his death. Photograph: Matt Sayles/AP.

series of shows at London's 02 Arena. Now, in keeping with the pattern established by the early deaths of Elvis and John Lennon, the comeback will be huger than anyone could ever have expected.

Expect next weekend's album and singles chart to feature the undisputed King of Pop at No. 1 as people rush to the shops to commemorate him in the only way they see fit: by listening again to the mesmerising sounds of arguably the most unique performer in popular music history.

Jackson had already postponed the opening night of his comeback in London by a week because he was concerned about his physical fitness and his ability to recreate his trademark exhilarating dance moves. It is not inconceivable that his strenuous fitness routines of the last few weeks precipitated yesterday's fatal heart attack. 'I don't know how I'm going to do 50 shows. I'm not a big eater – I need to put some weight on,' he said just

last week. All 750,000 tickets for his first live shows in over a decade had been sold.

For someone who set the bar so high in terms of the quality of his live performance and its stunning choreography, Jackson – as the professional he has been since six years of age – was determined that these new shows would not be anaemic imitations of his now legendary Thriller-era live appearances but performances that would somehow re-establish him as a global music phenomenon.

But the squeeze was always on: it's no secret that the star had severe financial problems ('he's a millionaire spending like he is a billionaire,' said one aide) and he needed to do this run of shows which would have netted him a minimum of €50 million. But he has had serious health problems.

His body had been ravaged by demanding dance routines and he had talked openly about his addiction to various prescription drugs. There was also talk of a serious lung complaint and continuing complications arising from his many plastic surgery procedures. When he last appeared in front of the media – to announce the comeback shows in London a few months ago – his frame was skeletal and his skin was pallid. He barely made it through the two-minute press conference.

Even the show's promoters were uneasy about Jackson's ability to carry off the shows – a complex insurance policy was drawn up and it is understood that the singer had to provide a medical report before any contracts were signed. Bookmakers offered odds that he wouldn't even make the first concert date.

All this will be forgotten over the coming weeks as the image of the unnaturally transformed and bizarre-looking 50-year-old is replaced by that of the fresh-faced young black man who reshaped the musical landscape. There simply is no gainsaying his massive musical contribution although some, both inside and outside the music industry, remain repelled by the allegations of child abuse that were made against Jackson.

Jackson's life, even as a child, never resembled anything approaching 'normality'. Born into a working-class family in Indiana in 1958, he was fast-tracked into the family business – the child pop group that comprised Michael and his siblings: The Jacksons. Defying the then colour bar in the US music industry, the wholesome-looking all-singing, all-dancing Jacksons were nationwide pop phenomena and at the age of six Jackson was a semi-professional who would be asked for his autograph by adult fans. Jackson has talked about how his father physically and verbally abused him as a child and how he developed an eating disorder (provoked by a fear of his father's discipline) by the age of seven.

Before he was a teenager, *Rolling Stone* magazine had singled him out as 'the main draw' in the now-named Jackson Five and remarked very favourably on the child's 'piping voice, grown-up

hoofer and vocal inflections similar to Sam Cooke, James Brown, Ray Charles and Stevie Wonder'.

Even at this stage his record company had decided that it would put all its chips on his solo career and he was assiduously groomed as a superstar-in-waiting. He began releasing solo albums which were musically innovative in how they fused soul, r'n'b and pop. His *Thriller* album of 1982 was a revelation – an edgy amalgam of diffuse musical styles, which became the biggest-selling album of all time (with over 100 million copies sold).

Thriller managed to satisfy both the musical purists and casual one-album-a-year fans. All pop is rooted in black music stylings and what Jackson and producer Quincy Jones managed to do was to join the musical dots between 'black' and 'white' music. *Time* magazine wrote on its release: 'Jackson is a one-man rescue team for the music business. A songwriter who sets the beat for a decade. A dancer with the fanciest feet on the street. A singer who cuts across all boundaries of taste and style and color.'

Though MTV never admitted this as official policy, the station at this time did not play videos by black artists. With the global success of *Thriller*, the station had no choice and Jackson became the first black musician it featured.

Jackson has talked about how it was at this time, with his face appearing on television screens and magazines all around the world, that he first became painfully self-conscious about his appearance. A pigmentation disorder (perhaps stress-related) called vitiligo caused his skin to form irregular white patches and the treatment for it effectively left his skin 'depigmented' – hence its ghostly look. It always distressed the man who could remember not being served in 'white-only' restaurants as a child that he was accused of trying to become white.

He first went under the plastic surgeon's knife after *Thriller*'s success – having a rhinoplasty procedure ('nose job') and a cleft (supposed to be 'cute-looking' but anything but) inserted in his chin. He had numerous follow-up 'corrective' plastic surgeries – to the extent that he became virtually unrecognisable from how he appeared on the cover of *Thriller*.

There was a concurrent deterioration in his behaviour: he developed 'eccentric' habits (although at least half of the more bizarre claims about his lifestyle are merely tabloid invention) and he desperately seemed to be trying, as an adult, to reclaim a childhood he never had.

He lived in a glorified amusement park, spoke in a squeaky child's voice (that's not his real voice by the way, it's an affectation) and surrounded himself with children.

In a music industry more used to the vices of drink and drugs, Jackson was indulged as being benignly weird. But 'eccentricity' spilled over into 'sinister' in 1993 when a 13-year-old boy, Jordy Chandler, accused the singer of child molestation. The charge was dropped, however, when Chandler later refused to testify against his 'best friend Michael'.

It is alleged that Jackson paid Chandler's family €20 million to have the charges dropped. His friends, who later quizzed him about why, if he was innocent of the charges, he paid out $20 million, report that Jackson said he just wanted the case to go away because a trial would do irreparable damage to his music career. In the wake of the Chandler incident, Jackson developed a drug addiction and his childhood bulimia re-manifested itself.

Janet Jackson, Randy Jackson, Tito Jackson, Marlon Jackson, Jackie Jackson and Jermaine Jackson, at Michael Jackson's public memorial service held at Staples Center in Los Angeles. Photograph: MJ Memorial/Kevin Mazur/AP.

Michael Jackson in concert, c. 1990. Photograph: Kevin Mazur/WireImage.

Shortly after, in what many at first took to be an April Fool's joke, it was announced that Jackson had married Elvis Presley's daughter, Lisa Marie. The unlikely alliance was believed by many to be an attempt at rehabilitating his image in the public eye. The couple divorced two years later. To this day, Lisa Marie Presley says the couple married out of love – telling this journalist once that she and Jackson enjoyed 'a normal sex life'. Jackson went on to marry a nurse, Debbie Rowe, with whom he had a son Michael, and a daughter, Paris.

When the couple divorced in 1999 she handed over full custody of the children to Jackson. Again, the rumour was that a large sum of money changed hands. Jackson also has another son, known as 'Blanket' (real name Prince Michael II), conceived through artificial insemination (he has never revealed the mother's identity). It was Blanket who he so recklessly dangled over a hotel balcony in Berlin a few years ago.

By this stage of his life, he had dried up as a creative force. He would never rescale the heights of his *Thriller* and *Bad* period and his last ever album, 2001's *Invincible*, was a tepid and unloved affair. Tours came and went and there were still coruscating stage routines but that was all soon to be relegated to footnote status by the screening in 2002 of a documentary in which Jackson was interviewed by the journalist Martin Bashir.

In the programme (an attempt to capture the 'real' Michael Jackson), the singer said that he shared his bed with a 12-year-old-boy, Gavin Arvizo. When Bashir expressed no little surprise – given previous allegations – the singer artlessly said these were just 'innocent sleepovers'. A few months later – after, according to Jackson, he stopped financially supporting Arvizo's family – he was charged with seven counts of child molestation on Gavin Arvizo. The trial was a media circus and Jackson was eventually acquitted of all charges.

A mental health professional who studied Jackson's psychological profile surmised that he was not typical paedophile material but instead had regressed to being a 10-year-old boy. It was some reflection of the celebrity culture we live under that during the trial all of Jackson's albums re-entered the charts due to huge sales and, even as he was walking daily into the courtroom, parents would be holding up their young children (normally white, normally young boys) and shouting: 'Please take him Michael; he will be your new friend.'

Only his die-hard fans (of whom there are many) believed that Jackson was a 'victim' – betrayed by those closest to him for financial gain. For everyone else there was the troubling evidence of a middle-aged man admitting he shared his bed with young boys.

He never toured or recorded anything of real substance following the Arvizo case. There were sporadic sightings of him in different locations around the world behaving strangely – in Las Vegas last year he was seen walking the streets in his pyjamas. There still was a way back musically after the court case (the music industry tolerates all forms of egregious behaviour by its main players) but Jackson was a busted flush.

It was the loss of his beloved Neverland mansion in California last year (due to financial difficulties) that by all accounts prompted his live comeback shows. With no new material to push, these shows were only going to be 'greatest hits' affairs, done out of economic necessity. But even the most cynical observer couldn't stifle the thrill that this magnificent performer could still dazzle and daze – that he somehow could recreate that moment of light entertainment shock and awe when he famously debuted his trademark 'moonwalk' dance at a Tamla Motown concert in 1983.

To the millions who applied for 02 tickets, his appearance, the state of his health and all the disturbing allegations simply didn't matter when weighed against the chance of seeing the most important and influential musical figure since Elvis Presley.

The music industry will now have its Princess Diana moment. Meanwhile, the record-pressing plants are already working overtime to service the public need for Jackson product, and before the weekend is out, all the over-priced 'commemorative' tat will be hitting the shelves to get one last return from a man who has been public property and a financial cash-cow for the majority of his life.

But do try to look again at that famous rendition of 'Billie Jean' at the Tamla Motown Concert of 1983. It is one of the most stunning and electrifying pieces of music television ever. As a writer, singer and dancer he was a genius. And this shy young man from Indiana was responsible for demolishing a reprehensible colour bar in the music industry.

As for all the assorted 'lifestyle' issues – to paraphrase Yeats: you simply can't separate the singer from the song or the dancer from the dance. Indeed, Jackson represented a 'beauty born out of its own despair'. F. Scott Fitzgerald got it right all those years ago: 'Show me a hero and I'll write you a tragedy.'

Doing What it Takes to Make a Star Perform

Brian O'Connor

Being in charge of the most valuable racehorse in the world isn't keeping John Oxx from his sleep these nights, although he could be forgiven a little restlessness at the sort of ground dilemma that still

Trainer John Oxx. Photograph: Tom Honan/INPHO.

makes Sea The Stars a less than definite starter in tomorrow's Irish Derby. Funnily enough, though, the Curragh trainer has noticed he is waking up earlier in the morning. 'But then maybe that's old age!' he laughs.

There's an ease to the quip that hints at the pay-off to such early starts. When a colt like Sea The Stars is outside, peering over a stable door and hollering for his grub, it must be difficult not to bounce out of bed.

Estimates as to how much Sea The Stars is worth right now fluctuate dramatically. A figure of €50 million has been bandied around, but there are plenty who will tell you that such a price is conservative with an extra large 'C'. Others venture that double that might not be enough to buy him.

The reasons are simple enough. As a racehorse, this hulking brute of a colt has already done enough to suggest he is one of the true greats of the modern era. Just three weeks ago he became the first horse for 20 years to complete the 2,000 Guineas-Derby double at Epsom. That he did so in a manner that suggests his best may be yet to come only emphasised the suspicion we are looking at a truly exceptional talent.

However, even if he wins tomorrow's Irish Derby by a furlong, it probably won't affect his intrinsic value much. That's because as a half-brother to Galileo – himself a dual-Derby winner in 2001 but, more importantly, currently the world's most lucrative stallion – Sea The Stars is a potential goldmine which runs on hay and water.

Such considerations, however, don't impinge on his trainer's thoughts. What happens after Sea The Stars finishes racing is not his problem.

During it, though, Oxx is the man with his hand firmly on the steering wheel. Right now the greatest challenge of all is to get this remarkable young athlete to deliver on all that talent. Come next winter, the worst thing of all will be to have some 'what if's' hanging over his head. It's easy, then, to understand Oxx's determination not to risk the horse on unsuitable ground.

That's the flipside of having Sea The Stars in your yard: the pressure not to mess up. Oxx might already have had a parade of champions through his Currabeg stables during the last three decades, but that doesn't mean he doesn't feel that pressure just as much.

'It's primarily a responsibility, training any horse. That's why when they pass the post in the front the main emotion you feel is relief: that they've done what you hoped and expected they would do.

'My responsibility is to have everything in place to allow them perform. If you want to call that responsibility pressure, then it's pressure. But to me, at this stage, it's work, what I'm paid to do,' he says.

Such a perspective is typical of the man who will be 59 in just over a fortnight. The slight figure doesn't appear substantially different to how he did when he first took out a licence to succeed his father in 1979. But it's not just physically that Oxx presents a reassuring constancy.

A resolute determination to maintain perspective on the horse game's heaving tide of opinion and fashion has run through his last 30 years. Never one to get carried away, whether the subject be beast or man, he remains a rock of sound thinking in what can be a ruthlessly self-interested industry. And yet there doesn't seem to be much doubt that Sea The Stars has managed to smuggle a way underneath his trainer's skin.

More than once this season, Oxx has described Sea The Stars as a 'great horse'. Without wishing to get all 'Dunphyesque' about the inflections that can be put on the word 'great', the phrase is significant. Oxx uses words with a care often lacking among some colleagues who prefer a more scattergun approach.

We are talking about a man who guided true champions like Sinndar, Azamour, Ridgewood Pearl and Alamshar, and didn't start tossing superlatives around until he had the perspective of their whole careers in front of him. But this horse has always been a little different.

No laughing matter as Ray Coady Snr, from Dunnamaggin, Co. Kilkenny, checks out the runners and riders at the Dubai Duty Free Irish Derby at the Curragh. Photograph: Brenda Fitzsimons.

'He has everything. He can go any speed and showed enough stamina to win at Epsom, even though there are some who say there is still a stamina doubt. I'm sure there will be a stronger pace on Sunday than there was at Epsom, and so questions will be asked and answered again. The stamp of the real greats is that they keep improving. We will see how this horse stands up to it, but so far he looks the real deal.'

That impression was first made in April of last year when Sea The Stars did his initial piece of fast work under Michael Kinane. With his pedigree and outstanding appearance, the embryonic champion was always a stand-out, but plenty of horses have boasted looks and relations and run like snails.

'The good ones usually show up straight away. The odd one might start slowly and come through, but as soon as Mick rode him in fast work he said he felt like a three-year-old,' remembers Oxx.

'We also came to the conclusion fairly early on that he doesn't really like any dig in the ground, even though he won his maiden on soft. When he ran in the Beresford, it was dead ground but the best we could get at the time and we were lucky to get it. He won, but got tired in the ground,' he adds.

So while the rest of the country has been baking in sunshine this week, one man has been anxious about the weather not being hot enough. Oxx's reading of ground conditions in the Curragh straight has not always been the same as the track's authorities, and the steel underneath the mild demeanour is seen in his determination to keep the options open for Sea The Stars.

Some will see that as an indication of concern about the Epsom winner lasting the mile-and-a-half at the Curragh, which is popularly believed to be a stiffer stamina test.

'I don't have a view on whether the Curragh is more of a stamina test. I just don't. Some people will tell you it is stiffer, but I met Willie Carson at Ascot and he simply said, how many Epsom winners have failed at the Curragh for want of stamina?

'His argument is that Epsom is very tough. They are blowing at the top of the hill, and, while they might freewheel down the hill, it's still a tough mile-and-a-half,' Oxx says.

What seems certain is that a stiffer pace will be guaranteed by Ballydoyle's platoon of runners. Kinane's decisiveness when faced with a comparatively mickey-mouse tempo at Epsom was enough to make the result seem almost inevitable from the time the field turned Tattenham Corner.

The 50-year-old former champion bows to no one in his admiration for Sea The Stars, and Oxx describes the veteran jockey's input as 'invaluable'. What happens once the gates open tomorrow the trainer is happy to leave to Kinane.

'Over the years all my jockeys have ridden fast work and they have a big role in what happens here. We work as a team,' he says.

'I think everyone was surprised by the pace at Epsom. It was the opposite of what we all thought it would be. The result was our fella was a bit over-eager. He didn't pull as hard as it might have looked, but if they'd gone faster he would have settled better.'

The inference is that going faster tomorrow might play into the hands of Sea The Stars. Going fast for a long time is all very well but ultimately it

AC/DC guitarist Angus Young on stage at Punchestown during the band's Black Ice world tour. Photograph: Alan Betson.

The remains of murder victim Tommy Joyce (20) leaving St Francis of Assisi Church in Priorswood, Clonshaugh, north Dublin, after his funeral Mass. Joyce, a known drug dealer, was shot dead on 17 June in the Grove Lane halting site on Malahide Road, Coolock. Photograph: David Sleator.

can leave you vulnerable to a class horse with a turn of foot. That's the Oxx runner to a tee.

'Years ago, practically all Derby horses ran in the Guineas, but these days we are inclined to pigeon-hole horses too much. I'm sure other good horses I've trained would have run well in a Guineas, but they wouldn't have had the speed of this one.

'It's not as if he won the Guineas after coming off the bridle three furlongs out and getting up on the line. He was going well the whole way.

'The Irish Derby is a race that means a lot to us. It's at our local track and it has been good to us. This time we have a great horse going there, and if he gets the trip he must have a great chance.'

Whether he gets the opportunity to even run now looks like being the sort of last-minute call that his trainer would rather avoid but is well able to make.

Media Proves Deaf to €1.87m Leech Message

Noel Whelan

This week a jury of ordinary citizens sent a €1.87 million message to the Irish media, but unfortunately it fell on deaf ears. On Wednesday, the jury found that a series of articles printed in the *Evening Herald* in 2004 damaged Monica Leech's reputation by wrongly suggesting that she was having an extra-marital affair with Minister Martin Cullen.

One would have thought a finding that our only national evening newspaper libelled somebody to that extent would have attracted a wave of media comment about the damage to her reputation. One might have hoped that with such a damning verdict, the media, always and rightly quick to hold everyone else to account, would have undertook some self-examination.

There has, however, been almost no media analysis of how such a story could come to be written, how such editorial judgments came to be made, and how and why it has become common practice to distort and doctor photographs of the type used to support the vulgar insinuations which formed the basis of the *Herald* stories.

Almost all media coverage of the outcome of the Leech case has focused on the size of the award and how the awarding of such an amount reinforces the need for libel law reform.

The National Union of Journalists issued a statement on the outcome on Thursday. It was posted on its website under the tabloid-like headline 'Big libel award against Independent Group blasted'. The NUJ did not denounce the stories in which Leech had been grievously libelled, but instead directed its anger at the level of damages. Having decided to comment on the case, even pending a Supreme Court appeal, it is very peculiar that the NUJ, which after all purports to be a professional body with a code of conduct to which journalists must adhere, had nothing to say about the quality of the work of the journalists who wrote and edited these *Herald* stories.

The short NUJ statement did describe it as 'unfortunate' that much of the media coverage in 2004 focused on Leech rather than on the decision to appoint an outside PR consultant to the Minister's department. It is shocking, however,

Monica Leech with her husband, John, leaving the High Court in Dublin after her libel victory over the Evening Herald *newspaper. Photograph: Stephen Collins/Collins.*

that the NUJ has so little to say about the substance of the jury's verdict. The import of the verdict was not only that the focus of the *Herald* reporting was out of place but that the stories contained a sleazy and inaccurate innuendo. What the NUJ should have posted was a statement headlined: 'Bad journalism in coverage of Leech story blasted.'

In the tone of their remarks on the verdict, the NUJ, the *Herald* and other media commentators have sought to characterise the jury's 'lottery-sized' award as the crazy, arbitrary decision of an amateur collection of citizens not working under judicial direction.

The amount of money awarded to Leech was clearly much greater than should be required to compensate her for the damage done, but the reason why a randomly selected jury of 12 persons with no axe to grind chose to award her this level of damages merits consideration.

On TV3 on Thursday night, Vincent Browne suggested one rational explanation for the size of the award, pointing out that an award on such a scale was necessary to re-enforce how wrong the story was, and that a smaller award might leave a suspicion in the public mind that there may have been some truth to the story. There may be something in that analysis.

The reach of the various stories suggesting Leech and Cullen had been having an affair was such that there may still have lingered a suggestion of no smoke without fire. It is a reflection of the impact which a false story given this prominence can have that, 4½ years later, a jury felt that an award of €1.8 million was necessary to extinguish any residue of the libel.

It may, however, also be that the majority of this jury, having been shown the articles in question, having watched the way in which the *Herald* sought to defend their publication, and being ordinary consumers of media in Ireland today, concluded that only an award on this scale could both adequately punish the particular media outlet and prompt change in the media generally.

The jury might not have been strictly legally entitled to be punitive in this way, but it says something about how annoyed they felt and what the evidence revealed about how sectors of the media operated.

New defamation legislation currently going through the Oireachtas will enable a judge to give a jury some guidelines on the amount of money appropriate where people are libelled, but even under the new law a jury will still be free to choose the amount. There is every likelihood that if such bad journalism persists, juries will still be minded to punish it by awards on this scale.

In an opinion piece in its Thursday edition, the *Herald*, with typical overstatement, described the award as a 'clear and present danger to press freedom'. It is, however, the failure of the media industry and the journalistic profession to recognise and check falling standards that poses the real risk to press freedom.

If an award of €1.87 million to a plaintiff won't make them sit up and take action – then what will?

THURSDAY, 2 JULY 2009

Unionism Must Take On Bigots in its Midst

David Adams

A few weeks ago, about 130 Romanian people had to take refuge in a church hall after being forced to flee from their homes in a unionist part of south Belfast. Scores of frightened men, women and children were bussed to safety, with belongings they could carry packed into plastic bin-liners.

Who could fail to have been moved by the images on our televisions and in our newspapers? Who in Northern Ireland could fail to feel anything other than sympathy, anger and a deep sense

A construction worker, suspended from a crane, rescues a woman who fell into the Des Moines River in downtown Des Moines, Iowa. Photograph: AP/The Des Moines Register, Mary Chind.

of shame? Lamentably, quite a few people if subsequent radio phone-in programmes are anything to go by.

At the time, senior unionist politicians and Protestant Church leaders were unequivocal in their condemnation. However, after windows were broken last week in an attack upon the church that had given refuge to the fleeing Romanians, the former were noticeably absent from media coverage of those calling to offer sympathy and support to the pastor and his congregation. They must have felt they had already done enough.

A few weeks before the expulsion of the Romanians, a Catholic man, Kevin McDaid, was beaten to death by loyalists in Coleraine in a sectarian attack.

Local unionist politicians condemned the murder of Mr McDaid, but were also at pains to point out that sectarian tension had been high in the area for some time. Whatever their intention (and I'm sure it was honourable), this was widely interpreted as offering 'mitigation'. The feeling was compounded when, disgracefully, no senior unionist politician saw fit to join local Protestant Church ministers at Mr McDaid's funeral.

What sort of message did their non-attendance send to the victims and the perpetrators of hate crime? Last weekend, Anna Lo, an Alliance Party MLA for south Belfast, was warned by police that her home was under threat of attack because of her vociferous condemnation of the intimidation of the Romanians.

Originally from Hong Kong, Ms Lo has lived in Northern Ireland for nearly 35 years, and is our only MLA from an ethnic minority. She is a shining example of everything a political representative should be.

In the early hours of Tuesday morning of this week, shots were fired through the window of a house in Ballymena. Apparently, it was the third attack within a month on the (Protestant) couple who live there. Their 'crime' was, as members of the local residents association, to challenge people engaged in hanging loyalist flags from every lamp post in the religiously mixed housing development.

Almost as an aside, there have also been threats made this week against the Belfast Islamic Centre, and against Chinese businesses in south Belfast.

The list of hate crimes perpetrated by members of the unionist community goes back as far as you care to look. It seems set to continue as far forward as we can imagine – if unionism doesn't decide to do something about it. The reaction of unionist politicians in particular to an attack is always the same: a few words of condemnation, and then move on.

To call this woefully inadequate is an understatement. It is long past time that unionists at all levels acknowledged that there is a major problem with bigotry within their community, and, more importantly, decided upon a comprehensive plan of action to eradicate it.

It's no good whingeing about getting an unfair press. The media doesn't invent what it reports upon. If the problems didn't exist in the first place, if horrific incidents weren't happening every other week, there would be no room for negative publicity.

Nor is it any good pointing the finger at nationalists and saying, 'They're just as bad.' In all honesty, that doesn't appear to be the case – and, even if it were, it's hardly an excuse.

Of course, all unionists aren't racist, sectarian, homophobic bigots; far from it. And of course there are those within the media and in politics who would like nothing better than to label them all as such.

But the people doing the real damage to unionists are not the media or political opponents, but the virtually unchallenged bigots within their own communities. Unionism is adding massively to its own negative image, almost colluding in it, by doing little or nothing to tackle bigotry.

Besides, image should not be a primary concern. This should not be reduced to a competition between nationalism and unionism. The safety and wellbeing of members of our society is all that matters. Individually and collectively, unionists must become relentless in their active opposition to the poison of bigotry.

Parents and political leaders, church ministers and schoolteachers, and every other unionist with a voice, must constantly be lecturing and hammering home a message of tolerance – especially to children. Unionists must make it clear that bigoted attitudes will no longer be tolerated within their communities. It is nothing short of shameful for politicians and others to make do with a few back-covering condemnatory remarks after each incident.

Bigotry is causing enormous pain and suffering within our society and must be tackled. It's long past time that unionists took up the challenge.

WEDNESDAY, 8 JULY 2009

Memorial Service Celebrates Life and Music of 'The King of Pop'

Denis Staunton, in Los Angeles

They had already heard tributes from Nelson Mandela and Diana Ross, and a specially written poem by Maya Angelou, and watched Mariah Carey performing 'I'll Be There', but it was a series of images on a video screen that first brought the crowd at Los Angeles's vast Staples Center to its feet.

The fast-moving compilation showed Michael Jackson as a child star, a handsome young black man and in the many mutations of his later years. But all anybody noticed was his soaring, soulful voice and his unparalleled dance moves which seemed to defy the laws of dynamics.

'The more I think about Michael Jackson, the more I think The King of Pop is not big enough for him,' Motown founder Berry Gordy had said a few minutes earlier. 'I think he is simply the greatest entertainer that ever lived.'

Before the memorial service began, images of Jackson flashed on a giant screen at the back of a stage laden at the front with banks of flowers. Jackson's brothers, each wearing a black suit, a white shirt, a yellow tie and a single, silver, sequined glove, carried the dead singer's casket to the foot of the stage.

In the front row, surrounded by 17,500 of Jackson's fans, sat his father, Joe, his mother, Katherine and his three children, Prince Michael, Paris and Blanket. Celebrities included Smokey Robinson, Stevie Wonder, Usher, Jennifer Hudson and actor Brooke Shields.

From the start, however, it was clear that the memorial service was not just a celebration of Jackson as an entertainer, but as a black man. A gospel choir performed a number of times during the event and one speaker after another stressed Jackson's role as an African-American pioneer. 'He never gave up dreaming. It was that dream that changed culture all over the world,' civil rights campaigner Al Sharpton declared in a fiery eulogy.

At every pause in the 2^1/$_2$ hour event, fans shouted, 'We love you, Michael! and Shields and Usher appeared overcome with emotion as they took the stage. The most affecting moment came at the end, however, when Jackson's 12-year-old daughter Paris broke down in tears as she gave the final tribute to her father. 'Ever since I was born, Daddy has been the best father you could imagine and I just want to say I love him very much,' she said.

An Orangeman at the Independents Orange Parade in Rasharkin, Co. Antrim. Photograph: Charles McQuillan/ Pacemaker.

*Michael Jackson's children, Paris Jackson (left), Prince Michael Jackson I and Prince Michael
Jackson II, on stage during the memorial service for their father.*

Nobody mentioned directly the child abuse allegations which dominated Jackson, but Sharpton had a pointed message for the dead singer's children. 'I want his children to know: there wasn't nothing strange about your Daddy,' he said. 'It was strange what your Daddy had to deal with. But he dealt with it anyway.'

The video montage that brought the crowd to its feet early in the service included images of lurid tabloid headlines about Jackson's cosmetic surgery and his private life and just a few spoken words from the star himself. 'I must say, it's good to be thought of as a person, not a personality,' he said.

WEDNESDAY, 8 JULY 2009

'There Ain't Ever Going To Be Another Michael'

Denis Staunton, in Los Angeles

As the 17,500 people who had won tickets to the memorial in an internet lottery filed into the Staples Center alongside celebrity guests, a hard core of fans waited outside. Near the arena, hawkers sold commemorative T-shirts, posters and buttons as a convoy of 16 black limousines carrying the Jackson family and friends drove up, followed by a hearse carrying the dead singer's casket.

Many of the fans waiting outside wore short trousers, white socks and black shoes in imitation of Jackson and a few wore his trademark sequined glove. Most were good-humoured, although there were a handful of protesters carrying placards about child abuse allegations against the dead star – and some fans were feeling disgruntled.

Hours before the first guests arrived at the Staples Center, Gwen Smith and her daughter Andrea were waiting behind a steel barrier nearby. Both large African-American ladies wore matching black Barack Obama T-shirts and Gwen was carrying a big black umbrella to keep the sun off.

Neither Gwen nor Andrea had tickets to the memorial service and neither of them was happy about the arrangements.

'I think it sucks,' Gwen said. 'We've already paid a lot of money to see Michael perform and buy albums and posters, T-shirts, jackets. Whatever Michael was selling, we bought it. We should be able to see him. I don't think it's right.'

Jackson's coffin had been driven from Forest Lawn cemetery in the Hollywood Hills to the Staples Center, but fans outside had no chance to see it. 'Why don't they put him in a glass casket and dress him up in his nice little outfit that he'd wear when he performed and parade him down the street for all the fans?' Andrea said. 'Why didn't they do that? We'd all stand on the side of the road and throw roses at him.'

'Right, like they do in Europe for the pope,' said Margie Fedor, a short, blond, middle-aged woman who had travelled from Canton, Ohio for the occasion. 'We could pay our respects like that and they could parade him all the way down to wherever he's going to be buried.'

Los Angeles city authorities decided against a public procession because it would cost so much to police, but Andrea wasn't having any of it, pointing out that a local basketball team had recently paraded in victory through the city. 'If they could do it for the Lakers, why can't they do it for Michael?' she said.

'How about the drag queens?' her mother butted in. 'In Hollywood, they had their little gay parade and they let them parade up and down the street half-dressed.'

If the fans outside the Staples Center were unhappy with the organisers of yesterday's event, they were furious about what they saw as the media's excessive focus on the child molestation charges against Jackson. 'We want to honour him,' Margie said. 'He didn't do anything to those little boys. He was a caring person.'

The music business has changed so much in recent years that nobody is ever likely to break

Brazilian Adelson Maia from The Rhythm, in Dublin Castle during the launch of Culture Night 2009. Photograph: Brenda Fitzsimons.

Jackson's record with *Thriller*, the biggest-selling album of all time.

Gwen, Andrea and Margie agreed that they were witnessing the passing not just of their favourite star but of the last of the great celebrities.

'There ain't ever going to be another Michael Jackson, ever. Never ever,' Andrea said. 'We'll always love Michael Jackson regardless of the things people said about him.'

THURSDAY, 9 JULY 2009

An Irishman's Diary

Frank McNally

I f ever there can be a happy funeral, it must be something like the one I attended last weekend in the north Monaghan village of Threemilehouse. The dead woman, Brigid McQuaid, had passed away peacefully aged 92. She was surrounded at the end by devoted children and grandchildren, some of whom had returned from Australia when the call went out. And among the many tributes paid to her was a fine old tradition whereby friends and neighbours dug the grave.

There were more than a dozen men involved in this task: Protestant as well as Catholic. The serious digging was left to the younger ones. But even bystanders contributed, in the form of conversation or other gifts deemed necessary to the occasion. I believe there were bottles of whiskey involved.

The deceased had been a famous dressmaker, who once drew customers from several counties on either side of the border. The concept of coat-turning survives now only as a metaphor for disloyalty. But it was economic necessity once; and in poorer times, Brigid's skill in turning coats, thereby making new coats, was much sought-after.

Her former customers, or at least their descendants, swelled the large attendance at the funeral mass. A heavy shower fell on the church during the service, by way of a blessing. Then the sun came out in time for the burial in a hill-top cemetery, where there was much conversation and laughter. I attended the Monaghan-Armagh football match in Clones later that day; and if either event could be described as grim, it definitely wasn't the funeral.

Communal grave-digging is a disappearing tradition, sadly. It is going the way of other funerary customs, like the one referred to in John McGahern's book *That They May Face the Rising Sun*: namely the arrangement of graves – indeed whole cemeteries – to point east, the expected path of the resurrection. (Not that Christians thought of this first; the architects of Newgrange had a broadly similar idea.)

For good or bad, probably both, the famous Irish wake is not what it once was either. In his

2006 travelogue-cum-memoir, *Booking Passage*, Irish-American Thomas Lynch wrote movingly about the phenomenon with the combined sensibilities of a poet and an undertaker (based in Detroit). In his professional capacity, he performed funerals for all faiths and none; but he thought his Irish ancestors had elevated death to an art form. 'Communal theatre' he called it.

Not all old Irish funeral customs were so healthy. One of them may or may not have inspired a famous sketch on Dave Allen's 1970s TV show, featuring a race between two funeral processions. Either way, there was a belief once widespread in Ireland and Scotland that the latest arrival in a graveyard was obliged to perform onerous duties for the other spirits.

When two funerals coincided, therefore, both sets of relatives would vie to spare their deceased loved ones such work, and trouble often ensued. *The Penguin Guide to the Superstitions of Britain and*

Annie, played by Nastasia Vashko, in the centre, and fellow orphans at a photocall to announce details of **Annie the Musical** *to be staged at the Olympia Theatre in Dublin. Photograph: Brenda Fitzsimons.*

Ireland mentions a case in Cork in 1897, where one party locked the cemetery gates beforehand to thwart the other, only for the rivals to 'throw' their coffin over the wall and celebrate victory with a 'wild cheer'.

It wasn't always as restrained as that. A similar case in Dublin in 1835, reported by the *London Times*, 'led to a full-scale riot, the deaths of two mourners and the serious injury of many more'. The last recorded mention of the custom here was 1923, so by now it can be presumed both late and unlamented, or so one hopes.

From Threemilehouse on Saturday, I finally made the short pilgrimage to another cemetery: the Church of Ireland one at St Molua's, Drumsnat, barely two miles away. This is one of the oldest Christian sites in Ireland, dating from 500 A.D. But I went there mainly to see the graves of Mary and Emily Wilde, half-sisters of Oscar, who died locally in tragic circumstances.

Their headstone was barely legible until we wiped the surface with wet grass. Then the names and ages – 22 and 24 – stood out along with the epitaph, which includes the line: 'They were lovely in life and in death they were not separated.'

This is poetic euphemism. The sisters were 'love-children' of Sir William Wilde, raised in Monaghan by his clergyman brother Ralph, away from the eyes of Dublin society.

They were attending a Hallowe'en Ball in a private house in 1871 when Emily's muslin dress caught fire. Whereupon Mary ran to help, and her dress caught too. Both died from their burns.

If Irish Catholics made an art form of wakes, Protestants did so with cemeteries. It probably helps that they tend not to be densely populated, although the judicious planting of trees is a big part of it too. But especially in rural Ireland, Protestant graveyards are invariably picturesque and profoundly peaceful places. St Molua's is no exception.

Under a yew tree nearby, I noticed what at first looked like a marble bust, sculpted in the Greek style. Then it moved. And on closer inspection it turned out to be a sheep: one of a small flock of ewes that (safely) graze in the old part of the cemetery, where all that was missing was a Bach soundtrack.

Very Vulnerable, Very Fragile

Kathy Sheridan

Ronnie McManus was not a man to defer to authority. His defiant court uniform of T-shirt and tracksuit bottoms was not designed to flatter

Fourteen-year-old Melissa Mahon.

his squat, burly frame. If demeanour matters to the men and women of a jury, it was probably ill-advised. But it sent a signal. The crude tattoos marking his temple, ears and neck and swarming over his powerful arms, the obsessive gym work and pit-bulls mentioned in evidence, all served the image of the hard man who kowtowed to no one.

If not scribbling interminable screeds for his counsel's immediate attention, he was officiously ticking off passages of evidence or rustling noisily through a plastic bag for his sheaves of notes.

The constant scribbling lent him an air of pro-fessional detachment as evidence mounted of a pitiless controller and manipulator, a muscular 44-year-old who claimed to care for a frail 14-year-old child, yet dumped her body like a dog; a father who never flinched as his young daughters gave heinous evidence against him by video link; a man who answered a flat 'no' when detectives asked if he loved his daughter, yet had boasted in media interviews of heroic custody battles in the UK.

He had no friends in court, no work-mates, since he wasn't known to hold a job for any length of time. Of a lengthy parade of soccer mates called to testify about kickabout times and places, only a few exchanged doleful greetings with him during breaks. Relatives on the witness list turned up for a day but when not called upon to give evidence they left and never returned. Since the defence chose not to go into evidence, no insights were offered into the forces that shaped the twisted, fantastical mind-set of 44-year-old Ronnie McManus.

'There's a new world coming and he's the king on the throne, and when it all kicks off there will be a battlefield. That's why he has his dogs. That's why he has to keep fit,' said a still-devoted Ruth Nooney, a 25-year-old who became engaged to him in 2007 after he helped to tune her television and now has a baby by him.

'He can be intense, obsessive, belligerent,' says a man who met him, 'but he can also do funny, vulnerable, charming, affable.' So when Angelique

Sheridan met him in a post-office queue in August 2006, it was 'brilliant' to begin with. The romance lasted six weeks, long enough for Sheridan to become acquainted with McManus's children and their ever-present friend, Melissa Mahon, a tiny, slightly-built 14-year-old, described variously as 'very vulnerable' and 'very fragile'.

McManus explained her presence by saying that Melissa had told him she was being abused and had asked for his protection. His daughter Samantha, however, said that Melissa was in love with her father and was three months' pregnant by him. Sheridan also claimed that McManus said in front of her and his elder daughter Shirley – who denied it – that he would strangle Melissa rather than go to prison for her. By the end of the affair, Sheridan was terrified of her boyfriend and con-vinced that Melissa was in serious danger.

It was Melissa Mahon's tragedy to come under Ronnie McManus's influence in her most vulner-able years. She was 'a great dancer' and loved country and western music, said her mother soon after she went missing. But she was also a child from a troubled background, uprooted from her native London at 13 to move to Ireland. Her parents, Mary and Frederick, met in Sligo in 1969 when Mary was in her mid-teens. They moved to London, where they had their 10 children. On a visit to Sligo in July 2005, Mary Mahon got a shared house and, when a second bedroom became available, summoned her family home to stay.

Life for the Mahon family was never smooth. There was contact with English social services while in the UK; two older daughters were on the child-protection register and three were taken into foster care, one overnight. Melissa alleged she had been sexually and physically abused by her father and mother respectively. In court, Mary Mahon said she was aware of the allegations and did not accept them, saying her husband had suffered enough. Asked why she had declined to make a statement to gardaí when her daughter went miss-ing for the final time, she implied that her daughter

Ronald McManus leaving the Central Criminal Court after he was sentenced to life imprisonment for the manslaughter of Sligo teenager Melissa Mahon in 2006. Photograph: Courtpix.

was no longer part of the family at that stage: 'It wasn't up to me. She wasn't in my care.'

On their arrival in Ireland, the family were already flagged to the HSE because of prior contact with British social services. Melissa's poor school attendance began to attract closer scrutiny from the HSE and social worker Catherine Farrelly become involved in mid-2006. That Melissa found common cause with McManus's daughters living nearby in the Rathbraughan estate was hardly surprising. They too had lived a chaotic, peripatetic life around the UK before moving to Sligo.

In the late 1970s, Ronald McManus left his native Sligo for England, where he met Lisa Conroy, the mother of his three daughters. In a

Sunday World interview before her father's arrest, his elder daughter described a life of abject poverty and violence at his hands and said they were on the 'at risk' register as a result. She and her siblings were placed in foster care for a year, she said, after which they were returned to their father's custody. Their mother, who had had another child, left the family home with the baby.

In 2000, a fight between McManus and a London drug dealer resulted in a gun attack on their home in which he and his then nine-year-old daughter sustained bullet wounds. They agreed to give evidence and were placed on a witness-protection programme (when he changed his name from Dunbar to McManus, his mother's maiden name), moving between various locations before ending up in Scotland. The return to Ireland in 2005 was because of 'racist abuse, no other reason', he told the *Sligo Weekender*. When it emerged he had actually been ejected from the witness-protection programme, he said it was because he had campaigned for better conditions for protected witnesses. His daughter said it was because he was 'constantly fighting' with the villagers.

Both families were only a year back in Ireland in summer 2006, and at this stage, Melissa was spending virtually all her waking hours with the McManuses. There was evidence of anti-social behaviour, shop-lifting and a house break-in by Melissa and the younger McManus girls.

McManus's daughter Samantha alleged that Melissa told her she was in love with McManus and they were having a sexual relationship.

On 4 August, Mary Mahon rang the gardaí to say Melissa had stayed out overnight but she was not unduly concerned; her daughter was probably hanging around McManus's house, she said, and she had decided to leave Melissa to come home in her own good time. No action was taken and almost three weeks elapsed before the HSE realised that Melissa was missing.

On 22 August, Catherine Farrelly, who had been pushing for a resolution of Melissa's school problems, became suspicious and asked Mary Mahon what was going on. Unhappy with her answers, Farrelly took her to a Garda station and then went with a garda to visit Ronnie McManus. He told them he had no idea where Melissa was but said he was worried about her and demanded to know why the authorities hadn't looked for her earlier – a constant theme of his exchanges with social services and the gardaí. He also invited them to search the house. They chose not to. If they had, according to his daughter, they would have found Melissa hiding behind the sofa.

Soon after, McManus contacted the HSE to say he had managed to make phone contact with Melissa, manoeuvring himself into a position whereby he became the HSE's sole conduit to the missing child. He could lay down the ground rules; thus the bizarre arrangement by which Catherine Farrelly was obliged to travel in his car with him and his daughter to a remote meeting place to see Melissa. There was evidence that to avert suspicion he ordered his daughter to greet Melissa as though she hadn't seen her for a long time.

As a 14-year-old runaway alleging abuse by her parents – about which she never made a statement – and refusing to go home, Melissa was finally placed into residential care by the HSE. But in her 16 days in the centre, she was absent as many nights as she was present. A social care worker testified to continuing high levels of contact between Melissa and Ronnie McManus and of finding a picture of McManus under Melissa's pillow. The HSE obtained a court order prohibiting contact between Melissa and Ronnie McManus.

Garda analysis of a phone owned by McManus would confirm grounds for concern. Between July and October 2006, more than 30 per cent of that phone's traffic comprised contacts to or from the 14-year-old child. By contrast, just 12 per cent comprised contacts with his then girlfriend, Angelique Sheridan.

Melissa's behaviour deteriorated. She and another resident were suspected of drinking and sniffing gas. Gardaí found both of them in bed with three older youths in a house in Cultragh, and when they tried to return them to the centre, the girls cut their arms with glass and threatened to slit their wrists.

After this, it was decided to try temporary foster care and on the evening of 13 September Melissa was taken to the Co. Leitrim home of Jane McCall, who described her as a charming, polite and pretty girl.

But at 11.30 p.m. that night, the child took a phone call that caused her to run out of the house in her bare feet and to knock on a stranger's door, asking him to ring Ronald McManus, her 'father'.

McManus – who was tiring of her neediness,

according to Angelique Sheridan – contacted the gardaí and social services, and Melissa spent the night in Manorhamilton Garda station with Catherine Farrelly, her social worker. The next day, back in Sligo, Farrelly persuaded her to try another foster family. The social worker also bought new clothes for her in Dunnes Stores and took her to the HSE offices to get changed and washed.

But sometime in the 15 minutes while Farrelly was out making arrangements, Melissa Mahon disappeared. She was seen heading towards the Rathbraughan estate by two women from the residential centre who were driving past. They called out to her but didn't follow her.

It was 14 September and the HSE's last sighting of Melissa Mahon.

Melissa survived another six days, according to Ronnie McManus's younger daughter. She said

Melissa was in their home on the evening of 20 September when gardaí called looking for her, but Melissa ran out the back door and jumped over a wall.

Only three people can say what happened in the next 24 hours. McManus chose not to take the stand. In their evidence, Samantha and her younger sister agreed on certain key points – that they saw their father in his bed that night, lying behind Melissa with his arm around her neck.

Samantha testified that Melissa's face was purple, her lips blue and that she was making a high-pitched noise as she struggled to breathe. They both agreed that McManus put her into a sleeping bag tied with a blue tie, and told of how they helped their father dispose of the body on the banks of the River Bonet, an area close to where the remains were found 15 months later, after a

Sheepdog pup Maury and three Bactrian camels from the Great European Circus on Garryvoe Beach in east Cork before a circus performance. Photograph: Daragh Mac Sweeney/Provision.

garda search triggered by information from Samantha. Her sister, who claimed to have seen the body in the sleeping bag before it was dumped, said that it had become half purple and half white.

However, the defence argued that the jury should focus on the divergences in the sisters' accounts, which, said Brendan Grehan SC, were 'radically inconsistent and inherently incredible'. Earlier in the trial, while cross-examining Prof. Marie Cassidy, the State pathologist, he drew attention to the sisters' evidence that they had seen their father lying in bed behind Melissa in a 'spoon' position, with his arm across her throat. Counsel wondered about that position 'as a mechanism for causing death'.

Prof. Cassidy replied that an arm on the neck or armlock can cause sudden collapse or death due to pressure on the sides of the neck.

'Could it happen in a potentially friendly situation?' asked counsel. 'It could happen without a person intending to cause harm,' she agreed.

Fifteen months later, the 14-year-old's skeletal remains would be found, chewed by animals and blown around the shores of Lough Gill, with only a few teeth in a jawbone to identify her. McManus's two younger daughters had finally reported her killing and led investigators to her dumping ground.

His younger daughter's confused feelings were evident in her early willingness to blame herself and her sister for Melissa's death.

Samantha told the court her younger sister was in love with their father and had been 'brainwashed' and terrified by him. They helped him dispose of the body because 'my dad was a very controlling man and we were scared of him . . . We were only young girls at the time'.

In the meantime, in October 2007, Ronnie McManus had been arrested and questioned by the gardaí about an alleged sexual offence and is expected to face further charges. Both his younger daughters were taken into care.

As for Melissa Mahon, we know little more about the lost, vulnerable child who believed she had found her saviour in Ronnie McManus. A few weeks after her daughter went missing for the final time, Mary Mahon told the *Sligo Weekender* she was at a loss to explain it.

Maybe Melissa had found it difficult to adjust to Sligo after London, she suggested: 'I don't know why she went away really. Young girls are sometimes hard to understand.'

MONDAY, 13 JULY 2009

Tree Image Provokes Mix of Devotion, Reserve and Scepticism in Rathkeale, Co. Limerick

Patsy McGarry

It was raining. Mud and puddles were all around. In the grounds of St Mary's church, Rathkeale, last Saturday afternoon, a solitary young man stood before the tree stump, his head hooded against the elements.

He contemplated the madonna-shaped piece of wood. He reached to it. He caressed it. A gust of wind blew a Padre Pio leaflet from the stump base where it had been placed with a St Martin de Porres card, an Our Lady of Lourdes medal, a miniature rosary, two earrings.

He reached into the mud and picked up the leaflet, lightly stroked the mud from it and put it back. He stood up to take a photo on his mobile phone.

He looked at it, studied it and then at the wooden object. He went to the tree stump again and furtively – as though he felt he shouldn't – began to pick at the remaining bark on the wood until a little came away. Discreetly he put the reward in his pocket as others began to gather. He walked away, speaking to nobody. What private agony there? What consolation sought from lines on a tree stump?

Cartoon by Martyn Turner.

At early Mass yesterday, Fr Willie Russell spoke about Mary. He pointed to her statue at the altar to his left. 'All it is is a statue, a reminder of Mary,' he told the congregation. There was 'so much evidence of the presence of Mary in the Bible', he continued, 'but in her humility she always remains in the background.'

He reminded the congregation that 'the only words she said in the Bible were at the wedding feast of Cana, when she said "do whatever he tells you".' It was also her message to us, he said. And he referred to Luke's gospel and all that Mary had stored in her heart. 'She remained in the background,' he repeated.

A man leaving the Mass later remarked how on one occasion last week there had been hundreds at the tree stump 'and just three in the church'.

Frank Marham (79) is not happy with Fr Russell. 'He's against it,' he said of the fuss over the tree stump. Frank is not. He regretted that candles and flowers left at the stump as offerings the night before had been removed overnight. It was the same yesterday morning. 'If it was left to Fr Russell it would be gone,' Frank said.

Standing by the tree stump, he told another devotee the story of how someone had gone to Fr Russell during the week testifying belief that the tree stump featured the madonna and child and the priest's response had been to hold up a piece of wood and say: 'Do you see Michael Jackson in that?' 'Sure that was hardly right at all?' said Frank.

Nora Sheridan spoke of the hundreds who had come to see the stump and that it was bringing 'all sorts together to pray, black and white, young and old'.

A more sceptical Eugene McNamara remarked that he had seen 'known criminals praying there this week. If it brings out the good in them, then what harm?'

A group of young Traveller girls placed hair bobs at the bottom of the stump which they had wrapped around stones. 'For luck,' one of them explained.

Helen Collins from Rathkeale could see 'what they're on about'. She felt, however, 'it might be a case of what you want to see'.

At the later Mass yesterday, parish priest Canon Joseph Dempsey spoke of scandals in the Church and the need for repentance and forgiveness. He did not refer to the would-be apparition in the grounds.

TUESDAY, 14 JULY 2009

'I'm not Sure about the Aubergine'

John Waters

Some years ago, a school-friend came back after decades on the foreign missions and, after we had talked for an hour, looked me in the eye and said he felt I was missing my destiny by a shade. After the initial irritation, it got me thinking. What might I be if not what I am? This idea soon became a liberation. I would gaze in the mirror into my Armada eyes and wonder if I might come from a long line of toreadors. I tried things out: maybe I should be a composer, an ice skater, a football manager . . . In such a mindset, I have fewer discomfort zones than once I might.

Still, sitting in one of the dozen seats reserved for press at an A-Wear launch for Peter O'Brien's summer collection in Dublin's CHQ Building, it is impossible to avoid noticing that I am one of just four men among a thousand women who is not a roadie or a photographer. I share the seating with a dozen older ladies, at the centre of a growing throng, as though trapped within a congregation of exotic birds as dusk falls, the chattering dying away from the edges to allow the elders to speak.

Sitting in the escalating hum of expectation, it strikes me that I am present for a ritual that, like much in our culture, suggests fixed, instant meanings, serving to transport us to a premature knowingness that misses the mystery.

It is 7.30 p.m. and the 1,000 women and four men have gathered around the catwalk/altar. Most of the women are aged between 30 and 50, approximately the target area. A few appear to be in pairs or groups, but many, although interacting, appear to be alone. By far the best-dressed women are the older ladies seated around me. Most of the others are dressed nondescriptly, with only a handful of trouser-suits or other ensembles suggesting a sense of occasion. Most are like the women I see in shopping malls, carrying paper bags with clothes and shoes I always assume must be infinitely more spectacular than what they are wearing.

In one of his writings, Pope John Paul II told a pointed story about two priests emerging from a church and being visited by the striding presence of a beautiful woman. One looked instantly away, recoiling from the temptation. The other looked squarely at the woman and even turned to admire her further as she passed. John Paul asked: which priest acted properly? His answer was that each had done the right thing for himself: one, being immature, had rightly avoided the danger of looking at the woman in a reductionist way; the other, having arrived at a point where he can see her in all her created beauty, was able correctly to enjoy this fine example of God's handiwork.

I fear I am going to have similar issues seeing beyond the dancers to the dance of Peter O'Brien's creations. But the models, although beautiful, are functional abstractions who barely insinuate themselves, though it is impossible not to note their extreme thinness.

Peter O'Brien's clothes are exceptionally striking in a way I do not expect. The colours are pure, vibrant, but in minor keys: navy and aubergine, and turquoise and duck egg – with and without polka dots – and a pale cream. There are white

John Waters at the Peter O'Brien for A-Wear summer collection 2009 in CHQ, Dublin. Photograph: Matt Kavanagh.

macs, poplin skirts and chiffons, blouses with bows, two-pieces you can mix and match. I'm not sure about the aubergine, but love the navy and even more the duck egg.

The clothes seem both nostalgic and contemporary, the materials as classy as the designs are classical. I am not surprised to hear O'Brien uses 100 per cent silks and cashmeres. His necklines are high and chaste. He is the same age as I am, and has tired, I intuit, of nothing being left to the imagination. The dearest items are the dresses (€190) and macs (€180); the cheapest, the blouses (€100) and skirts (€120). It doesn't seem excessive, especially as the styles promise to outlast the recession.

As the garments are walked out, I find myself instantaneously adapting them as costumes for a movie whirling up in my mind. I pan around the female faces and wonder if the same thing is going

on for them. Two young women have come to sit on either side of me. On my right is Sharon Keane, who looks like she might lately have been a model, but actually, as Keane Design building and project management, devises shop layouts and interiors. I want to use her as a sounding-board for my tentative theories, but she bashfully declines to be interviewed. She agrees, though, to check my speculations – so if anything of the following is ludicrous, it's all Keane's fault.

Fashion is really hope made material. The designer's gift is an understanding of the dynamics of desire, which concern the expression of harmony with the higher self.

Everything is predicated on sunburst moments poised between the ennui of waiting and the disappointment of realisation. Most women, and increasingly men, spend far more on what they will

Bono acknowledges acclaim from the fans at U2's August concerts in Croke Park. Photograph: Brenda Fitzsimons.

wear for fleeting periods of enhanced expectation than on what they wear for most of the everyday.

Peter O'Brien says women dress for other women, while Keane, forgetting her refusal to be interviewed, says most women ultimately dress for men. I think, after John Paul II, that both are right and wrong. The objective is not pleasing others but using them as mirrors for our innermost desires, daydreamed out as working scripts for the movies in our minds. I might buy a girlfriend one of Peter O'Brien's creations, because I think it will become her, yes, but more because I think it will suit my sense of myself, basking in the radiance of her presence.

In return for being my sounding board, I present Keane with a slogan I have been keeping for someone deserving. This, my most up-to-date apprehension of the dynamics of desire, literally came to me watching a TV advert for chocolate. Being some distance from the set, and my Armada eyes not being what they were, I misread the money-shot slogan as 'Forgive your happiness'.

When I congratulated the manufacturer, who happens to be a friend, he looked at me blankly and said: 'But that's not what our slogan says.' My Armadas had let me down, but I recognised my error as a given inspiration. It seems to articulate everything I have so far intuited about the moment at which all desire is pitched, though it also, in its intimation of total satisfaction, tells a white (chocolate) lie.

When Keane says my slogan is brilliant, I feel no necessity to be coy. I agree it could be used to sell anything that might fit in the reels of fantasy which roll within human minds, to nudge away the inevitable guilt that derives in part from the price to be disbursed and in part from the memory of previous hopes dissolved. The happiness we seek is always either vaguely ahead or achingly behind, splashes of pure bliss caught only in freeze-framed tableaus we call nostalgia.

I learn that the big sellers in the 'pop-up shop' afterwards are the stone macs and the cream lace silk dresses, followed by the turquoise silk ruffle dress – suggesting that the women present are pessimistic about the weather and harbour fantasies that are different from mine. I think as I walk back along the Liffey: so what else is new?

This was the first of a summer series, Discomfort Zone, in which Irish Times *journalists were dispatched to report on matters far outside their usual beat.*

MONDAY, 20 JULY 2009

Fallout from Zoe Collapse Poses Problems for Nama

Business Opinion, by John McManus

And so it begins. The unthinkable has happened. A significant part of the empire of one of the State's biggest property developers has collapsed into insolvency. It was suitably dramatic, with lawyers rushing into the High Court late on Friday to seek protection from creditors pending the appointment of an examiner.

And the reason? It's not that the Zoe Group – as this collection of six Liam Carroll companies is called – is insolvent all of a sudden. It has probably been insolvent for months if not years, but was kept on life support by its banks that have rolled up

Cartoon by Martyn Turner.

interest and not sought capital repayments on bank loans totalling €1.1 billion.

What brought things to a head was the decision of ACCBank – which is owned by Rabobank in the Netherlands – to pull the plug. It was threatening to seek to have the Zoe Group liquidated or placed in receivership on foot of its debt to ACC of €131 million.

There has obviously been a game of poker being played out over the last month or two, with the other banks in the consortium, led by AIB which is owed €489 million, hoping that in the end ACC would roll along with them on the basis that it had more to lose by collapsing the company now than by working with the other banks to try and salvage the situation over time.

ACC, or more specifically Rabobank, thought differently. It's pretty clear now that it wants to call a halt to a disastrous foray into Irish lending and get out.

As one of the few AAA-rated financial institutions left standing, it simply doesn't need it. There will be no happy ending to the Irish property bubble and if you are not in too deep, it's long past time to cut and run.

It raises some very interesting questions for our banks and more pertinently the directors of Allied Irish Banks (AIB) and Bank of Ireland. Given that their counterparts at Rabobank are better bankers than they are – having retained their triple-A status – why are they not doing what it is doing and liquidating Zoe and the other troubled developers?

The reason is obvious. Applying for court protection Zoe said that if the group of six companies, which have total debts of €1.2 billion, was liquidated, they would have a deficit of €900 million. Based on this write-down value, properties on which it has borrowed €1.1 billion from eight banks would fetch €275 million if they went on sale this morning.

That means a 75 per cent write-down for the banks. For ACC it means a loss of about €100 million, which is more than manageable for Rabobank.

For AIB it is a proportionally larger €367 million. For Bank of Ireland, which is owed €113 million, it is €84 million. But when you apply it across the rest of the distressed part of its commercial property book, which would be the consequence of liquidating the other insolvent property companies, you really are looking into the abyss.

Absorbing losses of that magnitude is simply not possible. Both banks would be destroyed and nationalised overnight.

It is in order to avoid just this that the Government has gone down the road of setting up the National Asset Management Agency (Nama) which in practice should allow the banks to absorb these losses over time. This should in theory also allow Nama to achieve better prices for the underlying assets and thus avoid the 75 per cent write-down scenario.

Nama has yet to decide what write-down will be applied to the property loans that will be transferred starting this autumn.

There seems to be a consensus though that it will be in the region of 20 per cent to 30 per cent, depending on the loans in question. It will be based on 'through-the-cycle' values – a guess as to what the property will be worth in the longer term – rather than the price you would get today if you put it up for sale, or 'mark to market' to use the jargon.

The figures given by Zoe Group in its application for examinership are as close as we have come to a mark-to-market event in the Irish market for some years. Even allowing for a bit of exaggeration to make a point, there is quite a difference between 75 per cent and 30 per cent.

This gap is particularly relevant because the presumption at this stage is that in an effort to keep the 'through the cycle' valuations used in the Nama process 'honest', they will be periodically checked against the mark-to-market data. It will have to be one hell of a cycle to bridge that gap.

This brings us to what is the real problem for the Irish banks. It's not whether they should be following the same hard-nosed strategy as ACC or

Rabobank. The real problem for them is what the fallout from the Zoe Group examinership is going to say about the logic and viability of the Nama process as currently envisioned.

Once AIB and Bank of Ireland start swearing affidavits supporting the Zoe Group examinership predicated on the sort of 75 per cent loan write-downs mentioned on Friday, it starts to get very serious indeed.

If the banks and their boards cannot convincingly reconcile the Zoe Group write-downs with the decision to start transferring similar properties and situations into Nama in three months time with write-downs of 30 per cent, then they have no business even thinking about raising money from shareholders. The way out?

Get a move on. Recall the Dáil, establish Nama and short circuit the Zoe examinership.

THURSDAY, 23 JULY 2009

When Science Is Reduced to a Game, Anyone Can Play

John Gibbons

This week marks the 40th anniversary of the historic first moon landing in July 1969. Or does it? Conspiracy theories have persisted over the decades, with books, websites and even organisations dedicated to 'uncovering' Nasa's gigantic hoax.

Laughable? Yes, but these theories are difficult to refute precisely because of the impossibility of proving a negative.

Buzz Aldrin, the second man to set foot on the moon, said last week he felt sorry for the 'gullible people' being taken in by this nonsense. The fact that millions earnestly believe this stuff is neither trite nor trivial.

Of course, if someone writing in a major newspaper were to dignify this hokum by endorsing it, they should expect to be on the receiving end of some well-earned ridicule.

Yet the mockery of evidence-based science by quacks, egoists, curmudgeons and ideologues is anything but marginal.

Earlier this month, *Daily Mail* columnist Andrew Alexander wrote a piece about global warming, reheating a hotchpotch of Junior Cert level science errors in a rambling assault on 'environmental fanaticism'. Yes, you've guessed it, the whole thing is a conspiracy theory, dreamed up by evil scientists involved in the largest conspiracy the world has ever witnessed. Their sinister agenda? The crazed pursuit of research grants, possibly. The author casually dismisses perhaps the strongest scientific consensus ever to emerge on any major issue.

Sadly, this is anything but unusual. Kevin Myers in the *Irish Independent* wears his non-understanding of climate science as a badge of honour, cheerfully recycling, in May 2008, wild claims produced by others of a similar hue, such as the *Sunday Telegraph*'s Christopher Booker. Paddy O'Keeffe's recent piece in the *Farmer's Journal* is so bizarre it's completely off the wall.

So what exactly is going on here? *Bad Science* by Ben Goldacre has some answers. It is a blistering exposé of the blight of science ignorance and the triumph of wilful stupidity. He lampoons all forms of quackery.

Among people working in the media, science literacy is the exception, not the norm. Some journalists, Goldacre reckons, feel intellectually offended by how hard they find science, and so 'conclude that it all must simply be arbitrary, made-up nonsense'.

Commentators thus feel free to 'pick a result from anywhere you like, and if it suits your agenda, then that's that: nobody can take it away from you with their clever words because it's all just game-playing, it just depends on who you ask'.

This may be harmless fun when it comes to Elvis sightings, but in the teeth of humanity's profoundest existential crisis in 100 centuries,

A top pro jump display team shows off some of its best tricks, courtesy of the Dairy Council for Northern Ireland. Pro jumping, also called powerbocking, involves acrobatics on spring-loaded jumping stilts. The stilts facilitate jumping 2 metres (6.5 ft) and running at speeds exceeding 40 km/h (25 mph). Photograph: William Cherry/ Presseye.com.

misleading the public is reckless. The real purpose of the scientific method, according to author Robert Pirsig, 'is to make sure nature hasn't misled you into thinking you know something you actually don't know'.

We humans reason anecdotally, depending heavily on hunches and intuition; it's an effective way of dealing with the constant deluge of information we have to process.

The price for this convenience is that we are susceptible to what are known as cognitive illusions. We see patterns in the genuinely random; we see causal relationships where they don't exist. We

seek out information and people to confirm our own biases, and reject these if they don't fit.

We can also be poor judges of our own aptitudes and limitations. Depending on intuition it may be appropriate when deciding what to watch on television, but it's the precise opposite to how the scientific method works. And for good reason.

In 1946, paediatrician Dr Benjamin Spock published the bestselling *Baby and Child Care*. It included one utterly wrong recommendation: that babies should sleep on their tummies – advice that led to thousands of avoidable cot deaths. That's why we do science: to weed out all those interesting hunches and replace them with rigorously tested scientific facts, however dull. Everyone now knows that cigarettes are dangerous; 50 years ago, everyone – including doctors – smoked.

The same goes for leaded petrol, ozone depletion, CO_2 and a host of other hazards that we have been alerted to over the decades by rigorous, scientific research. The media caricature of science as unfathomable, authoritarian and capricious is a dangerous fiction. It allows media-savvy showmen to set themselves up as 'experts'.

Self-styled nutritionist Patrick Holford bashed conventional medicine on *The Late Late Show* some time back, in favour of his hip 'alternative' methods. For instance, he says the anti-Aids treatment, AZT, is 'potentially harmful and proving less effective than vitamin C'. That's one serious claim. Supporting evidence? Nil.

When science is reduced to a game, anyone can play. Scientists say the Arctic ice sheet is in danger of disappearing; I say they're just stuffy old sausages and, besides, the world is actually getting colder. Maybe it's all about sunspots, or whatever other discredited theory can be shoehorned to match my intellectual whims.

We trusted science to deliver dramatic improvements in health and life expectancy, as well as genuine technological advances.

Now, at the time of our greatest peril, we've turned to the quacks, blowhards and snake-oil salesmen. As Samuel Beckett observed: 'We are all born mad; some remain so.'

SATURDAY, 25 JULY 2009

Of Moose and Men

Quentin Fottrell

We go to extraordinary lengths to get in touch with nature but Canada rewards the intrepid traveller with elegant outposts of civilisation deep in its vast forests.

The most foolhardy or, perhaps, adventurous among us will go to extraordinary lengths to catch a glimpse of a beast trundling along without a care in the world, minding its own business in its own natural habitat. Armed with binoculars, camera, insect repellent and a pair of hardy walking boots, we tell ourselves that there is something profound and life-affirming about it.

We will do almost anything to experience that moment: take a taxi to the airport, sit on a long-haul flight flicking impatiently through the *National Enquirer* or *New Yorker* – or the former folded discreetly inside the latter – then take a bus to a vast expanse of water, sit in a canoe and paddle like the bejaysus to get far away from human life or, at least, a mobile phone signal.

I did this and more. I flew into Toronto, stayed at three Ontario lakeside lodges in five days, before coming face-to-face with my first certified wild animal on my third day. It was a moose, so serene and handsome and pretty. And dead. Hit by a pick-up truck. Sadly, its lifeless body was lying in a ditch on the side of the road. That put my carbon footprint into perspective.

But hours later, canoeing in Opeongo Lake, one of 3,000 in Algonquin Park – 7,725sq km of forests and water teaming with wolves and moose and bears, oh my – I finally saw a couple of live ones. In a remote waterway called Hailstorm Creek, I glided quietly past a female moose in the water. Her calf stayed on dry land, wisely remaining close by her side.

There was nothing between me and the moose except a stretch of water, sunglasses and a generous slathering of factor 30. The moose had come out of the woods to bathe and cool down from the heat of the relentless midday summer sun. The mother first noticed our canoe when we were way off in the distance and, as we approached, she didn't take her eyes off us.

That's the price one pays for entering their world. I felt like an intruder. Adam, my canoe guide from Algonquin Outfitters, an outdoor

Canoeing past a moose in Algonquin Park, Ontario, Canada. Photograph: Doug Hamilton.

adventure store, told me a story about a couple who were cooking steak in these parts some years ago. The man was found alone, hysterical. His girlfriend had been killed by what Adam said was a hungry and, unfortunately, demented black bear.

Fear not. The Spring/Winter Algonquin Information Guide, a seasonal newspaper for visitors, says bears attack people only on extremely rare occasions. They are usually shy of humans. If you do see a bear, the guide advises not to turn and run, as this may trigger a predatory response. It adds, rather ominously, 'Do not climb a tree — bears are excellent climbers.'

I didn't see a bear, but a bullfrog hopped around the rocks, teasing me as I tried to catch it, always out of reach with a giddy bellyful of acro-

batics. Algonquin's waters have trout, splake and bass. Boreal chickadees and gray jays darted overhead. I half-wonder if the chipmunk I thought I saw lolling just below the water's surface was, in fact, my own toothy reflection.

My love affair with Canada goes back 10 years when I ate butternut squash soup at a friend's Thanksgiving dinner table covered in red and orange maple leaves in a cottage on Georgian Bay. Canada is as civilised a society as you will get anywhere in the world. It's true. Canadians are polite. They have enviable civic pride and, in 2005, introduced equal marriage rights for all.

So, I arrived at my lodgings with good tidings. First stop was Elmhirst Resort in Keene, 90 minutes east of Toronto. It started as a humble collection of cottages for American families, some

Sgt Maj. Tommy Murphy from the 17th Infantry Battalion and Mary Murphy (11) from Longford during the National Day of Commemoration ceremony. Photograph: Gareth Chaney/Collins.

of whom still come here three generations later. It's open all year around, even Christmas when the lake is covered in ice, and has branched into farming, boat plane training and horse riding.

The Elmhirsts go all the way back to the Battle of Trafalgar. As the jovial Peter Elmhirst told me on a barbecue boat ride along the lake, in 1818, King George IV granted to Phillip James Elmhirst, a lieutenant of the Royal Navy, 1,000 acres on the north shore of Lake Rice for his efforts against Napoleon. This was the family's entry into the land-owning class.

This resort's 340 acres and mile of lake shore were purchased in 1906 by Frank Elmhirst, the grandfather of current owner Peter Elmhirst. It is based near where the Elmhirst's original 1,000 acres were once located. The wooden split-level

cottages are basic enough, even if they do come with broadband, but there is nothing to obstruct the view between them and the lake.

Best of all, Peter has shrunk his own carbon footprint. He raises grain-fed Angus beef cattle. Chickens in the nearby farm lay eggs for breakfast. The orchard provides fruit and the greenhouse grows herbs, vegetables and flowers. Even the extensive wine cellar features only Ontario wines. Plus, you can cook in your cottage, or eat in their pub or restaurant.

Further north is the Canadian Canoe Museum in Peterborough. Once known for Quaker Oats and canoe-building, Peterborough is now primarily a college town. This museum boasts the world's largest canoe collection. There are 120 on view and another 500 in storage. Sounds impressive, doesn't it? In truth, I was dreading it. But the history of the canoe is the history of Canada.

First Nation men harvested bark and animal skins to build the crafts. Women were designated to do the stitching. Some things haven't changed. Museum worker Ipie, a good-humoured and remarkably Zen middle-aged woman, sat making garments like those worn by early European settlers. 'I used to build canoes. Then they found out I could sew,' she said, perhaps half-joking.

Later, canoes were given as wedding gifts to royalty (including Queen Victoria and Charles and Diana) and eventually manufactured for the middle classes. In 1904, the Cedar-Strip Comfort Courting Canoe or Canoe d'amoureux, en Lattes de Cèdre, had a built-in gramophone with a vinyl of an Indian love song 'By the Waters of Minnetonka'. And, yes, that song is on YouTube.

En route to our next overnight stay, we made a random stop in a quiet one-horse town on the Lazy Gull River called Minden. It's hard to believe now, but it used to be a booming and hell-raising logging town. Algonquin Park, where I saw the aforementioned moose, is only 45 minutes away, and if you were to stay here there is ample hiking and canoeing in the area.

I ate a hamburger for lunch in the backyard of the Dominion Hotel, which has been here since 1865. Our waitress said she saw a bear the other day while she was with her young son at a recycling centre on the edge of town. 'He was going through rubbish, so he was fine,' she said of the bear. Knowing her bear etiquette, she recycled first, and then slowly backed away.

Since the cancellation of Ontario's spring bear hunt to prevent too many bear cubs being orphaned, there has been a marked increase in the population of the black bear in these parts, according to local newspapers. Some, like the rummaging bear in the bins on the edge of town, have become increasingly brazen when it comes to humans. It is an inevitable role reversal.

The hotel, a modest establishment on main street, offers romantic getaways, yet the waitress told me about the ghost of a woman who died in childbirth after a relationship with a logger. (They're starting a ghost tour as spirits are good at drumming up tourism.) That was when Minden was a hive of activity. 'Unlike many others back then, Minden wasn't a dry town,' she explained.

When I arrived at my second destination, Pow Wow Point Lodge in Huntsville, I immediately went swimming with the fishes. How could I not? It has 1,500 feet of pristine lakefront with a southern exposure and 35 acres of open and wooded grounds. My one-room cottage was even more rustic than those at Elmhirst, and the warm, sparkling blue lake was even more inviting.

Pow Wow has a buffet lunch and dinner, and more upmarket cottages, too. The 1930s boathouse takes two people and has Cathedral ceilings and a whirlpool. There are deluxe cottages, some of which are lakefront and others nestled in the trees complete with Jacuzzis and stone fireplaces. But those fancier places are by the by. You really want to come here for the waterfront view.

And, finally, we arrive where I began this story of moose and men: the great Algonquin Park. This is the prize jewel of the Ontario province. After I took my previously recounted canoe trip, I had a special treat. Pilot Sebastien Marty, a Frenchman from Toulouse, flew me over the park in his yellow 1953 De Havilland Turbo Beaver. Trees, trees, trees, as far as the eye can see.

Sebastien is a happy man. He lives in a wooden cabin on the edge of Smoke Lake, on the outskirts of Algonquin, with his wife and children. This is one of those 'best jobs in the world' you heard tell about. He flies employees of the Ontario Ministry of Natural Resources on fact-finding missions like, say, tracking the survival rates and behavioural patterns of moose calves.

He spoke with a lyrical Franco-North American twang; he often said 'Yah! That's awesome!', or, 'Cool!' When I asked how fast we were going, as we swooped over a children's summer

Model Tara Chetty wearing a L'Wren Scott green gown, with Miu Miu shoes, Vinader bangle and Stephen Webster earrings at the Brown Thomas autumn/winter preview. Photograph: Alan Betson.

camp deep in the forest, Sebastien replied, 'I dunno! I can't read.' Pilot humour. In fact, he landed the float plane on the glassy water, a deceptive surface, without so much as a bump.

The flight gave me a glimpse of the unwelcoming terrain that black-robed missionaries contended with as they forged their way through this foreign land. Sainte-Marie Among the Hurons is a re-creation of a 17th-century Jesuit mission that lasted just 10 years. The mission brought God to the local Wendat tribe, plus deadly doses of smallpox, influenza and measles.

The earliest European settlement in Ontario and fourth oldest in Canada, it's built on the original site with wooden farm buildings with real furs drying over smoky fires, a locked waterway and Church of St Joseph. The interpreters are also method actors: Peggy sat quietly in her bonnet in one house. 'I'm making a pouch,' she told me. 'I'll probably attach it to a belt or something.'

The men in black robes and wide-brimmed felt hats wandered around speaking as if they all lived here nearly 400 years ago. 'We settled here in 1639,' one robed man in his 20s said. His tussled Zac Efron haircut could have been straight out of the 17th century. Another robed 'missionary' walked by in character. 'Hiya, Larry!' our guide chirped at him, as he passed.

The missionaries were well-intentioned, but their presence here was a disaster. The Wendat's sedentary rather than nomadic lifestyle made them good trading partners for the French and a favourite of the missionaries. Some Wendat converted to Christianity, some didn't. This caused deep divisions. War and disease eventually decimated the tribe of 22,500 by around 70 per cent.

It does seem macabre to celebrate this way of life when the interpreters themselves acknowledge how naïve and life-threatening the missionary presence here was. But having had a taste of this Little House on the Prairie puritanical way of life, Sainte-Marie does stand alone as a remarkable piece of social history. Certainly, it was far less luxurious than my next stop on the tourist trail.

My last overnight was at Severn Lodge. I liked that they didn't go with a token First Nation name. It has over 2,000 feet of shoreline and its own private bay and beach. A popular wedding destination, it is on the northern shores of Gloucester Pool, which is part of the Trent Severn Waterway in the Muskoka-Georgian Bay lake district. As a resort destination, it is stunning.

The Mordolphton Club from Pittsburgh, Pennsylvania, purchased the property sometime around the 1870s. In the 1920s, it was sold to George Barrick and Glen Crummel of Akron, Ohio, renamed Severn Lodge, and in 1936 sold to William H. Breckbill, who began working here as a student. In 1940, he married Jeanne E. Krammes. For years, husband and wife ran it together.

A black-and-white photograph of William and Jeanne, the sole owner-hostess when her husband was in Europe during the Second World War, still graces a wall of the lodge just inside the restaurant. Their sons Rick and Ron now run the lodge. Rick has the rounded, tanned look of someone who grew up in something close to paradise . . . in the milder summer months, at least.

My wooden, one-roomed, red-and-white cottage gave me a bird's eye view of the water's edge. Originally a lodge for loggers, it is now a refined and romantic retreat with an outdoor pool, 1922 mahogany motor launch on-hand to allow you to view the lakeside mansions and, if you and yours want some time for yourselves, the staff also organises group activities for children.

I travelled to the outback to see moose and marvel at distant horizons. On this my last day, I had found an elegant outpost of civilisation. Canada is a beautiful, socially progressive and, today at least, more welcoming land than what the early settlers faced. Severn Lodge would be the perfect wedding venue. Who knows, I may yet return here one day with the man whom I will marry.

The Public's Right to Know

Editorial

The belief that journalists should not reveal the identities of people who give them information in confidence is not fundamentally about the rights or privileges of the media. It is about the rights of citizens in an open and democratic society. Democracy is fuelled by information. If they are to hold those in power to account, citizens must first know what they are doing.

It is crucial, therefore, that people of conscience should be able to reveal unpleasant facts about important matters without being exposed and punished. It is equally essential that the general public should be free to receive that information in a timely manner, so that it can decide for itself what its implications may be.

This is a view which has been consistently upheld by the European Court of Human Rights, but not, until yesterday, by Irish law. It was in this ambivalent context that *The Irish Times* received, in September 2006, information from an anonymous source that the then taoiseach, Bertie Ahern, had accepted substantial payments from private individuals while he was minister for finance. This was, as the Supreme Court acknowledged yesterday, 'a

Patsy Gibbons from Columcille in Thomastown, Co. Kilkenny, with Gráinne, the fox he nursed back to health after it was found abandoned and malnourished as a cub two years ago. The pair are a regular sight walking the local streets. Photograph: Dylan Vaughan.

Orlagh Creamer, Lesley Dowdall and Aoife Creamer arrive at Dublin airport having survived the Bangkok Airways ATR-72 plane crash on the island of Koh Samui, Thailand. Photograph: Niall Carson/PA.

matter of public interest which a newspaper would, in the ordinary way, be entitled to print'. More importantly, it was a matter which the public was entitled to know.

The Irish Times was aware from the beginning that the ultimate source of the information was the inquiries of the Mahon tribunal. We fully understood the tribunal's need for confidentiality, and we did not lightly make a decision that this need was outweighed by the imperative of disclosure.

We were aware, however, that there was no certainty at that stage that these facts would ever be disclosed in public. We believed that the issue was not one of our right to publish, but of our duty to do so. The alternative scenario, that we would choose to suppress important information about the conduct of the taoiseach of the day, could not be contemplated.

Therefore, it is with relief as well as satisfaction that we welcome yesterday's Supreme Court decision to grant the appeal by The Irish Times against the High Court's ruling that the editor and public affairs correspondent of the paper be forced to answer questions before the tribunal as to the source of the leaked material. Had the judgment gone the other way, Ireland would have gone against the grain of European law and endorsed an extraordinarily narrow view of the public's right to be informed.

It is particularly welcome that Mr Justice Nial Fennelly relied very heavily on the precedents of the European Court and in doing so effectively adopted that court's judgments into Irish law. Unlike the position in the US, the European precedents are not concerned primarily with the rights of journalists or sources. They ask, as yesterday's ruling put it, 'Is there a pressing social need for the imposition of the restriction?'.

Contained in that question are two vital considerations – the needs of a democratic society and the belief that information should not be suppressed unless there is an overwhelming public interest in doing so. The full practical implications of the judgment may still have to be teased out and no right can ever be unqualified. But the criteria set out in the judgment are principles rooted in the assumption that information is the blood supply of the body politic. From that perspective, yesterday was a good day for Irish journalism which exists to serve the public's right to know.

WEDNESDAY, 5 AUGUST 2009

'The 19th Century is a Bit of a Blur'

Frank McNally

The one piece of advice I remember from my original Leaving Cert was that you should always read the exam paper carefully. So I do: and this is my first mistake.

It reveals that 20 per cent of the marks for honours history are allocated to a 'pre-submitted research study report'. My cruel Summer Living Editor had somehow failed to mention this during the breezy conversation in which he assured me that re-sitting an exam I last did when Jimmy Carter was US president would not involve the risk of humiliation.

For a moment, I consider a desperate plan involving the compilation of a 'post-submitted research study report'. One option might be to nip back to *The Irish Times* newsroom and interview the oldest colleague I can find about changes in the ethics of claiming unreceipted expenses in late-20th-century Irish journalism. But my allotted two hours and 50 minutes is ticking fast, so I abandon

the idea. Confidence already shattered, I plough on and read the questions.

The other shock of the modern Leaving Cert history paper – not exactly pleasant either, but more sympathetic to the prospects of success – is how much of the syllabus I have now lived through. Once upon a time, history was about long-dead people, such as Isaac Butt and Prince von Metternich. And sure enough, Butt and Metternich are still there in 2009: their conditions unimproved by the intervening years.

But large swathes of material that I remember as current affairs have slipped quietly from the news pages and into the history books while I wasn't looking. The Northern Troubles, for example. Margaret Thatcher. Jacques Delors. All suddenly sepia-tinted and staring back at me in the form of exam questions.

I sense Thatcher's broader influence on the history paper. She always talked about giving the consumer 'choice'. And by my calculation, apart from one compulsory question, the consumer of the 2009 Leaving Cert history exam is required to pick any three subjects from a bewildering list of 44. Just reading all the options saps my energy.

That said, an alarmingly high number of these automatically disqualify themselves on the grounds that the only detail I could now marshal to support them would fit on the back of a stamp. No ifs, Butts, or Metternichs: the whole 19th century is a bit of a blur. I could probably treat a few of the topics with broad brush strokes. But the history of French Impressionism is probably the only subject where the examiner would agree to stand well back from my answer and scrunch his eyes up; and incredibly this is not one of the 44 options.

Thus, frustrated at how little meaningful choice there is – damn you, Margaret Thatcher – I tick three of an estimated six questions that could be attempted with any confidence. Then I start writing.

Next to not having attended school for 30 years, the other problem facing a middle-aged

Frank McNally has a second go at the Leaving Cert. Photograph: Alan Betson.

Leaving Cert student is a technical one. Like most of my generation, I learned joined-up writing in the era of ink-wells and blotters. At best, I was no calligrapher. Now, thanks to my subsequent mastery of such journalistic techniques as two-fingered typing, it has been decades since I used legible long-hand for anything bigger than a Christmas card.

It should be something you never forget, like riding a bike. But not wishing to take any more chances, other than the risk of hand-cramp, I make another quick decision: to do my entire paper in block capitals.

The compulsory question – on Martin Luther King and the Montgomery Bus Boycott – is almost too easy. The student only has to read two texts and compare them. It's so simple I suspect a booby-trap. But circling the question several times and prodding it here and there does not set anything off. So I complete the answers and proceed to my first chosen subject: 'Why were the [1921]

Anglo-Irish Treaty negotiations controversial?' Forty minutes later, with both my penmanship and Éamon de Valera hung out to dry, I find myself warming to the whole Leaving Cert thing again.

The years fall away and, emotionally involved now, I plunge into my second chosen question – on the social and economic effects of the modern Troubles – with something bordering on enthusiasm. Then the effort drains me, and by the Good Friday Agreement, I badly need some form of stimulant to keep going.

As luck would have it, there is a canteen next door. Strictly speaking, a real Leaving Cert student would not be allowed to nip out mid-exam for a takeaway coffee. But strictly speaking, his teachers would have warned him about the pre-submitted research project. So taking advantage of lax security, I complete my last question – on Thatcher and Europe – over a strong Americano.

Like a bedraggled marathon runner, my right

The hospitality stand at the Dublin Horse Show. Photograph: Alan Betson.

hand has already hit the wall. Now it's operating on instinct, and I just hope the examiner can still read the stuff: except, of course, the bits where I use indecipherable writing as a strategy.

Suddenly, my time is up. On the other hand, the Editor has not arrived yet to collect the paper, and I realise that only a sense of honour prevents me from taking advantage of the extra few minutes. So I do just that, ruthlessly: going back over my answers and inserting footnotes.

Finally, the Editor arrives and I hand up my paper. Then, a little ruefully, I head back to the newsroom, remembering what Harry Truman once said: 'There is nothing new in the world except the history you don't know.'

In resitting his Leaving Certificate for a series of summer feature articles with colleagues, Frank McNally was adjudged thus by an independent marker: 'With more

effort and development … has the potential to achieve a high C/low B grade.'

SATURDAY, 8 AUGUST 2009

Beached at the North Border

Derek Scally, in Travemünde

In a silent green wood, a concrete monster lurks among the trees. Rainwater and ivy are going about their business, wearing away the speckled concrete façade of the watchtower which hasn't served its purpose for 20 years and, slowly, is returning to nature.

This is the northernmost lookout point of the inner-German border that wound its way south like a giant snail track through 1,400 km of woods, fields and villages, dividing the country and the world for three decades.

From the tower, guards could watch the starting point of the border on the nearby beach of the Priwall peninsula in Travemünde, on Germany's Baltic coast.

Pictures from the 1970s show a demarcation in three steps: a series of poles linked by a plastic red-and-white chain, followed by Halt signs and then a tall, wire-mesh fence.

Today the only warning sign is for the nudist section: at the point that was once the end of the western world, a few elderly, leathery Germans are letting it all hang out.

'We used to hang our towels on the chain. That's how unthreatening it all was,' says Travemünde-born Holger Walter, now head of the cultural office in the nearby city of Lübeck. 'We couldn't see the mines. We simply had no idea what came after the border. It might just as easily have been a sheer cliff face.' After the fence came watchtowers, spotlights and guards. Then came snapping dogs, barbed wire, and tripwires triggering automatic spring guns. Beyond that was the tiny village of Pölenitz and then the empty rural landscape of Mecklenburg.

Travemünde, a pretty seaside town of red-brick Hanseatic buildings, has been attracting tourists for a century. It features in Thomas Mann's first novel *Buddenbrooks* (1901). Pictures from the time show a smart tourist resort with spotless villas, a race track and even an international airport on the Priwall peninsula, a three-minute ferry ride away.

Then came the war and the ban on civilians on the peninsula; soldiers followed, as did a new submarine harbour. In 1945 came the British soldiers, patrolling up to the point where their zone met that of the Soviets.

Although it stuck out into the highly militarised Baltic Sea, the Priwall peninsula was of little strategic importance. The divide sliced the head of the peninsula − West German territory − off

from the East German mainland. The border, just a few hundred metres wide, ran along the old historical border between Schleswig-Holstein and Mecklenburg.

It didn't tear apart as many families and friends as the Berlin border. Half of the people in this region were wartime refugees from further east. As locals say, they had enough to do integrating the new arrivals without worrying about the people behind the border in Mecklenburg.

That much was clear in the autumn of 1961, when Lübeckers raised a flag at half mast in solidarity with their 'brothers and sisters behind the border of shame'. They were referring to the Berlin Wall, 300 km southeast, and the border in their own back garden.

It was an indication of things to come: nearly half a century after it was erected, the Berlin Wall has become the symbol of Germany's division. The barrier that turned west Berlin into an island in the communist east has supplanted in popular memory the other, inner-German border, even though that was created almost a decade before, in 1952.

Its first iteration was a metre-high, barbed-wire fence, designed to stop the flood of people from east to west that would top 2.5 million people by 1961. As in Berlin, this border was fortified continuously, first with landmines, and then, in 1966, with wire-mesh panels which would eventually rise as high as four metres.

The border fortifications stretched across a band at least 200 m wide. A five-kilometre-wide restricted area was created on the eastern side. Residents within this zone were given special papers to show every time they came and went. Visits were highly restricted.

Anyone considered 'politically unreliable' or likely to flee was removed from the restricted zone in two waves of forcible resettlement, in 1952 and 1961.

Nearly 50,000 East German guards were charged with watching − day and night − what East Berlin termed the 'anti-fascist protection wall'

A Grafton Street, Dublin mime artist has even the birds fooled. Photograph: Matt Kavanagh.

A piece of work by Steven McGovern from Celbridge in Co. Kildare is reflected in his sunglasses during the People's Art 2009 exhibition at St Stephen's Green in Dublin. Photograph: Cyril Byrne.

(although all fortifications were directed against the east) and, later, the 'state border west'.

On the other side, another 20,000 West German border police and customs officials monitored the 'zone border', a name reflecting Bonn's official line of refusing to officially recognise the division or the other German state to the east.

When the two states signed a 'basic treaty' in 1972, the basis for chancellor Willy Brandt's Ostpolitik, the border was rechristened the 'German-German border'. But the divide remained and was made even more impenetrable with the passing years.

It was around this time that the notorious automatic spring guns were introduced: mounted on the fence and triggered with tripwires, they sprayed would-be escapees with tiny metal splinters.

The first recorded death on the inner-German border is journalist Kurt Liechtenstein, shot in 1961 after crossing the border, reportedly to interview East German farmers about conditions.

Another 370 deaths would follow, until the East German authorities caved in to popular protest and opened the inner-German border on 9 November, 1989.

Two decades on, memories are fading fast about the 1,400 km border, memories historians suggest were lopsided to begin with.

'For westerners the border was not part of their own culture but the embodiment of the other,' writes Maren Ullrich, author of *Divided Views*, a history of the border.

'In the east, meanwhile, there is no image of the border in people's minds because of the

US President Barack Obama presents former president Mary Robinson with the Presidential Medal of Freedom in the White House. Mrs Robinson received the award in the face of a campaign against her by pro-Israel groups in the US. Photograph: J. Scott Applewhite/AP.

exclusion zone. How can there be a memory if there is no image?' As a result, she says, the popular memory of the inner-German border is exclusively a West German one, and often confused with the history of the Berlin Wall.

As in Berlin, little physical trace of the border remains: in their euphoria, Germans up and down the border area tore down the fence and the watchtowers in 1989.

Back in Travemünde, local historian Rolf Fechner produces old albums of photos and documents of the border. The history of his hometown – in particular the Cold War era – is one of his two passions in life. The other is the music of Rory Gallagher.

Flicking through the photo albums, it's extraordinary to see how, by the late 1960s, tourists ignored the Cold War divide and returned to Priwall.

'It was completely normal on the beach, with people as far as you could see. Then it just stopped,' remembers Fechner. The eastern beach was completely empty and untouched while, in the west, the nudist beach went right up to the border.

'This lookout post was very popular with the eastern border guards,' jokes Fechner. 'Occasionally teenagers would get drunk and wander over the border, between the chains on the fence, until they were warned by guards over loudspeakers to go back.' Westerners became so used to the beach border that it took Travemünde four months after the Berlin Wall was breached to get around to opening its own border crossing.

Even then, the euphoria was short-lived: three months after the first easterners headed west in Trabants belching out petrol fumes from their two-stroke engines, westerners took to the streets to complain about the air pollution.

City officials in Lübeck dreamed of a chance to shake off regional obscurity, uniting the divided regions of Schleswig-Holstein and Mecklenburg. Today, the states remain separate, and local officials laugh at the grand plans of 1989.

'Politicians thought unification would make Lübeck the Queen of the Baltic but all we got were 20,000 yokels from the Mecklenburg countryside,' laughs Holger Walter in his Lübeck office.

As the 20th anniversary looms, the former exclusion zone has been rechristened the Green Band, a nature reserve of 17,000 hectares which, in some cases, has been untouched since 1949.

'The section of the Green Band in Priwall comprises 150 hectares of untouched countryside,' says Thomas König, a nature reserve ranger here. 'It's home to cormorants, wild geese and many other rare species.'

In recent years a cycle lane has been installed through the territory and, slowly, Germans are rediscovering the forgotten border as a glorious green lung running through the middle of their country.

Along the way are tiny border villages such as Rüteberg, cut off from the world for 30 years, or Mödlareuth, Germany's answer to Spike Milligan's *Puckoon*, where the inner-German border ran through the centre of town.

Here in the north, Travemünders are blasé when asked about the division. 'I really never registered the border,' says pensioner Klaus Gropig on the ferry from Priwall. 'Some people from the old east come over here to work but, besides that, I can't say I see the two sides growing together much.' He was annoyed to see Travemünde lose its

West German border-town subsidies in 1989, particularly when Mecklenburg received 20 years of extra funding.

'I suppose we had our time getting money, then they had their subsidies,' he says. 'Now I'm old enough to know that things always even out in the end.'

FRIDAY, 14 AUGUST 2009

Pricewatch Daily

Conor Pope

Almost every time Pricewatch refers to Ryanair in anything but the most flattering of terms, its head of communications Stephen McNamara sends us an angry letter.

Even broadly positive references annoy McNamara. Recently, we wrote about airlines losing baggage and said 'for all its faults' Ryanair had a good record on baggage handling. Cue another missive in which McNamara asked if there was 'any possibility you could write an article on anything to do with air travel without having a dig at Ryanair'. He claimed it 'doesn't have a "good record"' but 'the best record in the industry' and asked us to 'indicate what you mean by "all its faults"'. When we put details of this on our blog, the response from readers was immediate, with many choosing to highlight what they believed were Ryanair's faults.

'Ryanair does not provide what the consumer wants,' said one reader. Customers 'want to be treated like a human being, to get to their desired destination (not 50/60 miles away), to be seated in comfort, and to be allowed to bring luggage without persecution'. Or 'How about a complete and utter lack of communication when flights run late and infuriating jingles when the planes arrive on time/early', said another. A third questioned why Ryanair charged passengers to check-in using their own computers and to print their own boarding

Cartoon by Aongus Collins.

cards, and asked why infants were charged €20 and given no hand-luggage allowance.

'I'm sick of that miserable "booking charge/service charge/admin charge" system,' complained another, while several gave out that Visa Electron cards, which would allow people to avoid credit-card fees, were almost impossible for Irish residents to get.

The charge of €100 to change a name on a ticket and the €40 fee for printing a boarding pass if you forget yours were highlighted, while uncomfortable seats, on-board advertising, the lurid yellow livery, and talk of charging for access to toilets were also referred to.

We forwarded the comments to McNamara who dismissed them as 'subjective and inaccurate rubbish' and even implied Pricewatch had made them up to further some class of anti-Ryanair agenda.

He said claims the airline 'does not provide what the consumer wants' were absurd, and insisted there was no lack of communication 'during rare flight delays'. The on-time jingle is infuriating only because it is 'played so regularly' and passengers who don't want to pay a web check-in fee should 'just travel on one of our promotional fares (€10 one way or under)'.

Apparently, Visa Electron is used by 'many thousands of Irish residents' and the name-change fee is a good thing because it's 'designed to allow passengers who have bought non-refundable pro-motional fares the opportunity to transfer it to friends or family'.

The €40 boarding card re-issue fee is only levied on passengers who fail to arrive at the airport with their boarding pass, which 'is a better alter-native than not allowing these passengers to travel at all', McNamara claimed. He concluded by suggesting Ryanair's airline seats were 'extremely comfortable and our onboard advertising and yellow livery are much beloved by our passengers'.

The final word goes to a 'reader' called Jean who said our spat was 'like a bad romantic comedy, where you start off as enemies but then realise that you love each other. You're Meg Ryan and Ryanair is Tom Hanks'.

TUESDAY, 25 AUGUST 2009

Young Faces Fill Church in Farewell to 'Awesome Dude'

Kathy Sheridan

Hundreds of young people were among the overflowing congregation at the funeral yesterday of Sebastian Creane, the 22-year-old student who was stabbed to death at his Bray home on 16 August. His assailant, Shane Clancy, who took his own life after the stabbing, was buried last Thursday.

Row upon row of young faces, pale, tearful, bewildered, filed into the Church of the Most Holy Redeemer on Bray's Main Street, in their formal black suits, casual bright hoodies or shirt sleeves to say farewell to a friend they characterised as calm and gentle, an 'awesome dude' with a 'ridiculous' sense of humour and a magnificent moustache.

The clothes they had chosen reflected the part of Sebastian's life they shared. Purple Converse trainers — some obviously brand new — were worn by several of his fellow students from Dún Laoghaire Institute of Art, Design and Technology, a collective homage to the distinctive 'basketball squeaking' of Sebastian's own well-worn Converse on the photographic studio floor. Others saluted his bohemian style with their purple hoodies and black and white scarves.

The simple wicker casket, wreathed in garden flowers and foliage along with the single red rose placed there by Sebastian's girlfriend Jennifer Hannigan — who was wounded in the stabbing incident — bore photographs of a characteristically ebullient Sebastian, 'radiant, forever young', in the words of chief celebrant Fr Brendan MacHale.

More than an hour before the 10 a.m. Mass began — heralded by 'Bridge over Troubled Water' sung by Tommy Fleming and accompanied by Phil Coulter — many of Sebastian's old friends from St Gerard's, Bray, and from college in Dún Laoghaire, huddled in the porch around the scrapbook of memories, tributes and photographs they would later present as offertory gifts.

The offerings also included a guitar, 'a symbol of his love of music, one of the many bonds between him and [his brother] Dylan'; a camera; and symbols of the 'fun times' — a Nintendo console and a collection of photographs, including one of Sebastian sky-diving with his mother, Nuala. Phil Coulter followed these with his own offertory gift — a specially composed, sweet piano lament.

Later six of Sebastian's friends walked to the lectern to offer prayers for the faithful, thanking God for their friend's creativity, for his 'contagious enthusiasm', for his willingness to take time out for those around him, for his music, skateboarding and photographs; they honoured his brother Dylan's courage 'in coming to the aid of Sebastian'.

Fr MacHale added a prayer for the family of Shane Clancy, making a brief reference to that time 'when beauty disappears and only the demonic takes over'.

In his homily, Fr MacHale referred to Sebastian's parents, James and Nuala, as people who summed up 'very vividly' the depth of the psalm 'The Lord is my Shepherd'.

'On Thursday, James said, "It's like I'm in a tsunami but I'm okay." And then here on Saturday, as we prepared this liturgy . . . Nuala said, "I

Friends of Sebastian Creane (22) carry the wicker casket containing his body from the Church of the Most Holy Redeemer in Bray, Co. Wicklow. Photograph: Julien Behal/PA.

grieve. I don't suffer. I don't believe we're sent here to suffer.'"

Fr MacHale described Sebastian's love of music as his act of thanksgiving and quoted from the writings of the poet and philosopher John O'Donohue: 'Though your days here were brief,/Your spirit was alive, awake, complete:/Now you dwell inside the rhythm of breath,/As close to us as we are to ourselves.'

Sebastian's music lives on from inside that rhythm of life and binds him to his parents, to Dylan, Laura and Jen and all his friends, Fr MacHale said, quoting another John O'Donohue prayer: 'Let us not look for you only in memory/ Where we would grow lonely without you,/You would want us to find you in presence.'

One of Sebastian's closest friends, Daragh Coulter, read from the *Book of Wisdom*: 'Length of days is not what makes age honourable, nor number of years the true measure of life . . . They have been carried off so that evil may not warp their understanding or treachery seduce their souls; for the fascination of evil throws good things into the shade, and the whirlwind of desire corrupts a simple heart.'

The second reading from St Paul urged its listeners to 'fill your minds with those things that are good and deserve praise, things that are true, noble, right, pure and lovely and honourable'.

At Communion, 'Something Inside so Strong', the Labi Siffre song written about Nelson Mandela and apartheid, was sung by Tommy

Fleming, followed by a recording of Neil Hannon's 'Songs of Love', during which tears fell freely: 'So while you have time/ Let the sun shine down from above/And fill you with songs of love.'

At that point, Nuala Creane, accompanied by her surviving son Dylan, who was also severely injured in the incident, rose to deliver a eulogy rich in faith and encouragement, much of it clearly directed at the many young people in the church.

'The light that shone in Seb shines in you also, in its own special way. Let it shine and be at peace,' she said.

To the strains of Phil Coulter and Tommy Fleming singing 'Steal Away', the coffin was borne from the church and from there to Sebastian's final resting place at Leigue Cemetery in his parents' native Ballina, Co. Mayo.

Sebastian Creane's parents, Nuala and James, at their son's funeral in Bray. Photograph: Garry O'Neill.

This is a slightly edited version of what Nuala Creane said at her son's funeral:

What is my God . . . saying to me about this incomprehensible act?

Seb's body is back in a Moses basket. It's a little bit bigger than the one he began life's journey in, but it serves the same purpose: a place to rest.

We are faced with a grim reality today, burying my youngest son. Reality for me is the sum of all my experiences, my beliefs, my thoughts, which I project out into this world and with which I create my story.

In Ireland we have a great tradition of story-telling. Firstly, we tell stories to try to make sense of the human condition and secondly, when we share our story, we connect with one another. We come to know each other.

This morning, I am going to tell a story. In my story, my God is the God of Small Things. I see God's presence in the little details.

My beloved J. [her husband James] and I decided to have a second son — we didn't know it was going to be a boy then of course — because we didn't want D. to be an only child. And I knew also that my expectations of Dylan, if he was on his own, would be too high.

Seb was eager to be born. He arrived three weeks early at 10 minutes to two in the afternoon.

Do you remember the old days when the clock faces in the haberdashery window all read '10 to 2' because the face of the clock looked like it was smiling? If you've never seen it, look at Ledwidge's window in Main Street. My God of Small Things was telling me this would be a happy child. And he was.

Seb has 45 first cousins. What a bountiful table to sup from throughout one's childhood. Seb was also the youngest child in the Grove and he did his best to be as good as the rest of them.

At 2 1/2, he could cycle his bicycle without stabilisers on which at every opportunity he would disappear around the corner, abandon the bike at the door of Pauline's shop and stand with his curly head peering round the door, brown eyes trained on Pauline, waiting until she relented and gave him a sweet.

Still as a nipper, he was with me in Hickey's one day when I was buying curtain hooks. As I queued to pay, I realised I needed another one. Showing the hook to Seb, I asked him to get me one from the shelf. When he brought me back the correct one, I stored the information away. He had a good visual memory. It would stand him in good stead.

Contrary to popular perception, academia for Seb was not easy, but fortunately, he met teachers in St Nicholas's Montessori, St Cronan's, St Gerard's, Sallynoggin Senior College and Dún Laoghaire Institute, who challenged him, tested his mettle, supported him, praised him, so that he became a fine young man.

The last gift Seb gave to J. and me was during our summer back in June. One Sunday morning, Seb informed me that he fancied a swim down at the seafront. I didn't pay much heed.

He asked J. and J. said 'Yeah', he'd walk down with him. I was asked a second time. I gave in. So around midday Seb threw the towel over his shoulder and the three of us traipsed down to the beach. We sat on the pebbles and watched him as he went in for his dip . . . As I watched Seb I thought the child in that fella is still alive. It's a memory we treasure.

Maybe my God of Small Things is saying let the child inside each of us come to the surface and play or, as a point of fact, that I was blessed with a sunny child. Or as a parent I know that the one gift each of us would want for our child, is that they are comfortable in their skin . . .

Cancer survivor Rosa Melvin Caird, aged 9, meets professional cyclist Lance Armstrong during rehearsals for the opening of the Livestrong Global Cancer Summit at the RDS in Dublin. Photograph: Brenda Fitzsimons.

And now I ask what is my God of Little Things saying to me about this incomprehensible act which took place in our home on Sunday morning of August 16th? This tragic incident which caused mayhem in all our lives and robbed D. of a younger brother he was proud of. As D. himself said, Seb was like him but with swagger.

D, Seb, Jen and Laura faced a presence of demonic proportions that manifested through Shane Clancy. How do I, Seb and Dylan's mother, even try to rationalise this one? We live on Earth in a world of contrasts – big, small, hard, soft, good, bad, dark and light, but one can't paint a picture without at least two shades.

It is the dark which gives definition to the light. Darkness is just the lack of light.

Through my God of Little Things, I notice that both boys who died were 22. Both had the same initials. Both were entering their final year in college and looked set, even in these recessionary times, to have fruitful careers.

So many similarities, yet on the morning of August 16th, my God of Small Things said to me, one boy represented the light, the other the darkness, as they both played their parts in the unfolding of God's divine plan.

And as a result we, my beloved J. and I, and all of you, are faced with a choice: do we continue to live in darkness, seeing only fear, anger, bitterness, resentment; blaming, bemoaning our loss, always looking backwards, blaming, blaming, blaming, or are we ready to transmute this negativity?

We can rise to the challenge with unconditional love, knowing that we were born on to this earth to grow . . .

Our hearts are broken but maybe our hearts needed to be broken so that they could expand.

And now that we have our attention on our hearts, please bring to mind a happy moment in your lives – the happier the better. Now let that happy feeling fill your whole heart. Now bring your attention to Jen. She feels so responsible. She blames herself. Bathe her heart in that happiness.

Let our happy thoughts wash those feelings out of her. Keep sending her your happiness. And then forgive yourselves.

I am so conscious of all you young people who came in contact with Seb. I know you're bewildered and want to do something to make it right. The best way you can honour Seb's life is to co-create the most enlightened lives you can. The light that shone in Seb shines in you also, in its own special way. Let it shine and be at peace.

THURSDAY, 27 AUGUST 2009

15 Houses for €1m – One's a Mansion

Michael Parsons, in Goresbridge, Kilkenny

An 18th-century mansion on 47 acres, in the heart of Co. Kilkenny's bloodstock belt, is for sale for €1 million to include a completed holiday home development in the grounds. Duninga House, near the village of Goresbridge, is the former home of the Mullins family whose son Willie is one of the country's leading trainers.

The estate is being sold on the instructions of receivers at accountancy firm KPMG, after its owner, Cork developer Oliver O'Dwyer, failed to complete plans to convert it into a luxury hotel and tax-break holiday home destination.

The €1 million price tag includes 14 newly-constructed holiday homes with Section 23 tax breaks; numerous stables and outbuildings; a derelict gate-lodge; and attractive woodland. It also includes exclusive fishing rights and river frontage onto a gorgeous, navigable stretch of the Barrow.

Even with the downturn in property prices this is an astonishing price for assets of this quality. And thereby hangs a tale which is about to become very familiar. The sales brochure unexpectedly quotes Thackeray, the English novelist and travel writer who serendipitously visited Duninga over 150 years

Duninga House at Goresbridge in Co. Kilkenny, which comes with 47 acres by the River Barrow, on sale for €1 million.

ago and wrote enthusiastically of arriving via 'a pretty avenue of trees leading to the pleasure grounds of the house – a handsome building commanding noble views of river, mountains and plantations'.

Not much has changed. But the writer's next comment – which does not appear in the brochure – was uncannily prescient: 'The gentleman who . . . owns the house, like many other proprietors in Ireland, found his mansion too expensive for his means, and has relinquished it.'

History now repeats itself because Duninga, which was acquired by its developer owner four years ago, must now be sold, with joint agents Savills and Dominic J. Daly Auctioneers of Cork seeking 'serious expressions of interest no later than October 12th'.

Although 14 holiday homes have been built in a former walled garden, the hotel project has stalled.

The renovation of the 997 sq m (10,732 sq ft) 14-bedroom house is described as 'quite advanced' and outside there are abandoned foundations and walls – constructed to first-floor level – for a new block which was to provide 23 extra bedrooms.

According to the estate agents handling the private treaty sale, suitable uses for Duninga include use as a private residence, completion of the hotel concept or adapting the property for use as a language school, nursing home, retirement village, or, indeed, its reinstatement as a commercial stud. The hotel project was always viewed with some surprise by local people. Although Kilkenny

Some of the 14 holiday homes, once valued at €412,000 to €545,000 each, which were included in the Duninga House sale price of €1 million.

city is just 18 km away, the area, while noted for its wonderful scenery, is not a major tourist destination. It is better known in horsey circles – the famous Donohoe horse sales take place a short furlong away and Gowran Park Racecourse involves a drive of just 5 km.

Not a single one of the 14 Section 23 holiday homes – which were initially launched at prices between €412,000 and €545,000 – was sold. Those prices seem almost surreal now.

A visit to Duninga today is not unlike visiting Pompeii. It's as if a terrible and sudden catastrophe had taken place in the middle of a working day and the builders had just dropped their tools on the spot and fled.

You half expect to come across a yellow fluorescent-jacketed labourer hunkered down with his jumbo breakfast roll and a copy of the *Daily Star* – frozen forever in the lava and ashes of the boom meltdown.

A few kilometres away, in the even more remote townland of Ullard, the Zoe Group's Liam Carroll has also built a small complex of holiday homes.

He had also applied for planning permission to build a 144-bedroom three-storey hotel, a car-park for 252 vehicles and a leisure centre on adjacent land. The fields lie empty – save for a flock of sheep grazing amidst the thistles. A sign on the gate reads: 'Beware of Bull'.

THURSDAY, 27 AUGUST 2009

An Upbringing that Groomed the Clan for Public Service

Kevin Cullen, in Boston

It all started in the dining room in London, because old Joe Kennedy believed that kids learned most of what they needed to know not in school but at the table, when the family shared food and ideas and even some good-natured slagging.

Imagine being a Kennedy kid and you're sitting in the ambassador's residence in London and your father starts grilling you on world events.

What do you think of Chamberlain? Why is Germany so aggressive? How did Mussolini rise so fast in Italy?

The kids were expected to know what they were talking about and, if they didn't, someone, usually a sibling, sometimes the father, called them out. Being a Kennedy meant being in perpetual competition, at the dining-room table, at school, during an impromptu game of pick-up football. Politics seemed easy after growing up a Kennedy.

There was never any question that Joe Kennedy was grooming his kids for big things, all to do with public service and public life. And not just Joe jnr, Jack, Bobby and Teddy. The girls – Kathleen, Eunice, Pat and Jean – were expected to be well-read and well-spoken and not just so they could marry and marry well.

Senator Edward Kennedy surrounded by family members. Left to right: son Patrick, stepson Curran Raclin, son Edward jnr, daughter Kara, his wife Vicki and stepdaughter Caroline Raclin; in a family room at the Massachusetts General Hospital in Boston after his brain tumour diagnosis. Photograph: AP/Boston Globe.

Senator Edward Kennedy in June 2002. Photograph: AP/Doug Mills.

Imagine being Teddy Kennedy. You're still in short pants, you're living in London, it's 1939 and you're holding the hand of your Irish governess, Luella Hennessey.

Teddy told Mrs Hennessey that an English boy was teasing him and punching him in the park and Teddy pointed at the English kid and asked Mrs Hennessy if it was okay if he hit the English boy back. And Luella Hennessey, speaking more as an Irishwoman than as a governess employed by the US ambassador to the Court of St James, told young master Kennedy to 'go for it'. And so he did. So did they all. They all went for it. All except Rosemary, who suffered from some form of mental disability which was made permanently worse by a partial lobotomy.

But even Rosemary's life became profound, touching millions of lives for the better when her sister Eunice became a champion for those with mental and developmental disabilities.

'I was young, but I remember those dinners,' Ted Kennedy told me two years ago, after I had gone through his mother's collected papers at the library named for his brother, the assassinated president.

'My father was like a game-show host asking questions. I was lucky. I was the baby, so I was exempt. But, boy, oh boy, were they entertaining.'

Old Joe Kennedy made a ton of money in Hollywood and the Kennedy kids could have easily coasted into a private life of luxury. But old Joe Kennedy wouldn't hear of it and, in the end, neither would any of them.

Exuberant Rose of Tralee finalists. From left: Lisa Dunne, South Australia; Katherine Quirke, Edmonton; Romy Farrelly, Sydney; Stephanie O'Dwyer, Kilkenny; Maeve Gallagher, Liverpool; and Ashling Colton, New York, on Banna Beach in Co. Kerry. Photograph: Domnick Walsh/Eye Focus.

'We grew up in this atmosphere that, you know, "of those who have much, much is expected",' Ted Kennedy said.

'When we were at that dinner table, there was no ideal higher than public service. The conversations were about history and current events and world leaders and this and that, but the whole point of the exercise was to talk about public service, about the importance of it.'

Joe jnr was the chosen one, but his navy plane exploded above the English Channel in 1944.

Kathleen, the most beautiful, gregarious and maybe the most intelligent of the Kennedys, could have been anything, even in that day and age. But, she, too, died in a plane crash, two years after her husband, an English aristocrat, died at the front within weeks of her brother Joe.

Death haunted the Kennedy kids and it often pressed those into service before they were ready or able. With Joe jnr dead, Jack became the family standard-bearer.

His election as president fulfilled old Joe Kennedy's dream, the ultimate revenge of an Irish-American Catholic whose family had first arrived in a Boston when there was systemic discrimination against Irish Catholics.

But it also cast young Ted Kennedy, just 30, into a run for a US Senate seat when his resume consisted mainly of being a Kennedy.

His opponent, Massachusetts attorney general

Edward McCormack, ridiculed Kennedy's inexperience, saying during a debate: 'If his name were Edward Moore, with his qualifications – with your qualifications, Teddy – if it was Edward Moore, your candidacy would be a joke.'

Leave aside for the moment that McCormack himself was the nephew of the US house speaker John McCormack, the fact of the matter was Ted Kennedy was a Kennedy.

Jack Kennedy's election as the first Catholic president and his subsequent assassination, followed by Bobby's political career and assassination, ensured that being a Kennedy was in itself a qualification.

It was poignant and not a little tragic that Ted Kennedy fell ill last year at the Kennedy compound in Hyannisport, the same spot where his father suffered a stroke 48 years ago. It was there also that Ted Kennedy died.

They are creatures of habit, these Kennedys, and like tourists they cross the Sagamore Bridge and return to Cape Cod when the weather turns good. They have always returned to Hyannisport, in good times and in bad.

Teddy's father was 73 when he had a stroke, three years younger than Teddy was when the brain cancer was diagnosed.

Old Joe Kennedy lived another eight years in a wheelchair and it drove him mad with frustration. He was in the wheelchair when he found out that someone had shot his Jack and he was in the wheelchair when he found out that someone had shot his Bobby.

Ted Kennedy remained fairly robust in the 15 months he outlived the cancer. He lived long enough to see all his kids and grandkids and long enough to see a man, a black man, who reminded him of his brothers, be elected president.

Vicki, his wife, said they had more than a few good dinners in Hyannisport, with all the kids and all the grandkids gathered around the table. And, sick as he was, Teddy was pumping them with questions.

Government Must not Fall until Crucial Measures Implemented

Garret FitzGerald

So far at least, loss of confidence in the Government does not seem to have affected the swing in public opinion in favour of the Lisbon Treaty, which has, I believe, been a consequence of growing recognition of the importance of Europe to Ireland in our present crisis.

To date, the European Central Bank has provided us with domestic liquidity support estimated at well over €50 billion – having allocated to Ireland, with our 1 per cent share of euro zone population, some 7 per cent of its total crisis assistance.

However, this collapse of public confidence is clearly making it increasingly difficult for us to tackle effectively both our fiscal and banking crises.

It was this Government that destroyed our competitiveness through an irresponsible promotion of public spending, and thus inflation. It then aggravated instead of damping down our housing bubble. So it was never going to be easy for it to win public support for the drastic measures required to resolve the crisis to which it had contributed.

It might have been better if there had been a change of government around or shortly after the time when the crisis declared itself last autumn.

A new government, not inhibited from explaining the origins of a crisis for which it had no direct responsibility, might have been better able to mobilise support for the very tough measures needed to resolve it.

However, that did not happen, and now the Government has the very difficult task of mobilising public and parliamentary support for huge

Ballycastle goat catcher Seamus Blaney (left) hands over the 2009 King Puck, Billy, to Killorglin goat catcher Frank Joy at Killorglin's Laune Bridge. Photograph: Don MacMonagle.

Jamie Rochford with her horse Charlie at Puck Fair in Killorglin, Co. Kerry. Photograph: Julien Behal/PA.

spending cuts and tax increases. And it must also take very unpopular banking measures that are all too easily misrepresented as being designed to bail out developers and bankers who share with the Government responsibility for the crisis.

I have hitherto avoided any comment on the relative merits of Nama vis-a-vis other possible approaches because I have not felt competent to comment on the finer points of what is a highly technical issue.

However, my concern about maintaining our recently improved credibility in international financial markets has persuaded me today to comment.

I am concerned – whether because of loss of nerve or because of failing to secure Dáil support for these two key elements of its programme – that the Government may fail to get through the Dáil by early December either or both its budgetary proposals and its measures to deal with our banking crisis. This could undermine our capacity to borrow the huge sums we need to keep going. After these two measures have been successfully implemented, if the Dáil or the electorate so decided, there could then safely be a change of government. But in my view it would not be helpful for that to happen within the crucial three months ahead.

The Opposition parties should be the first to recognise this. No worse fate could befall an opposition than to precipitate themselves into government by defeating measures, the rejection of which could throw our State into the hands of the IMF.

One can readily imagine the relief many in government might feel at finding themselves freed of their responsibilities in circumstances that could then provide them with an unexpectedly good chance of returning to power if their successors failed to resolve the situation.

Nevertheless, the temptation to reject what is bound to be a very tough budget will be strong.

Moreover, the present populist anti-Nama mood, currently intensified by the manifesto of the 46 economists, could all too easily lead to the Opposition overplaying its hand – and there are signs of this happening.

Fine Gael has said it will vote against the Nama Bill. Labour's stance seems recently to have hardened on this issue. And the Green Party appears to be prepared to have its Dáil position on this highly technical issue decided by a popular vote of party members.

The article (Opinion and Analysis, 26 August) by 46 economists (from which, however, I note the significant absence of the names of some highly qualified members of that profession) raises three issues.

The first is the issue of transparency and Oireachtas oversight – but they accept that the Minister has stated his willingness to take amendments in this area.

Their second point is that the duration of Nama is 'opaque' – but this does not seem to be a key issue, for no one knows how long it may take for these loans to recover their value – so the Government cannot at this stage sensibly fix the duration of Nama.

The economists' final point, however, is one over which there is widespread and legitimate concern: how far will Nama go in rating above their present value some properties in respect of which major loans have been made – and how will Nama assess 'the fair economic value' of such loans?

The economists propose that bank shareholders take some of the 'hit' – a view that is widely shared – but also that bondholders do likewise.

However, these economists fail to distinguish between subordinated and senior debt, despite the fact that an attempt to resile from our commitment in respect of the latter could prejudice our capacity to continue to borrow from international markets.

Who would want to lend any more to us if we repudiated the senior bonds of our banks?

A similar apparent failure to make this distinction was also a worrying feature of last weekend's Fine Gael statements on Nama. Fortunately this confusion was clarified by Richard Bruton on this page yesterday. A similar clarification by the 46 economists would be helpful.

TUESDAY, I SEPTEMBER 2009

The Law, it Appears, Is Unable to Protect Us

A Dad's Life, by Adam Brophy

I have hummed and hawed over this topic. I would rather not write about it because to do so will make it real. I don't want it to be real, in many ways it feels unreal, so maybe writing about it will solidify it. Because right now, I can't get my hands or my head around it.

We have discovered a man has been watching our house. Neighbours advised us shortly after we moved here that a man with a past history sometimes hung around the area. We took their warnings on board and insisted the kids stayed within calling distance of the house at all times. But, to my embarrassment, I felt no immediate concern.

Something about the way the cautions were delivered, as if we couldn't possibly be talking about a subject as serious as child abuse in such calm terms. It made them theoretical.

You live in the city. You presume there are threats all around. You watch. As a father in playgrounds, often the only one present, I have become aware of the suspicion and caution of others. Not all, of course, but mother hens are wary. I absorb it but also share it.

I watch for the lone man shadowing children's areas. It's not a comfortable thought, it's rarely made conscious, but I watch closely.

Munster's Marcus Horan dives over for the opening try in the 32nd minute of a Magners League match against Cardiff at Thomond Park. Photograph: James Crombie/Inpho.

Yet, even in the past five years more dads have appeared on the kiddie radar. For economic reasons, or social ones, there are more of us visibly present at the front line. The wariness begins to recede.

The city family moves to the country. Very quickly your preconceptions and prejudices are shattered. It's not all that different, but there is more space. Oh, loads more space and space is great.

That's the big swap – convenience for space, and you soon forget how nice it was to have a shop 10 doors away as you tie a couple of cats together and swing them rampantly around your new living area.

Once the cat abuse has lost its lustre you shoo the kids outside, tell them to find themselves something to do. There is, after all, a whole country to explore.

We found the man crouched behind a tombstone in the old, disused graveyard situated yards from our front gate.

The elder, in a fury at a perceived slight from a friend, had stormed off and disappeared, refusing to answer our calls. As concern mounted, the search widened. Across the road, we discovered the man, crouched, observing. We approached and he turned on his heel and sprinted away.

Panic began to rise. Where was the child? Hidden inside the house, enjoying the drama she had created with no real idea of our mounting fear. She wondered why we were so relieved to find her.

Later, I checked his vantage point. From there he could see directly into our back garden where that day five children, seven and under, had been playing.

Former Danish MEP Jens Peter Bonde (left) and former Green Party MEP Patricia McKenna at the launch of an anti-Lisbon Treaty referendum campaign in Dublin. Photograph: Dara Mac Dónaill.

I returned to the neighbours and this time took all details of the potential threat that they could provide. This time I took them seriously. I described our peeping Tom and gained confirmation that we were discussing the same person.

Armed with as much information as I could muster, I reported the incident to the Gardaí. This went against my instinct which was to arm myself with something blunt and heavy and visit the man myself, but an ingrained belief that the law will help forced me to go to the authorities.

Now. Will the law help? A garda visited the man whose name I provided. The man admitted he had been spending time around our house. He was warned to stay away. We were advised to contact the Gardaí should we see him in the vicinity again. This is, it appears, as much as the law can do for us.

Here we have a man who was in trouble for 'an incident' in the past. Local information suggests that there has been far more than one incident. This much I was told but I am unable to check his history as there is no register available to the public for this sort of sick activity.

This man has admitted to watching our house. A man has been watching my house, my children. How safe would you feel? What are we supposed to do? Sit back and wait for something to happen? At which point we will at least be sure of the perpetrator.

Anyone with the smallest understanding of an abuser's mind knows that they do not want to walk away from what attracts them. Yet that is what our system thinks is enough. To advise them to walk away. This is not right. This is not right.

MONDAY, 7 SEPTEMBER 2009

Mere Heroism Cannot Stop Kilkenny

Tom Humphries

History. Legend. Pantheons. Those things aren't for the meek. Then again black and amber stripes aren't for the meek either.

With seven minutes of this wonderfully and robust All-Ireland final left, Henry Shefflin stood over a penalty at the Hill 16 end and stared at the Tipperary goal.

A moment of calm in a day of thunder. Tipp men standing big on the line. One small goal behind them. Pressure in its purest form.

By Henry's standards he had played a good game if not a great game but now history hinged on his nerve. Kilkenny were two points down, with the momentum of the game seeping away from them. The sheer weight of his county's desperate hunger for four in a row must have been pressing him into the Croke Park turf.

On days when great athletes bottle things the simple mechanics of the game escape the memory that lives in the muscles.

There are a million tiny variables in the act of lifting a sliotar, raising it to a spot a few yards in front of you and stepping to meet it with perfect violence.

Or maybe there aren't.

Henry bent. He lifted and drove the ball to the Tipperary net with such fury and precision those on the line barely had time to flinch.

Kilkenny's Martin Comerford scoring his goal in the final quarter of the GAA All-Ireland senior hurling final in Croke Park, despite the efforts of Tipperary's Brendan Maher (on the ground). Photograph: Alan Betson.

Joe Sheridan from Mayo springs into action at the All-Ireland Road Bowling Championships on the Baltray Road in Drogheda, Co. Louth. Photograph: Ciara Wilkinson.

Perfection. It wasn't the most beautiful moment in a game spangled by wonder and genius but it was the ultimate match of man and moment.

The penalty (regardless of its disputed validity), in its timing and its execution, summed up Kilkenny's day. It described, too, the personality of this team which has claimed a lease on hurling history. It was a moment which advertised the very character of greatness.

So, four in a row. Seven All-Irelands this decade for Brian Cody and his lieutenants Henry Shefflin and Michael Kavanagh. There can be no quibbles. No asterisks in the record books. No complaints. Kilkenny have moved the game on to a new level. While other humans are still struggling to find ways to cope with life at that altitude Kilkenny are comfortable at the peak.

They have absorbed the best of what everybody has thrown at them these past four years. They have been rattled but more often they have hummed. When the chips are down, when the backs are to the wall, when the going gets tough, whatever, they refuse to flinch.

They have redefined hurling. After the 90s, a decade of uprising and novelty in the beautiful game, Kilkenny have reclaimed hurling and made it their own.

Yesterday in front of 82,106 white-knuckled customers they faced down an extraordinary challenge from Liam Sheedy's young Tipperary team and won in the end, pulling away, stretching the margin to five points, the greatest it had been all day.

'The scoreboard only matters once in a game,' said Brian Cody afterwards, 'at the end.'

It's a long time since Kilkenny saw a scoreboard freighted with the sort of regret which Tipperary felt after 72 minutes or so of hurling yesterday.

'I'm hurting. Proud but hurting,' said Sheedy

afterwards, his words surely reflecting the mood of an entire county.

'The lads have given it everything today and just come up short. We were facing the best team, possibly, in the history of the game. We just needed a goal at some stage to push on.'

Goals. All year we noted how Kilkenny had been leaking them and we wondered coming to Croke Park to what extent Tipperary's spry full-forward line could exploit that small fissure in Kilkenny's excellence.

It was Tipp's misfortune to find PJ Ryan suddenly armed with the powers of a comic strip superhero yesterday. Ryan made five extraordinary saves, making himself the game's single most influential figure. His prominence was adequate testimony to the heroic quality of Tipperary's challenge.

He spoke afterwards with extraordinary modesty of his contribution. One save from Eoin Kelly carried the sort of brilliance which often goes unappreciated. Kelly wound up from close range to drive the ball into oblivion and beyond. Ryan braced himself as best he could. At the last second Kelly slipped and his shot was relatively tame but Ryan had to readjust himself in a split second and get his hurley down low to his left to turn the ball around the post. An extraordinary reflex.

'You get a bit of luck, really,' was all he would say of the moment. 'That second, Eoin Kelly slipped. If his feet hadn't gone from under him he would have busted the net out. You get a bit of luck on the day.'

Kilkenny have had bits of luck along the way to this epic achievement but mainly they have been of their own making. The penalty which Shefflin converted may have been a soft award in the context of such a bruising math as yesterday's but its conversion was an act of almost routine excellence as were Ryan's saves and Martin Comerford's cool finish for Kilkenny's second goal.

The final whistle offered Kilkenny a release which the GAA's plans for a staid presentation were never going to contain. Cody crossed the border onto the field, briefly dancing a manic jig. For a minute or two we watched the giants at rest embracing and celebrating. Then the dam burst and a stripy sea flooded the Croke Park turf.

'Plan B,' said the tannoy. 'Plan B.'

Kilkenny, who had just consummated the only plan they were ever interested in, carried on regardless. Plan A was unrelenting excellence and achievement. They had no Plan B. Such contingencies are for ordinary mortals.

MONDAY, 7 SEPTEMBER 2009

Who Needs Fireworks after Explosive Final Display?

Seán Moran, at Croke Park

Kilkenny 2-22 Tipperary 0-23

The crowd at yesterday's GAA All-Ireland hurling final was denied the promised fireworks display, as the intended new on-field presentation disintegrated amidst crowd invasions and urgently-intoned declarations of 'Plan B', 'Plan B'.

But no one in the capacity crowd had gone short of fireworks, as an enthralling final unfolded. Tipperary, underdogs by circumstance if not temperament, put up a fantastic display, dictating the course of the match up until the dramatic closing minutes, but in the end there was no denying Kilkenny's rendezvous with history.

The All-Ireland four-in-a-row was completed and Cork's 65-year-old record emulated. It was fitting that an achievement of such historical magnitude should have taken nearly the entire 70 minutes of a wonderfully absorbing final to be decided and when the match was there and available, Kilkenny got the scores that clinically unpicked the challenge of the Munster champions.

Kilkenny manager Brian Cody celebrates the final whistle. Photograph: Alan Betson.

There may have been a perceived ominous inevitability about what was going to happen, given the champions' remorseless ability to put away opponents no matter how disturbing the challenge posed. But Tipperary pressed and threatened to the extent that a sensational upset was drifting into the realms of reality when the explosive events of the 64th-minute dramatically realigned the tie.

For Tipp, and most neutral observers, the crucial incident was unfortunately a refereeing error when Diarmuid Kirwan awarded a penalty for a foul on Richie Power by Paul Curran that took place outside of the area.

At that stage, Tipperary led by two points – a pretty endangered margin when Henry Shefflin is striding through the smoke to attempt the shot.

It hadn't been his best of afternoons, even though a final total of 1–8 left him just three short of Eddie Keher's all-time championship scoring record. But Shefflin was ruthless with the chance, declining to be satisfied with the plausible safety of taking his point and instead blazing it high into the net.

Still, there was only a point in it, but the coming seconds, reminiscent of Offaly's later knockout blows on Limerick 15 years ago, saw Michael Kavanagh – like Shefflin pocketing a seventh All-Ireland medal, just one short of the Christy Ring and John Doyle benchmark – hurtle past Lar Corbett to keep the ball in play and clear it to Eoin Larkin.

Martin Comerford, dropped on Friday night to the surprise of many but making a major impact when introduced in the 55th minute, made the run and Larkin spotted him. In an instant Brendan Cummins was taking the sliotar out of the net for the second time in a minute.

Still Tipperary came, but the match was beyond them as Kilkenny sensed victory, and attempts to get the margin to within a score foundered in a late burst of point-scoring, with Jackie Tyrrell venturing up from corner back to swing over one and Larkin, after a couple of wides, finding the range and supplying two of his own.

So in a few business-as-usual minutes, the champions wrote themselves indelibly into history. But for so long that conclusion had looked far from certain.

The first task for Tipperary was always going to be to avoid the sort of catastrophe that had befallen Kilkenny's most recent All-Ireland opponents Waterford and Limerick – the concession of early goals and a resulting surge in panic levels.

This they managed in an opening quarter not for the squeamish. Tyrrell charged Seamus Callanan, switched into full forward before the throw-in, shoulder into chest and pole-axed him without even the sanction of a free. Referee Kirwan enthusiastically let play flow but, as generally happens in such cases, occasionally at the expense of the rules.

Otherwise the match was a terrific spectacle. Tipperary's young defence played superbly.

Pádraic Maher overcame a ninth-minute error that let in Shefflin for a shot that Brendan Cummins crucially saved, but the full back went on to have an exceptional first senior final – recovering from his error within two minutes to stand his ground well with Shefflin under a dropping Aidan Fogarty delivery.

Less anticipated was the competitiveness of the Tipp half backs where Declan Fanning, no sign of his reportedly damaged hamstring, hurled a lot of

Libertas leader Declan Ganley speaking at a press conference in the Shelbourne Hotel in Dublin to announce his decision to enter the No to Lisbon campaign, despite saying after his defeat in the European elections that he would not. Photograph: Dara Mac Dónaill.

ball as Power roamed and Conor O'Mahony locked the rearguard together.

One problem that continued to haunt the Munster champions was the ball-winning deficiencies of the half forwards. Pat Kerwick did some good things, but John O'Brien had a disappointing afternoon. The situation was partly remedied by the locating of Corbett at centre forward from where he ran Kilkenny ragged at times and ended up with four points from play.

On the wings, though, John Tennyson and Tommy Walsh were in control, the latter outstanding in his familiar ability to magic high ball out of the air and hit telling deliveries up the field. In the 16th minute he hit a wonder point from around his own '65' line.

Tipperary might have had more of an attacking platform but the scoring was tit-for-tat and seven times the sides were level in the first half. If Shefflin wasn't firing on all cylinders the rest of the attack were ticking over and Eddie Brennan excelled with three first-half points from play.

Eoin Kelly made a huge contribution to Tipperary, shooting 13 points in all and providing nearly-flawless (one wide) scoring from dead ball opportunities and managing to get away a point from play amidst a thicket of three defenders to tie up the match at 0–11 each going into injury-time; but Kilkenny still added two before the break for a half-time lead.

Although the Croke Park surface wasn't as much of an ice-rink as it had looked a week previously there were occasional slip-ups.

Just as Tipperary survived the initial first-half exchanges without suffering a blitz from the champions, they came out on the restart and showed renewed application.

Kerwick set up Callanan for a shot that PJ Ryan – who had claims on the Man of the Match accolade for two important saves – turned away for a '65'. None the less emboldened, Callanan scored two points within a minute and Shane McGrath,

who went on to have a better second half, restored the lead shortly afterwards.

Tipp kept pushing and by the end of the third quarter led by two, 0–17 to 0–15.

Disaster however lurked. Replacement Benny Dunne was red-carded in the 55th minute for a crazy swipe at Walsh and the match swung to Kilkenny.

For a while it looked like the dismissal had driven on Tipperary, suddenly giving them an alternative focus to the daunting prospect of closing out the match.

Three points from Kelly and Callanan put them as much clear, 0–20 to 0–17 with 10 minutes to go. But the countdown to history was about to begin in earnest.

SATURDAY, 12 SEPTEMBER 2009

Chairman who Guided Expansion of *Irish Times*

Obituary: *Major Thomas McDowell*

Tom McDowell, who has died aged 86, did not set out to become involved in newspapers but became a major architect of *The Irish Times* of today via an accidental route which took him from his native Belfast to the British army, to London as a lawyer and to Dublin temporarily as an industrialist.

As chief executive and chairman of The Irish Times Ltd – the positions he held with considerable success for almost 40 years – he oversaw the greatest expansion in the newspaper's 150-year history during which its circulation trebled to more than 105,000 copies a day and it was transformed from an ailing company into a trust that guaranteed the independence of its journalism.

Born in Belfast in 1923, the only child of a Protestant and unionist couple, Tom McDowell finished school at the Royal Belfast Academic Institution in 1941 as the second World War was

Major McDowell, former Chairman of The Irish Times Trust Limited and Chief Executive of The Irish Times Limited, at a special unveiling of his portrait at **The Irish Times** *offices in Dublin in June 2008. Photograph: Bryan O'Brien.*

under way. He was dissuaded from enlisting immediately in the British army by his parents: his father, also Thomas, had been gassed in the first World War and suffered serious lung problems which led to his early death in 1944. The young Tom went instead to Queen's University in Belfast to study commerce but, a year later and still uncertain about his long-term plans, he joined the Royal Ulster Rifles with an emergency commission.

A knee injury during a night training exercise in Omagh made him ineligible for active military service and he became a weapons instructor. The accident also led to him meeting his future wife, Margaret Telfer, the physiotherapist who treated him in hospital in Bangor, Co. Down.

He rose to the rank of major and was part of the Allied forces in occupied Austria following the end of the war, taking part in joint patrols in Vienna with Russian, American and French officers. In the post-war period, he was given two years to finish his college course and spent a summer studying law with a tutor before passing the English bar and returning to the British army.

After a further military posting to Edinburgh, his legal qualification brought him to the army legal service in the War Office in London. With little prospect of further promotion and every chance of being posted abroad without his young family, he decided to leave the army. He was offered a job as legal adviser in London to James North Ltd, a company which made protective clothing; with no experience of industry, he asked to be given a managerial role at first.

The company suggested a managing position in its operations in Dublin. He slotted easily into the city's old business establishment, joining the Kildare Street club, becoming a director of Pim's department store, and setting his career firmly on a commercial rather than a legal path.

His involvement with newspapers came about through the recognition of his business acumen. He was asked by some acquaintances to take a look at the financial troubles of the *Evening Mail*, which was bought subsequently by The Irish Times, adding to the latter's own financial difficulties.

He was asked later by The Irish Times to see if Roy Thomson, the Canadian-born British press baron, might be interested in taking it over. Thomson passed and the company then asked McDowell himself to take charge as chief executive in 1962.

Among his first actions were to close the *Evening Mail* and the *Sunday Review*, a short-lived tabloid that was ahead of its time. A year later, another problem was resolved when Douglas Gageby, who had been hired as managing director of The Irish Times shortly before McDowell's arrival, took over as editor.

Thus, what had begun as a slightly awkward relationship turned into a highly successful partnership as Gageby set about broadening the newspaper's editorial appeal and McDowell set it on a successful commercial course.

McDowell always credited Gageby and his successors as editor with the success of the newspaper, pointing out in an interview last year for the newspaper's archives that 'people buy the paper to see what the editor has said, not to know how it is printed or what kind of paper is used'.

Bedrock's Garage, *a living breathing installation, performed by Dominic Thorpe and Amanda Coogan, in a window of Arnotts department store in Dublin. Photograph: Alan Betson.*

Although he had a close relationship with editors, especially Gageby, he did not interfere in the editorial running of the newspaper. He did not share Gageby's republicanism but believed that the minority in the North had been treated badly by the majority.

When the North erupted in violence in 1969 – a time when there was little or no real communication between nationalists and unionists or between Irish and British politicians and bureaucrats – he tried on his own initiative to interest the then British prime minister, Harold Wilson, in talks with all the other parties involved.

His efforts came to nothing but irritated the then British ambassador to Dublin, Sir Andrew Gilchrist, whom he had bypassed.

In a briefing letter about McDowell's approach, Gilchrist wrote that McDowell had described Gageby as 'a renegade or white nigger'. McDowell strongly denied the charge when Gilchrist's letter was published in 2003: 'I never used that phrase, nor would I have thought of using it, about Gageby,' he said in last year's interview. 'Other people [in Belfast] called him a renegade, but I never thought he was a renegade. Douglas never made any secret of what he was. There could be no doubt about him turning or changing or anything like that.'

By the early 1970s, the circulation of *The Irish Times* had almost doubled in a decade to 60,000 and it was making money. Some of the directors indicated an interest in selling the company and McDowell proposed instead that it be turned into a trust. It was a period when several newspapers in Ireland and Britain had changed hands or were seen as being vulnerable to takeovers.

His aims were to protect the newspaper's independence, make it as difficult as possible for anyone to take over, and formalise its aims in a guiding trust.

McDowell's primary interest in the arrangements was in drawing up the terms of the trust, using his legal expertise and drawing on a wide range of media models including the *Guardian*, the *Observer*, the *Economist* magazine, and the *New York Times* as well as other documents ranging from the Constitution to the American Declaration of Independence.

He worked on the trust document for many months, going through 28 drafts before he was satisfied with the result. Among the issues he had to consider was the mechanism for appointing trustees: various options that would allow public bodies or interests to name members were considered but ruled out because of fears that the appointments would become politicised.

In the end, he opted to appoint them himself, with the help of each one selected to appoint others. When he had finished the draft trust document he showed it to Gageby who suggested that a proviso requiring the newspaper to reflect minority views be included, which it was.

The five directors of the company, including McDowell and Gageby, transferred their shares in the company to a solicitor in the autumn of 1973 in anticipation of announcing the trust at the end of that year.

Further delays in finalising the trust terms resulted in its announcement in April 1974, on the eve of the introduction of capital gains tax.

The timing gave rise to suggestions that the directors were taking their cash (£325,000 each) out of the company before the new tax took effect.

McDowell always denied that this was the case, maintaining that the timing was coincidental: he was also adamant that the motivation behind the formation of the trust itself was altruistic. The formation of the trust left the newspaper with a large bank debt, used to buy out the directors/shareholders, at what turned out to be a difficult economic period after the first oil crisis hit the western world in the autumn of 1974. McDowell successfully guided The Irish Times' financial fortunes through the subsequent recession and into further periods of growth throughout the 1980s and 1990s.

He stood down as chief executive of the company in 1997 and retired from the chairmanship of The Irish Times Trust in 2001: he was given the title President for Life in recognition of his huge contribution to the newspaper.

Tom McDowell was a private person and never sought or exploited the public status or limelight that goes with being a newspaper publisher. But he was an extraordinary presence in 'the bunker', his office in D'Olier Street. He always dressed formally and though he was somewhat aloof, he knew every employee.

During his visit to the new *Irish Times* offices on Tara Street in June 2008 for the unveiling of a portrait of him by Andrew Festing, he described the newspaper and his family as the two loves of his life.

His wife, Margaret, predeceased him in 1992. He is survived by his daughters Penelope and Karen, sons-in-law, five grandchildren and four great grandchildren.

Thomas Bleakley McDowell, 'The Major': born 18 May, 1923; died 9 September, 2009.

WEDNESDAY, 16 SEPTEMBER 2009

Boxing's Ready-Made Poster Boy with Talent to Dazzle

Johnny Watterson

(On 14 September, Irish Olympic bronze medal boxer Darren Sutherland was found dead at his flat in London. He was 27 years old and had apparently taken his own life.)

In late November of last year professional boxing promoter Frank Maloney was asked why, of all the fighters at the Beijing Olympics, he pinned his dreams on Darren Sutherland. Then looking across the table in DCU's Helix Theatre to the physical grace, the diamond ear stud and shaved eyebrow of 'The Dazzler', the question fell redundant.

The Olympic bronze medal-winning middleweight hungrily sat forward in his chair, begging that someone would ask him a question so that he could bewitch them with the buzz of his patter. A talent and a ready-made poster boy, the charismatic Sutherland was, 10 months ago, Ireland's latest gift to the professional ranks.

He was the fighter who broke moulds. In one of his first meetings, when he was signing up to be part of Ireland's High Performance amateur team some years prior to the 2008 Beijing Games, he made his first small impression.

'Darren was a completely different personality to the rest of the boxers,' said an official with the Irish team. 'There were lots of aspects to his personality. He talked, talked, talked, talked, came in and one of the first things he said was, "I'm going to write a book about the story of my life." Later on he would say: "I'm going to get a degree. I'm going to be world champion."

'He was very bright. He had a good brain and had broad interests in things like music, technology, hip hop.'

Darren O'Neill, who has just returned from the World Championships in Milan, knew Sutherland as a friend and middleweight rival. He recognises that same personality.

'He was always in good form,' says O'Neill. 'There'd be times when we'd all finished up and Darren would still be going. He'd break your heart.'

Sutherland was born in Dublin but moved to London when he was very young. His father, Tony, was from the island of St Vincents in the Caribbean and his mother, Linda, from Dublin. At one point as his reputation grew, the Caribbean island approached his boxing club, St Saviours in Dublin, and asked if Sutherland would box in the Commonwealth Games for them, offering to fly two coaches with him to Australia. He declined.

Darren Sutherland lands a punch on Bulgarian Georgi Iliev, during his professional debut at Dublin City University Sports Centre in December 2008. Photograph: Morgan Treacy/Inpho.

The family came back from Britain to settle in Navan and a young Sutherland began to box in St Brigid's gym in Blanchardstown before ambition took him to St Saviours OBA in Dorset Street in Dublin's inner city.

'He came to us at about 15 years old. In recent years the young lads in the club saw him as a star,' said St Saviours secretary Martin Power. 'He came back here five or six weeks ago like he was still a member of the club. He was still messing. He'd three or four kids in the ring with him, all on top of him. There was a bit of a Cassius Clay about him, the manners of a gentleman.'

As a teenager Sutherland went over to Brendan Ingle's professional gym in Wincobank, Sheffield, but returned to Ireland disillusioned with the sport. But by 2002 he was back competing as an amateur in the light middleweight division.

It was about then that he decided to reinvent himself and at 20 years old studied in St Peter's College, Dunboyne, with kids three years younger than he was. At the age of 22 he passed his Leaving Cert and began a sports scholarship in sports science at DCU, which dovetailed with his full-time training with the Irish amateur team.

He had come through disappointment in 2006 when an eye injury sidelined him for a long time, but his career was on the up. The Olympic medal further enhanced his profile and his appeal. There was no question that he would turn professional; just a matter of who he would sign with.

The Dazzler was a tee-totaller, and also a free spirit. He was infectiously upbeat and never afraid to tell us how he saw the world he lived in.

In his last press conference in Ireland, Sutherland said he was fulfilling a life-long dream pursuing a professional world title. Nobody can comprehend how that optimism of just months ago dissipated to the extent of him taking his own life in an apartment in south London.

'It's very strange what happened,' says Power. 'No, it just doesn't square off with his personality at all.' Yesterday that was a common sentiment.

'I'm like a sponge and I know that will help me. I'm a fast learner. I soak up information,' said the 27-year-old casting his spell 10 months ago. 'By the time the next Olympics comes around, I want to be challenging for the world title. That's the sort of time frame I'm thinking.' Beside him then Maloney sat grinning. Maloney had spent his early years striving to be a jockey and a professional footballer as well as spending time in a Catholic seminary.

'The four rounds in amateurs were like a sprint to me. I'd spar for an hour. They had to tell me to get out of the ring,' explained Sutherland then. 'Now,' he said as he finished the sermon, his eyes widening, 'it's time to show my full repertoire of skills.'

THURSDAY, 17 SEPTEMBER 2009

Nama Day Signalled by Arrival of Distressed Assets

Miriam Lord

And so came the day, Nama Day, when all the Distressed Assets were gathered together for the first time since their world collapsed around them. Or since Leinster House closed for the summer holidays.

What value would you put on them now? Would you even buy them for tuppence at a cake sale, never mind at a general election? Biffo and his Distressed Assets trooped into the Government benches at 2.30 in the afternoon, a sorry collection of Fianna Fáil and Green deputies. Many already sported new session haircuts, but there were no indications of an upside in their worried expressions.

They know they face a very real risk of further generous discounts when they go to the market for support. Judged on current value, many would not survive.

Confronted by such a large collection of impaired deputies – the opening Dáil session was televised live – the depth and gravity of the situation facing the nation hit home.

This depressing picture wasn't helped by the sight of the Ceann Comhairle ascending the chair to kick-start proceedings by reading out a prayer. John O'Donoghue, despite the fact that he is now in a role that is Above Politics, is one of the most Distressed Assets in the House.

There they were, backbenchers and Ministers, back from the holliers and propped up on the counter of the Dáil chamber, with the biggest liabilities gazing glumly across the floor like a pair of doggies in a pet shop window.

Brian Cowen and Bertie Ahern – the Allied Irish and Anglo Irish of the 30th Dáil – sat in the outside first and last seats, neatly bookending the grim Government balance sheet from top row to bottom line.

Minister for Finance Brian Lenihan ran the show yesterday. According to the experts, he's one of the few who might still realise his potential if he plays his cards right. In economic parlance, Lenihan might be lucky to emerge from this debacle with his face wiped. Most of the rest can only look forward to having their eyes wiped on election day.

So many strands to this distressing story – an unsavoury tale that keeps on giving.

Sinn Féin's Arthur Morgan added to the air of helplessness when he treated television viewers to a taste of the sort of antics that give parliamentary politics a bad name and give worried taxpayers a fit of the vapours.

This Dáil session was billed as one of the most important ever in the history of the State. The

Nama legislation was about to begin its final journey, and its impact on the country will affect citizens for decades to come. A day for getting the head down to some serious debating and legislating. A day for showing why the calibre of our elected representatives is so important, and why the results of the work they do is of such magnitude in the lives of ordinary people.

Step forward, Arthur Morgan, and take a bow.

He chose this occasion to pull what Labour's Eamon Gilmore labelled 'a parliamentary stunt'. With Lenihan ready to deliver the results of his Government's 'exhaustive, bottom-up process' of finalising the Nama legislation, and the Opposition ready to engage in meaningful discussion, Deputy Morgan decided to engage in a bottom-up exercise of his own. Under the guise of

a point of order, Arthur called on the Taoiseach to apologise to the people of Ireland for lying about the property bubble, and called on the Government to apologise for robbing the taxpayers.

To howls of frustration from deputies on all sides, and wails of protest from the poor beleaguered Bull in the chair, Arthur refused to shut up. Perhaps the fact that his party leader, Gerry Adams, was beaming down from the visitors' gallery had something to do with his outburst.

Twice, the House was suspended. This was not the sort of attention needed by John O'Donoghue. (On the plus side though, it might have given The Bull a chance to take in a couple of horse races on the telly.) Following protracted negotiations with the Superintendent of the House and the Captain of the Guard, bolstered in the closing moments by

Caleb Folan of Ireland tries to take the ball off Aaron Mokoena of South Africa, during an international soccer friendly at Thomond Park. Photograph: Donall Farmer/Inpho.

Brian Friel under a portrait of himself during a tribute event in the Abbey Theatre. Photograph: Aidan Crawley.

the arrival of Big Martin, the beefiest of Dáil ushers, Arthur finally stopped playing to the disgusted gallery.

'Following discussion with my colleagues, we have decided that I will withdraw,' he said huffily, before taking his leave. Gerry hopped out of the gallery ahead of him and the two exited together.

The incident provided the day's only example of cross-party unity, when Government deputies applauded Enda Kenny and Eamon Gilmore after they called on Arthur to cop himself on.

With this being such a big day, Bertie Ahern graced the chamber with his presence. He chatted outside the railing with deputies Tom McEllistrim, Timmy Dooley and Frank Fahey. They seemed engrossed in what the former taoiseach was saying – perhaps he was giving them a sneak preview

of his sports column in next Sunday's *News of the World*.

Young Tom is swanning with the greats this week – he was also spotted at Listowel races with the Ceann Comhairle, who was cruelly deprived of a fourth day at the Kerry track due to the demands of office.

Meanwhile, Gerry Adams had to suffer his own punishment after his political protegé's juvenile carry-on in the chamber. Senator Donie Cassidy, glimpsing the Sinn Féin leader in the VIP seats, bounded over and sat beside him, talking into his ear for what must have seemed like an eternity.

Donie managed to force Gerry from the House far more quickly than The Bull managed with Arthur. When the honourable member for West Belfast returned, he found himself sharing the small gallery with Julian King, CMG, Her Majesty's ambassador to Ireland. Mr King was visiting the Dáil for the first time in his new role, and he chose a good day.

Finally, Brian Lenihan got down to his exposition of the bottom-up process that is Nama.

In a nutshell, €77 billion of distressed assets – Biffo, Bertie, The Bull, Cabinet and backbenchers not included – are to be bought at a 30 per cent discount.

Sounding like an amateur plastic surgeon, Brian envisaged a less than 10 per cent uplift in Nama's assets over a 10-year period. He spoke for three-quarters of an hour, as the Distressed Assets tried to keep up. Bertie buried himself in the accompanying document, looking less than overjoyed.

Across the floor, the Opposition number-crunchers got to work with their highlighter pens, calculators and notepads. Pat Rabbitte loosened his tie, shaking his head and sniffing. There appeared to be smoke coming off George Lee's pen, while Richard Bruton wrote in different coloured ink on a blizzard of paper. Joan Burton had a sheaf of papers on the go, the contents of a stationery cupboard beside her elbow and the ear of Eamon Gilmore.

The Distressed Assets applauded their man when he finished his speech, which the Opposition would later say was very short on specifics. It was heavy on Barack Obama references though, which these days is rather lazy. 'Nama is our bold, upfront action,' he concluded, to snorts of derision from across the way.

Richard Bruton was good. So good that quite a few of the Distressed Assets remained in the chamber to listen to him. Joan was even better, despite the fact her voice kept giving out because she forgot to bring her Strepsils.

The Distressed Assets escaped to their offices and to the bar, there to hide from the people from Nama. But it's only a matter of time before they too are hoovered up and given a shave.

Same as it ever Was for Kerry

Tom Humphries

Cork 1–9 Kerry 0–16

The more things change, the more they stay the same. A decade that began with the stirring of a northern revolution and mutterings from the south about 'puke football' ended yesterday with Kerry once again in the ascendant, having done what they have always done. They adapted to football's new style and then outlasted their rivals.

Kerry! In the end we all bow to their eminence. They began the year looking as if the arrival of championship football had caught them by surprise. They finished yesterday by outplaying a Cork side who had looked as if they were growing inexorably toward greatness. Poor Cork. Yesterday they hit the pitch carrying that great weight which we in the GAA call the burden of favouritism.

Whatever they felt about that, they opened up in the first 10 minutes exactly as we might have expected them to. They looked like men with a point to prove.

When Colm O'Neill got in behind the Kerry defence after 10 minutes and beat Diarmuid Murphy at his near post, the sceptics in the Kerry side of the congregation rubbed their chins and nodded. Kerry full back Tommy Griffin had been skinned. The goalie hadn't wrapped himself in glory. Cork would push on surely.

Instead Kerry just took the goal as an affront to their standing. Jack O'Connor had his tactics just right. Colm Cooper did what he usually does when he meets Anthony Lynch in Croke Park, tortured him. Declan O'Sullivan on Kieran O'Connor was a mismatch. Tadhg Kennelly at centre forward kept Graham Canty so busy in his own kitchen that he never got to venture upfield.

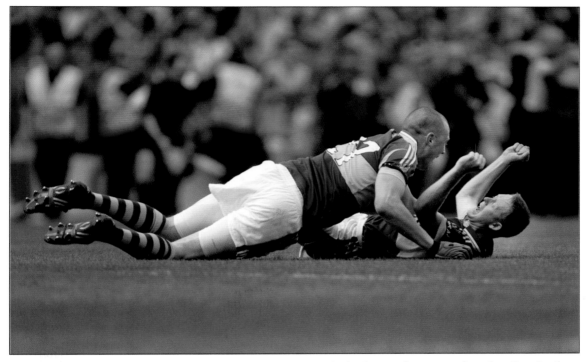

Colm Cooper and Kieran Donaghy of Kerry celebrate at the final whistle, after beating Cork in the All-Ireland senior football championship final in Croke Park. Photographer: Dara Mac Dónaill.

Tommy Walsh's performance on Michael Shields was a bonus which brought points just about every time Kerry needed them.

Kerry pressed on and by half-time had turned the five-point deficit into a two-point advantage. The concession of the goal had scarcely winded them. Teams like that are scary to play against.

By the time the second half was underway Cork had hurler Eoin Cadogan in one corner of the full-back line, full back Shields in the other corner and John Miskella had moved from wing back to full back. Mixing and mending on the run is a dangerous process.

Kerry started the second half with a free which Colm Cooper converted as part of his flawless day of free-taking and a point from Darren O'Sullivan at the end of a mesmerising solo run.

For O'Sullivan it was a special day. He played his first All-Ireland final a few years back as a late

sub on a bad day against Tyrone. This year Kerry chose him to be the county captain and tomorrow night he will carry the cup home to picturesque Glenbeigh. He confessed afterwards the final whistle had brought a wave of emotion that he hadn't expected.

'I just didn't know what to do. I was overcome. To be captain of this great team and to get to lead them out in Croke Park and then to lift the cup. It's a time I will never forget.'

And this was an All-Ireland win the people of Kerry will never forget. Much of the decade was spent fending off the irritation of the northern dominance and there are those who say Kerry never beat Tyrone in their three championship meetings.

If there has to be a team of the decade, however, the laurel has to go to the team that outlasted and outperformed all others. The journey that

Kerry's Seamus Scanlon and Cork's Patrick Kelly and Alan O'Connor in action during the All-Ireland senior football championship final at Croke Park. Photograph: Alan Betson.

Kerry completed yesterday was remarkable if viewed just as the story of one season. If you go back, however, to the jaded and demoralised Kerry side that Jack O'Connor took over at the start of the 2004 season, their story is wondrous. Six finals in a row. Four wins.

For O'Connor, after a two-season hiatus during which Pat O'Shea took the team, yesterday was a personal triumph. Despite an astonishing record of managing teams to success at club level, schools' level and all age grades of intercounty football, there has been a persistent Greek chorus of doubters who question what the Dromid man actually brings to the table. O'Connor doesn't have to explain what he brings to the table. What he brings home is the bacon.

This year he knew his side hadn't the legs left to start the summer at spring pace and keep that going till September. So they limped out of Munster and shambled through the qualifiers

before reassuring themselves by devouring the startled earwigs of Dublin in the All-Ireland quarter-final. After that it was business as usual. When it comes to one-off big games, O'Connor is virtually peerless, tactically.

Yesterday Pearse O'Neill, the Cork centre forward, entered the game as virtually a certainty to win an All Star. He was erased as a presence in the game though by Mike McCarthy and his story was replicated in several key areas.

'We were in trouble earlier in the summer,' said O'Connor, 'and written off. We get our energy from enjoying each other's company and working hard.'

Enjoying each other's company? They do that and enjoy the company of Sam until Christmas. Then thoughts will turn to the idea of making a seventh final in a row.

Who would bet against them?

Index

Page numbers set in *italic* indicate a picture or material referred to in a caption.